STRATEGIC CONUNDRUMS

STRATEGIC CONUNDRUMS

RESHAPING INDIA'S FOREIGN POLICY

RAJIV SIKRI

An imprint of Penguin Random House

EBURY PRESS

Ebury Press is an imprint of the Penguin Random House group of companies
whose addresses can be found at global.penguinrandomhouse.com

Published by Penguin Random House India Pvt. Ltd
4th Floor, Capital Tower 1, MG Road,
Gurugram 122 002, Haryana, India

First published in Ebury Press by Penguin Random House India 2024

10 9 8 7 6 5 4 3 2

ISBN 9780143464570

Typeset in Garamond by MAP Systems, Bengaluru, India
Printed at Replika Press Pvt. Ltd, India

www.penguin.co.in

To Veena, my wife and colleague

Contents

Preface

Foreign policy is not an elitist, esoteric activity that is conceived and executed in a separate silo, disconnected from what happens within a country. It is an integral and critical element of an overall strategy to serve national goals and priorities, including social and economic development and defence preparedness. Unlike the situation in the first four or five decades after its independence, India's growth and prosperity now depend to a considerable extent on the state of its relations with other countries. An increasing number of Indians have global interests. Millions of Indians, including workers, students, professionals, businessmen and tourists, live, study and travel abroad. It is natural that Indians, especially the younger generation, wish to have an informed understanding of the country's foreign policy issues. This book seeks to make a modest contribution in that direction.

India's relations with its neighbouring countries are treated in detail, as I believe that its security and development depend, in large measure, on the existence of a peaceful and prosperous neighbourhood. India's strategic neighbourhood in the Indian Ocean and in the surrounding regions, in the Persian Gulf and South-east Asia are covered at some length, as also India's relations with the United States, China and Russia. I have tried to analyse the underlying compulsions, rationale and limitations of India's relations with different countries and regions. It is my hope that this book will stimulate an intelligent discussion on India's foreign policy challenges.

New Delhi
June 2024

Chapter 1

The World Today

After the fall of the Berlin Wall in 1989, which signalled the end of the post-World War II era and the defeat of the Soviet Union in the Cold War, the world has been in flux for more than three decades. This momentous event started a process that led to the breakup of the Soviet Union a couple of years later. It also emboldened the United States towards triumphal and unilateral behaviour. A 'new world order' was proclaimed. Long-established principles of international relations—like the sovereignty of states, equality between states and non-interference by states in the internal affairs of other states—were cast aside in the name of 'humanitarian interventionism' or of tackling the problem of 'failed states'. International treaties and agreements were given the go-by if they did not suit the United States.

Sadly, the world today is in worse shape. It is less safe and more uncertain. Witness the wars and devastation in Ukraine, Gaza, Syria, Iraq, Libya, Afghanistan and Yemen. European unity has unravelled. There is growing right-wing nationalism, xenophobia and racism in both Europe and the United States. In East Asia, there are heightened tensions in the South China Sea and over Taiwan, and North Korea remains defiant and combative. The global reach of religious-terrorist organizations has increased. Nuclear deterrence no longer seems to work. All Cold War-era agreements between the United States and the Soviet Union/Russia to minimize the risks of nuclear confrontation have been jettisoned. There is zero trust between the two nuclear superpowers. The confident and naive prediction of the well-known American political scientist, Francis Fukuyama, that the fall of the Berlin

Wall in 1989 and the collapse of the Soviet Union in 1991 signified the 'end of history' has turned out to be wishful. As the world changed over the next decade and a half with the rise of China and India, and the resurgence of Russia, the changed geopolitical scene signalled, as the US neo-conservative scholar Robert Kagan ruefully observed, 'the return of history and the end of dreams'.[1] The same logic of hard power, which converted, briefly, a bipolar world into a unipolar one, is now gradually and inexorably giving way to a multipolar world. US global dominance is under challenge not only by a rejuvenated Russia under Putin and an aggressive, self-confident China, but also by middle and small powers who are asserting themselves more confidently.

The international order established after World War II is on its last legs, but a stable balance of power and a new global structure to regulate inter-state relations is not on the horizon. One sees a constantly changing pattern of the global kaleidoscope, and it is difficult to say when, if at all, it may stabilize. It is likely that what may eventually emerge is only an informal arrangement, not a new structure. Whatever its exact pattern, the twenty-first-century world will be different from that of the twentieth century. A few years ago, most observers envisaged a more open, more integrated and more interdependent world. In the wake of globalization and the end of the Cold War, as severed relationships and long-frozen borders reopened, new opportunities for economic cooperation emerged. However, the law of unintended consequences has been at work. The self-serving assumption and hope of its early advocates that globalization would lead to Americanization of the world has turned out to be misplaced. Globalization is now hurting the West and has triggered a backlash. Deeply worried by China's control of a huge chunk of global manufacturing, its geopolitical rivals are now working to develop alternative supply chains that are secure, not merely the most economically profitable. The unprecedented sweeping sanctions by the West against Russia have given a further deadly blow to globalization and divided the world as the West engages in a losing effort to coopt the rest of the world against Russia.

Many countries are in a bind as they grapple with the challenge of reconciling their quest for optimal and integrated economic and social development, which pushes them towards regional cooperation with their neighbours, with their political compulsions like preserving their national sovereignty, independence and dignity. For developing countries, the challenge is to find viable substitutes for the colonial-era economic ties that have outlived their utility. In the immediate aftermath of decolonization, the links of the former colonies with their erstwhile imperial masters were invariably stronger than their associations with their neighbours. Today, however, the Commonwealth and the Francophone group of countries are mere shadows of their original avatars, in part because Britain and France no longer have the resources to sustain their respective colonial-era linkages. But regional cooperation is not easy, since artificially drawn colonial borders have disrupted traditional economic, social, cultural and family linkages and created territorial disputes among the former colonies.

All countries, whether developed or developing, are becoming increasingly multicultural. This has exacerbated social tensions. The gap between the rich and the poor is widening, both within countries and in the world as a whole. Inequality, of course, is nothing new. What is new is that throughout the world, the information revolution has created an unprecedented degree of awareness and high expectations among the poorer and disempowered developing countries, now collectively called the 'Global South'. Weaker sections of society and smaller countries that have for long remained frustrated, alienated and humiliated, feel empowered today. With socialism and communism no longer the philosophies that motivate leaders and inspire the youth (as they did during the twentieth century), disillusionment with existing political systems finds new outlets. Unless societies develop the political institutions and social attitudes that take cultural diversity into account, they could become dangerously brittle. The world's marginalized, who cannot aspire to a hedonistic cornucopia of material comfort, have tended to fall back on religion. Regrettably, today's religious leaders and intermediaries continue to exploit people by spreading fundamentalist and intolerant versions of religion. Islam is the religion most affected, but Christianity, Judaism, Buddhism and Hinduism are not immune to these trends.

Technology is increasingly driving many changes. All countries realize that it is the mastery of new technologies such as artificial intelligence, nanotechnology, biotechnology, materials sciences and information technology that will determine the technological edge and economic competitiveness of companies and countries. Cyber warfare, cybercrime and problems of governance in a digitally interconnected world are new areas of concern, both for governments and for ordinary people. Strenuous efforts are being made by the leading countries to retain or develop a technological edge in critical areas like semiconductors and to have reliable and cost-competitive access to rare earths and metals.

There is a worrying mismatch between the mindset, structures and institutions set up after World War II and the complexity, dynamism and volatility of the twenty-first-century world. Unfortunately, former Soviet President Gorbachev's sensible plea for a 'new thinking' in the nuclear age did not gain traction. The United Nations Security Council (UNSC) reflects the mid-twentieth-century power balance rather than today's realities. Seeing the growing rivalries and animosities among its permanent members (P-5), it is hardly surprising that the UNSC is ineffective in its core purpose of ensuring peace and security. But the solution is not a brazen might-is-right approach or an arbitrarily determined, so-called 'rules-based world order' that many rightly view as a euphemism for neo-colonialism. On various occasions, the West has undertaken military operations without UN authorization under various pretexts, such as 'humanitarian intervention' (Yugoslavia), 'war on terror' (Afghanistan), 'search for weapons of mass destruction' (Iraq), or simply 'regime change' (Ukraine, Libya and Syria). Where the United States could not or did not want to act on its own, a supine European Union (EU) or an obedient North Atlantic Treaty Organization (NATO) was brought in. Russia and China have not lagged behind. Russia took over Crimea in 2014 and invaded Ukraine in 2022, while China has almost taken over the South China Sea and is engaged in aggressive behaviour towards India.

There are similar anachronisms on the economic side. Just over a couple of decades ago, the International Monetary Fund (IMF) was at the forefront in leading a bailout of Russia, Argentina and stricken Asian economies. Today, the role of the IMF as the lender of last resort has atrophied. The IMF and the World Bank no longer reflect today's economic realities, which is why India, during its chairmanship of the G-20 in 2023, set up an independent expert group led by Lawrence Summers (former US Treasury Secretary) and N.K. Singh (chairman of the fifteenth Finance Commission of India) to give suggestions for the reform of multilateral development banks.[2] With their share of global economic power having come down, the G-7 countries (the United States, Canada, the United Kingdom, France, Germany, Italy, Japan) no longer set the global economic agenda. Global economic issues cannot be credibly tackled without the full involvement of large economies like those of China and India. Thus, the G-20 has emerged as a more representative, and therefore a more credible, organization, though it is yet to show that it is an effective one. The West is no longer able to impose its views on global trading rules on the rest of the world, and the WTO has been weakened. Western multinational companies no longer dominate global investments as before, and their share of the global economic pie is steadily shrinking. The rise of national oil companies of the non-West oil producing countries is much larger than that of the so-called independent Western oil companies that dominated the global oil business for decades. An increasing share of global wealth is in the hands of companies and individuals from India, China, Russia and the Arab world, who are snapping up businesses in the West. Citizens from these countries make up a significant proportion of the world's billionaires. Thus, it is evident that the current and looming foreign policy challenges are radically different from those of the twentieth century.

Troubling paradoxes remain in the way the world is organized and managed. New states and statelets, acutely conscious and protective of their sense of national identity and sovereignty, continue to mushroom, even as many states, both old and new, are losing control of their destinies, even their identities. Their predators are not only the large and powerful states but also non-state actors, like terrorist groups, drug mafia, non-governmental organizations (NGOs), multinational corporations, technology giants and a ubiquitous and invasive international media. However, the essentially nineteenth-century European construct of the nation-state retains its legitimacy as the basic political unit in the world. The UN has 193 members today, sharply up from just fifty-one in 1945. For their self-preservation, modern nation-states impose restrictions on migration, even though such restrictions go against the natural historical trend of unrestricted migration across the globe. Besides, falling birthrates in affluent countries and the unwillingness of their local populations to do low-end jobs creates a demand for migrant labour. Thus, migration across borders continues, much of it illegal, often creating humanitarian crises, spawning criminal activities and giving a boost to human trafficking. One cannot but be concerned about the alarming tendency of the major powers, in the name of self-determination, to break up established states and indulge in territorial aggrandizement. This flouts the accepted UN principle that self-determination applies only to states under colonial rule and should not be a legal fig leaf for the big powers to dismember states and create new fictitiously sovereign and unviable entities. These trends also disturbingly discount the model of the tolerant multicultural state, which in today's world is often the only safeguard against potential instability and strife. Such policies only validate renowned US political scientist, Samuel Huntington's pessimistic theory of the 'clash of civilizations',[3] which argued that in the post-Cold War world, conflicts in the world would be between civilizations rather than inter-state or ideological.

The world has, unfortunately, not tried to analyse the root causes of the depressing phenomenon of 'failed' and 'failing' states dotted around the world, surviving only with the help of economic, financial and military life-support systems provided by the major powers and international aid agencies. This state of affairs is not sustainable in the long term. Fragile states are like dormant volcanoes that may erupt any time, bringing destruction and misery in their vicinity. At the same time, the cooperation of these small, seemingly insignificant states is crucial when it comes to tackling new global threats like piracy, terrorism, arms smuggling, money laundering and drug trafficking, as well as the key issues of human survival (availability of water, energy and food, and climate change), over which war could break out among nations. The disruption of commercial shipping in the Red Sea as a consequence of attacks by the Houthis in impoverished Yemen brings this out dramatically. Any quest for a stable new world order will have to squarely deal with these contradictions.

US Power Plateau

It is questionable whether the United States can retain its 'full spectrum' domination of the world for too long. Even though it remains the preponderant and uniquely global power, the United States implicitly does acknowledge that its influence has noticeably dropped. Countries are no longer afraid to defy or ignore it. US inability to prevail in Vietnam, Afghanistan, Iraq and Syria has brought out the limits of US military power. The overwhelmingly large US military arsenal (its military spending overshadows that of all other major powers) is being threatened by the development of new weapons systems and asymmetrical capabilities by Russia and China to neutralize US military superiority. American political influence around the world is also on the decline. Cracks are developing in the US alliance structure. Hitherto obedient allies in Europe are deeply troubled by the US intention to fight a war to the end in Ukraine. They are seemingly helpless to do anything about it for the moment, but it wouldn't come as a surprise if they raise their voice against US policies that are hurting them economically and have flooded Europe with Ukrainian refugees and unaccounted lethal weaponry. Japan, no longer very confident about US security guarantees, has taken a policy decision to significantly strengthen its indigenous defence and security capabilities. There is even talk that Japan and South Korea are contemplating acquisition of nuclear weapons. A traditionally loyal ally like Saudi Arabia no longer obediently accedes to US demands to ramp up oil production to bring down oil prices. In a remarkable act of defiance, US allies like Jordan and Egypt cancelled their meeting with US President Biden during his visit to the region in October 2023 after the Hamas-Israel conflict erupted. Even Latin America, the United States' traditional backyard, is wriggling out of the hitherto tight US grip over it.

The situation is no better on the economic side. While the US economy remains the world's largest, its share in global economic output has come down. The gap between the US economy and fast-rising economies like those of China and India is narrowing. Sanctions against Russia and weaponization of the instruments of global finance controlled by the United States have made many countries wary about parking their foreign currency reserves largely in the US dollar. Many countries are quietly diversifying their enormous foreign exchange holdings, international transactions (including oil) and currency pegs away from the dollar. If these tendencies pick up momentum, the dollar could be at risk of losing its status as the world's reserve currency. Then there is the rising clout of sovereign wealth funds in the hands of the central banks of geopolitical rivals like China and Russia and the plentiful petrodollars in the hands of the Organization of the Petroleum Exporting Countries (OPEC) nations. The United States remains the world's largest debtor. All this is evidence enough that the long-dominant economic position of the United States is under threat. The United States is unlikely to be able to indefinitely retain its global dominance on the basis of its military and technological superiority in some areas. Even though the United States still arouses more admiration as well as envy than any other country, US soft power has lost some of its attractiveness. Global awareness about environmental challenges, climate change and health have made growing numbers of people realize that the US lifestyle is both unattainable and unsustainable. Thanks to the mindset generated by 9/11 and the resultant US obsession with security, the image of the United States in the world has changed. Instead of being regarded as a welcoming beacon of hope, refuge, freedom and prosperity, the United States is now viewed more as an armed fortress that seeks to protect an insecure and self-absorbed society. Bereft of the ideological cloak of the Cold War, the legitimacy of US hegemonic policies has eroded. The credibility of America's self-anointed 'leadership' role and as 'a force for good' is waning. Its platitudinous concern for democracy and human rights is increasingly viewed with suspicion and mistrust across the world.

From the perspective of its own national interests, the United States is, understandably, searching for a strategy that would preserve its unquestioned primacy in the world. It is looking for ways to counter these disturbing trends that are credibly threatening to dislodge it from its lofty and safe perch, and to hedge against looming uncertainties. It is therefore pursuing a foreign policy course that would enable it to retain its global domination (euphemistically termed 'leadership') in all respects—political, military, economic, technological and cultural. Although most Americans would recoil with horror at the thought, the United States is an empire, but now a declining one. As with most empires, the decline is likely to be long, bloody and messy.

Rising China

Will China dominate the twenty-first-century world? China is now openly acknowledged as a peer competitor and challenger to the United States. China-dominated organizations like the BRICS and the Shanghai Cooperation Organization (SCO) have expanded to include other powers. At the same time, many dark clouds hover over China too. For the last couple of decades or so, China has been growing impressively and seemingly inexorably, but there are signs that its economic miracle could be running out of steam. Its model of development requires an ever-expanding availability of raw materials and commodities as well as markets that cannot be taken for granted. China's growing demands are also bringing it into conflict with competing countries also seeking access to limited and fast-depleting natural resources. It is extremely doubtful if the Chinese have developed a superior management technique that has eluded all other societies and have managed to evolve a model of economic development that successfully overcomes irreconcilables. Today there is enough evidence of fundamental weaknesses in the Chinese system that would seem to rule out a linear upward graph of China's economic growth—declining population; a rickety financial and banking system; curbs on successful entrepreneurs; unprofitable state-owned enterprises; a property bubble; simmering discontent in the rural areas; growing economic and regional disparities; and looming environmental disasters. China's much touted but inherently exploitative Belt and Road Initiative (BRI) has run into many roadblocks; countries across the world have become wary as they realize that the unviability of BRI projects could result in their national assets falling into the hands of China. If, despite the odds, China proves the sceptics wrong and continues to grow, this would be deeply problematic for many countries, including India.

Nor does China's recent political history give cause for comfort. Political change in China over the last century has come about through violent means. China's dilemma is that the political legitimacy of the Communist Party of China depends on its ability to deliver a high level of economic growth. There are signs of a pushback against Xi Jinping, who has concentrated all power in his own hands, eliminated his political rivals and managed to ensure that he can remain in power for life. This makes for an inherently unstable political system. No country as large as China has been able to combine consistently high economic growth over a long period with an authoritarian political system. In the absence of a reliable mechanism to transfer political power from the Communist Party of China to a more broad-based coalition of interest groups, the danger of destabilizing political violence cannot be brushed aside. China suffers from a 'pressure cooker syndrome'. A pressure cooker is safe only when the whistle blows periodically as steam is released. China does not seem to have any pressure-release mechanisms. It seeks to create an impression that all is well in the country, but that is far from true. Public protests against China's zero-Covid approach compelled the authorities to abandon this failed policy. Other festering sores in China's social, economic and political systems are likely to erupt. Will China's pressure cooker one day explode with a bang?

Taiwan is an obvious flashpoint. Tensions with Taiwan have sharply risen as it makes it increasingly clear that it is not in favour of reunification with China, which has meanwhile ratcheted up its military posture and pressures on Taiwan. However, despite the fiery rhetoric,

China is likely to exercise caution lest it should draw the United States into a China–Taiwan conflict. An important factor weighing on the minds of all actors would be Taiwan's global dominance in the manufacture of semiconductors. Yet the biggest potential threat to China may not be from Taiwan, but from Tibet and East Turkestan (now called Xinjiang), non-Han areas that have been colonized by China. Although China has managed to put down the upheavals in Tibet that have periodically erupted over the last fifteen years, the Tibet story is not over. The disaffection of the Tibetans extends deep into the interior of Tibet. Similarly, the authorities' heavy-handed policies in East Turkestan aimed at eradicating Uighur culture and traditions have only deepened the alienation of the local population. Although brutally suppressed, the Tibetans and Uighurs refuse to be cowed down. In the twentieth century, between the fall of the Manchu dynasty in 1911 and the communist takeover of China in 1949, both Tibet and East Turkestan functioned as de facto independent states and were recognized as such by other states. The unpleasant reality about China is that, like other imperial powers, it too will find it nigh impossible over the long term to hold on to its conquered domains—the sprawling buffer zones of East Turkestan, Tibet, Manchuria and Inner Mongolia—unless all sections of its population, including the dominant ruling Hans as well as the non-Han conquered peoples, like the Buddhist Tibetans in Tibet and the Muslim Uighurs in East Turkestan, feel that they are equal stakeholders, not rulers and subjects. A truly serious problem would arise if myriad revolts across the country involving the Tibetans, Uighurs and other disaffected groups like the Falun Gong coalesce into a common movement.

Russia's Resurgence

Defeated though it may have been in the Cold War and its Soviet and East European empires dismembered, Russia is not to be underestimated. In the twenty-first century, under President Putin, Russia has got back on its feet, rebuilt state structures and regained its badly dented self-confidence. High oil prices facilitated Russia's economic recovery and growth. With its debts repaid and with huge foreign exchange reserves in its kitty, Russia today is in a combative and chauvinistic mood. For the last couple of decades, Russia has given priority to rebuilding its military through an ambitious programme of expansion and modernization. Russia is once again forcefully resisting aggressive US intrusions into its strategic neighbourhood. Russia's blitzkrieg against Georgia in August 2008, its takeover of Crimea in 2014 and its ongoing 'special military operations' in Ukraine emphatically demonstrate the resurgence of Russian power. Russia remains a technology leader in many critical areas and will do its utmost to ensure that it retains the unique capacity to be able to threaten the physical destruction of the United States—the principal reason why the United States is compelled to take Russia seriously.

Even though Russia has regained its appetite to be an assertive global player, especially as an energy superpower, it faces formidable challenges, such as a declining population, threats to its internal cohesion and stability, and an immature political system. The harsh sanctions imposed by the West, which are unlikely to be lifted any time soon, have adversely impacted Russia's economy, but much less than what the West had hoped.

Rise of Asia and Africa

Till recently, it was believed that the twenty-first century would be an 'Asian century' where China and India would play increasingly decisive roles in world affairs. The fulcrum of global politics and economics is indeed inexorably shifting towards the Asia-Pacific. However, new nuances have emerged. One is growing India-China mistrust and rivalry, which is unlikely to abate in the immediate future. The second is the rising profile of the Persian Gulf region and Africa. After five centuries of being dominated by Western colonialism and imperialism, the world is now in a post-colonial era. A resource-poor West has lost its comfort zone. It can no longer predicate its growth and development on exploitation of natural and human resources across the world, nor treat the developing countries as a mere market for its manufactured products. This is hardly surprising. Historically, China and India have led global economic growth. Today, they are the second and fifth largest global economies respectively, and are rapidly growing. Nearly 60 per cent of the world's population lives in Asia and the Pacific.[4] Other influential countries in Asia include Japan, South Korea, Taiwan, Vietnam, Indonesia, Iran, Saudi Arabia and Turkey.

Sometimes the question is raised as to whether there is really a single 'Asia', and whether what is called Asia is only many regions that have little in common with one another. Such an assertion begs the question as to whether there can be a 'Europe' despite the centuries' old tradition of inter-state rivalry and conflict among its constituents. How can one deny that Asia has some factors that give it a civilizational unity? Just as European civilization is based on Greco-Roman and Judeo-Christian traditions, democracy and individual rights, Asian societies have their roots in the common spiritual and philosophic traditions of Hinduism, Buddhism, Jainism, Sikhism and Confucianism, which stress collective social harmony and obligations over individual rights. It is noteworthy that Asia has no history of religious or sectarian conflicts involving Hinduism, Buddhism, Jainism and Sikhism. Islam's religious moorings derive from the same traditions as other religions of the Book, though its social mores are more akin to those of other Asian countries. It is Europe's experience of divisiveness and conflict that led its constituents to pursue, during colonial times and even today, policies that created divisions where none existed earlier. This is not to minimize other differences among Asians, nor to suggest that Asia can become a European Union clone. Yet there is a definite Asian identity, admittedly somewhat elusive, based on a common heritage and colonial experience.

Africa's importance will also grow in the twenty-first century. Its rich natural agricultural and mineral resources, as well as its size, its growing population (currently almost one fifth of the global population) and critical geographical location are attracting the attention of the rest of the world. China, India and Russia are increasingly influential in Africa while the footprint of the West is reducing. One thing is reasonably clear: the geopolitical tussles of the twenty-first century will play out in Asia and Africa, because of geography, demographics, and economic strength. This is not to ignore the serious problems facing Asia and Africa, such as militant Islam, terrorism, drugs, piracy and failing states. It is in Asia and Africa that hope springs and, equally, where fears arise.

Whither India?

If the world has changed, so has India's geopolitical situation. As a result of the Partition of British India in 1947, India has both lost (Pakistan, Bangladesh) and regained territory (Hyderabad, Junagadh, other princely states, Nagaland, Tawang, Goa, Sikkim and Pondicherry). Thus, India's neighbours have changed after 1947. To India's northwest, Afghanistan, Iran and Central Asia are no longer geographically contiguous with it. Across the Himalayas, instead of a benign Tibet and East Turkestan, India has an aggressive China as a neighbour. Moreover, fluid frontier regions have given way to hard borders on maps and messy ground realities. India now has to deal with immediate neighbours who are very sensitive about their sovereignty and independence. Outside powers, first the British, then the Americans and now the Chinese, have been trying to keep the Indian subcontinent divided and fractious, as that prevents India from realizing its potential as a global player.

Another important change in India is worth noting. Till a couple of decades ago, foreign policy was not seen as a matter to which the country needed to give special attention or an area where it needed to work out a careful strategy. In the first quarter century after India's Independence, Prime Minister Nehru's assessments and policies, with the exception of his China policy, were widely accepted by the country. As a relatively weak state striving to build a newly independent nation, and subject to the considerable influence of foreign powers, India's foreign policy was basically defensive, except in the matter of its immediate neighbourhood. In the post-Nehru era too, India's interactions, both political and economic, with the rest of the world were relatively limited. India did pursue with some success, and often at considerable cost, an independent foreign policy. Today, in a complex and challenging geopolitical environment, India is much stronger, more confident, increasingly influential and better able to resist outside pressures. A new generation of Indians is not content to see India as an 'also-ran'. It has the ambition to see India become a major global player. The formidable challenge before India is how to ensure such an outcome.

Chapter 2

'Akhand Bharat?'

Why does India have so many problems with its neighbours? The short answer is: the baneful effects of the politics of cultural identity throughout South Asia, arising out of a collective failure to recognize and acknowledge that this region has a distinctive personality, and its nations an intertwined history, arising out of its definite geographic identity. Virtually cut off from the rest of the world by the Himalayas to the north, the Indian Ocean to the south, thick forests to the east and barren lands to the west, its inhabitants traditionally had relatively little contact with the outside world. At the same time, the absence of any significant internal geographical barriers, other than the central Indian forests and mountains (accounting for the somewhat different histories north and south of the Vindhyas) created an inevitable geographical, cultural, economic and ecological interdependence of all parts of this vast expanse of territory. These circumstances gave to the heartland of the Indian subcontinent—covering the bulk of the territory of present-day India, Pakistan and Bangladesh—a broadly common history and led to the evolution of a unique civilization and culture. Remote and insulated in the pre-modern era from the cultural influences of the mainland by jungles, mountains and the ocean, the periphery of the subcontinent (Sri Lanka, Maldives, Nepal, Bhutan, Baluchistan, the North-West Frontier and tribal regions of Pakistan and India's North-east) had a more autonomous development and therefore more distinctive cultures. But even these regions had considerable interaction with the heartland and were greatly influenced by it.

Generally, culture is the most important component of an individual's personality. It is also, for most countries around the world, the prime component of their national identity. This is even truer for a land as steeped in culture and tradition as South Asia, where religion is the key element that has shaped the collective personality of the people and governs their daily lives. South Asia's religions have many common elements. An offshoot of Hinduism, Buddhism rejected the evils of the Hindu caste system but retained its moral and ethical codes, and the principal features of its philosophy. Buddha is revered among Hindus as an avatar of Vishnu. Islam, as practised in south Asia, has a distinct subcontinental character, very different from the Islam practised in the Arab world, in South-east Asia and Africa. It has not been able to transcend many Hindu traditions, including the caste system (whence the unique category of 'Dalit Muslims'). This is not so surprising, considering that the overwhelming majority of the Muslims in the subcontinent are converts from Hinduism. For the same reason, there are Dalits among South Asia's Christians and Sikhs too. Despite the fundamental anti-caste character of Sikhism, the caste system has carried over into Sikh traditions as well. The dividing line between Hinduism and Sikhism, at least in the popular perception, is somewhat blurred. Hindus and Sikhs freely visit gurudwaras and temples, and intermarry. Some Hindu families have a tradition that one son becomes a Sikh while the others remain Hindu.

In South Asia, neither religion, nor race, nor language constitutes the basis of its identity. On the other hand, there is commonality in dress, food habits, marriage and social customs and, most importantly, ways of thinking. The South Asian obsession with cricket reflects a common culture. Popular films, music, songs and dance transcend political frontiers. All South Asian countries have an uncanny common political culture. Bandhs, gheraos, hartals and other street protests as a means to seek redressal of grievances are widespread throughout the region. Other commonalities are the political legitimacy of heredity and kinship, the ability of women to become political leaders and, regrettably, political violence. Probably no other part of the world has seen so many political assassinations. All these common characteristics can be explained by the deep cultural and psychological bonds, a kind of emotional unity, among people across south Asia, arising out of their subconscious recognition that they have common civilizational roots.

Outsiders too have regarded India—not the modern nation-state of India but the geographical entity of South Asia—as a distinct civilization. Tales of India's fabled wealth and rich culture fascinated them and aroused their curiosity. Soldiers and plunderers, traders and travellers, strove to reach *India*, whether it was the Macedonian Alexander or the Chinese travellers Xuan Zhang and Fa Hien, the Arab Ibn Batuta or the Turks and Mongols from Central Asia. When the Spanish and the Portuguese started their voyages of exploration in the fifteenth century, it was in search of a sea route to *India*. While Vasco da Gama actually reached India in 1498, Christopher Columbus, who reached the shores of the American continent a few years earlier, thought he had reached *India*. In the pre-modern era, Europeans understandably initially mistook other parts of the world with which they came into contact to be India since they were aware of only the Indian civilization as another flourishing, developed civilization, apart from their own. Thus, the European immigrants to the Americas called the indigenous people of the Americas *Indians*, be it the 'Red Indians', or the 'Indians' of the Mayan and Inca civilizations of Central and South America. The West Indies and the East Indies got their names in a similar fashion. The impact of 'Indian civilization' extended to countries on the Indian Ocean rim, and even across the Himalayas to Central Asia, where the fascination for India continues unabated. It is worth recalling all this to emphasize that throughout history outsiders recognized and admired India's unique civilization and culture. British colonial rule gave rise to a shared elite culture in undivided India. The thinking and attitude, even the language (a mix of English with the local languages) of the elite in India, Pakistan, Bangladesh and Sri Lanka in the immediate post-colonial period, were common. So were the institutions and laws. In countries where the British impact was not so direct, for example Nepal and Bhutan, their respective elites are distinctive.

Historically, the dividing lines between the different religious, linguistic, ethnic and other South Asian communities were never sharp or clear-cut. All modern South Asian countries are multi-ethnic and multi-religious societies, and attempts to repudiate the reality that religious and cultural roots extend beyond national frontiers lead to many inconvenient and illogical contradictions. The holy Vedas of the Hindus have their origins in the territory of present-day Pakistan. The subcontinental Muslim culture and the Urdu language, which Pakistan claims as its cultural heritage, have their roots in Delhi and western Uttar Pradesh. The holy places of Buddhism, the dominant religion in Bhutan, Sri Lanka and northern Nepal, are in India and the Terai belt of Nepal, where Buddhism does not have any strong roots or a large following. Nankana Sahib, the birthplace of Guru Nanak, the founder of Sikhism, and many major Sikh shrines are in present-day Pakistan. The word 'Hindustan', which means the abode of the Hindus, derives from the word 'Hind' or 'Sindh'. To invaders streaming down the Khyber Pass, 'Hindus' were the inhabitants of the land beyond the first major natural barrier, the river Sindh, or Indus. Pakistan's attempts to find a new identity for itself, by clawing at tenuous linkages with West and Central Asia, while denying its deep historical, cultural and other links with the South Asian sub-continent, have proved futile. It is not easy to uproot or disown a cultural inheritance going back many centuries.

The question of cultural identity is not merely theoretical but has profound practical relevance. It has affected South Asian inter-state relations as well as the internal politics of all South Asian countries. Differences over culture have retarded development in all these countries. The creation of Pakistan was a manifestation of cultural separatism. The essence of Pakistan's ideology is a denial of its common cultural roots with India. Cultural identity figures high in the politics of other South Asian countries too. For Bangladesh, its War of Liberation in 1971 was about preserving its cultural identity against West Pakistani, specifically Punjabi, political and economic domination. However, in reasserting Bengali nationalism, it has excluded the other cultural and social groups like the Adibashis, the Chakmas and the Garos.

In recent years, it has been understating its Bengali character, which it has in common with West Bengal, and overstating its Islamic character. For decades, Nepal retained its sense of identity by emphasizing the role of the Hindu monarch as a factor of unity in the country, as well as by observing small but telling practices, like a unique time zone, a unique flag shape and a unique official dress. Bhutan's deliberate policy of remaining in isolation is intended to preserve its cultural identity. The origins of the internal war in Sri Lanka that lasted more than two decades lie in the attempt of the Sinhala community to evolve a Sinhala-Buddhist cultural identity to the exclusion of the country's Tamil heritage. The Maldives, isolated from the mainland, developed a unique national identity created out of the interplay of influences from India, Sri Lanka, as well as the Persian and Arab world, but it has become a fundamentalist society after Islam was designated as the official religion and the citizens of Maldives prohibited from practising any other religion.

Common Heritage vs Modern Identities

The modern nations of South Asia have emerged as separate entities just over seven and a half decades ago, a relatively short period in the history of this ancient land. As sovereign and independent countries, they have acquired new political and juridical personalities, taken separate paths of development, and understandably sought to project a distinct cultural tradition as an expression of their nationalism and separate identity. Without that, their very raison d'être would weaken. South Asian leaders who routinely and grandly proclaim that poverty alleviation and people's welfare are the foremost concerns for them should first analyse why the whole of South Asia is so backward. Obviously, it is not because of paucity of resources (no other part of the world is so blessed with abundant sunshine and water) or because people are not talented or hard-working (south Asians seem to do very well when they migrate abroad). South Asia has not developed or progressed as much as it could have because the people of South Asia over-emphasize their newest identity as citizens of one country or another and underplay their shared cultural heritage and traditions with other South Asians. South Asia's tragedy is that its people have been artificially divided on the basis of ethnicity, caste and religion, first by their colonial masters and then by their own political elites.

A major challenge before all South Asian countries is the question of how to reconcile and harmonize the common cultural heritage of the South Asian subcontinent with preserving their separate modern political identities. Questions arise. How long can a country keep alive its artificially cultivated identity by a selective emphasis on some, and a deliberate denial of other, elements of its past? Are centuries-old traditions less important than decades-old ones? Is religious identity more important than regional or cultural identity? Is modern experience more relevant than ancient inheritance?

The way it has been handled in South Asia so far, culture has been a divisive and debilitating factor. It need not be so. The common cultural heritage of South Asia can, and should, promote unity, harmony and mutually beneficial development. South Asia has had a long tradition of communal harmony and peaceful coexistence through the centuries, at least till the colonial era. Rulers may have been intolerant, but at the popular level South Asia was spared prolonged bloody religious wars like the Crusades or the Catholic–Protestant enmities of medieval times. However, since the birth of new nations in South Asia in the second half of the twentieth century, this region has been beset with enormous violence and killings.

Modern South Asia's political borders are colonial, not natural. True, South Asia has never been a homogenous political unit. But never in its history has it been divided along such irrational lines. It is not possible to have mono-religious, or ethnically or linguistically homogenous states in south Asia. The idea was tried through the creation of Pakistan in 1947, but has failed. In Sri Lanka, despite the elimination of the LTTE in a civil war that lasted more than two decades, Tamil grievances remain unresolved, and it is evident that a Sinhala-Buddhist-dominated Sri Lanka will remain inherently unstable. The Nepali ruling elite, dominated by people from the hills, cannot wish away the Madheshis of the Terai who constitute nearly half the population of Nepal. Unfortunately, many South Asian countries have wrapped their respective national flags around an exclusivist, somewhat artificial, identity based on religion or ethnicity. Therein lie the roots of many of South Asia's political and economic problems. Is South Asia one of the poorest regions in the world because South Asian political leaders have deliberately chosen to underplay the interdependence, complementarities and commonalities of the region? Instead of taking advantage of their common cultural heritage and natural synergies (including institutions and interconnected physical infrastructure inherited from the colonial times) to collectively play their rightful role in the world, South Asians are a divided lot working at cross-purposes. Instead of using their common traditions to increase their collective strength and bargaining power, South Asians are enfeebled by internal rivalries and jealousies.

Most of the controversies, agitations, violence and killings in South Asia have been over cultural identity rather than over economic issues. Some of the key factors that have shaped India's political life in recent years have been communal problems involving Hindus and Muslims (and lately Christians too), the issue of 'secular' vs 'communal' parties, the controversy over 'Hindutva', and the rejection by the Dalits and the other backward castes (OBCs) of the idea that they share a common cultural legacy with the upper-caste Hindus. Pakistan broke up over the inability of the system to accommodate Bengali nationalism. Punjabi Sunni political, economic and cultural domination in Pakistan has continued to provoke widespread Shia-Sunni violence and separatist movements in the North-West Frontier Province (NWFP), Baluchistan and Sindh. Sri Lanka was wracked by debilitating ethnic violence over the Tamil issue for over two decades. In Nepal, the grievances of the people in Terai are ethno-cultural, reflecting the resentment and anger of the Madheshis over continuing domination of the hill people in all aspects of life in the country. A democratic polity is the only effective long-term way to tackle secessionism, communal violence, sectarian conflict and fundamentalism, and to ensure peace, prosperity and stability in South Asia.

Regional Cooperation in South Asia

Across the world, countries generally have a substantial percentage of their overall foreign trade with neighbouring countries. This is not so in South Asia. South Asia's forays into regional cooperation have been unimpressive. It was only in 1985, nearly four decades after the modern nations of South Asia came into being, that the South Asian Association for Regional Cooperation (SAARC) was set up. Despite so many agreed areas of cooperation, innumerable institutional mechanisms and a permanent secretariat, it has not taken off as a meaningful framework for regional cooperation. Since its founding, SAARC has held only eighteen summits, the last one a decade ago. The absence of any substantive results is masked by an exaggerated emphasis on hyperbole, public rhetoric, formalism, protocol and pomposity. So far, SAARC has been basically a talk-shop, or at best a consultative body, with few successful concrete collaborative projects. The relatively low level of regional trade and economic activity in the region only underlines the large untapped potential.

SAARC suffers from some fundamental structural flaws. Mutual suspicion and political hesitation have been the biggest stumbling block. Without a shared political and strategic perspective, the necessary trust and goodwill for meaningful regional economic cooperation is missing. Secondly, India is overwhelmingly dominant in South Asia but has had difficulty in convincing its neighbours that it is a true regional leader rather than the neighbourhood bully. The list of items that its SAARC partners can competitively export to India is very limited, which means that trade in the region is heavily balanced in India's favour. That does not go down well with India's neighbours. Thirdly, intra-South Asian connectivity is woefully inadequate. Apart from Pakistan and Afghanistan, land connectivity among all the other non-Indian South Asian countries is only via India. Air connections frequently require transit via India. Fourthly, the smaller countries of South Asia have more in common with the neighbouring regions of India than with other geographically distant South Asian countries. Fifthly, many members of SAARC have do not have just a South Asian history and culture; they also have non-South Asian connections, which they try to over-emphasize—Pakistan with Central and West Asia; Afghanistan with Central Asia and Iran; Nepal with Tibet; Sri Lanka and the Maldives with the Indian Ocean. Sixthly, SAARC decisions require unanimity, which means that it is easy for any one country to block decisions. Finally, as SAARC has not shown itself to be meaningful to the lives of ordinary people, there is no domestic constituency for it in the member countries. Unsurprisingly, SAARC has floundered, even though it is self-evident that cooperative, trustful and harmonious relations between South Asian countries could make this region a truly dynamic engine of growth and global influence.

India, Pakistan and Bangladesh, the three largest countries in South Asia, bear collective responsibility for this situation. The remaining five SAARC member countries are, in geographical, demographic and economic terms, on the periphery of SAARC. Three (Nepal, Bhutan and Afghanistan) are landlocked, and the other two (Sri Lanka and the Maldives) are islands. Despite periodic bouts of tension, so far India has had no serious security problems with any of these five smaller states, which are happy and eager to take advantage of India's proximity and economic dynamism. When President Zia-ur-Rahman of Bangladesh first proposed the setting up of SAARC in the early 1980s, it was not born out of any genuine desire for regional cooperation but to create a mechanism for India's smaller neighbours to gang up against India. As for Pakistan, its obsession with trying to bring India down, including by fomenting terrorist activities against India and harbouring a mindset of seeking 'equality' with India, engenders a competitive and hostile rather than cooperative approach. Contrary to its WTO obligations, it does not grant Most-Favoured-Nation (MFN) treatment to India and has linked normal trade relations with India to a resolution of the Jammu and Kashmir question.

Given this situation, India has understandably not been enthusiastic about SAARC. Although it does not, and cannot, openly oppose SAARC, it has tended to regard its summits mostly as a venue for bilateral diplomacy with Pakistan or to signal unhappiness with a neighbour. India, under Prime Minister Modi, appears to have given up on SAARC as a meaningful vehicle of regional cooperation. Bilateral cooperation with willing neighbours, sub-regional cooperation through structures like the BBIN (comprising Bangladesh, Bhutan, India and Nepal) and alternative regional organizations like the Bay of Bengal Initiative for Multi-Sectoral Technical and Economic Cooperation (BIMSTEC) have become India's preferred regional mechanisms to deal with its neighbours. For the moment, the prospects of SAARC are bleak, and it is likely to sputter on aimlessly.

The uncertainties of SAARC have given added importance to BIMSTEC, which brings together the countries around the Bay of Bengal: Sri Lanka, India, Nepal, Bhutan, Bangladesh, Myanmar and Thailand. India's North-east region lies in the middle of the BIMSTEC region. Unlike SAARC, BIMSTEC is a geographically coherent and logical grouping with a better balance of power than the former since the dependence of India's North-east region on Bangladesh and Myanmar considerably reduces India's preponderance in the grouping. BIMSTEC is seen as a practical and desirable bridging mechanism between South Asia and its eastern neighbours. From a long-term perspective, India's North-east region and Bangladesh could be potentially converted from relatively poor regions on the periphery of the South Asian subcontinent into the fulcrum of a thriving and integrated economic and cultural space linking India and South-east Asia. BIMSTEC also complements and supplements India's engagement with ASEAN, since BIMSTEC members Myanmar and Thailand are also members of ASEAN. Bangladesh's attitude is the key element that will determine the success of BIMSTEC. It seems to have realized that by coming on board India's 'Act East' train, it could benefit enormously from its integration into a wider Asian framework.

BIMSTEC was set up in 1997 as an economic cooperation group consisting of Bangladesh, India, Sri Lanka and Thailand. Myanmar joined it in 1997, and Nepal and Bhutan in 2004. It held its first summit in Thailand in July 2004, but over the next decade only one more summit (in India in 2008) was held. BIMSTEC lost momentum because many of its members were distracted by their own domestic political preoccupations. Under Prime Minister Thaksin, Thailand was an enthusiastic proponent of BIMSTEC, but its interest in BIMSTEC flagged after Thaksin was ousted and a military regime took power in that country in 2006. India has been the other key driver of BIMSTEC. Under the Congress-led United Progressive Alliance (UPA) government, India was more focused on SAARC (as part of its policy of engaging Pakistan). As SAARC has floundered, BIMSTEC has become more important in India's regional diplomacy. Over the last decade or so, BIMSTEC has acquired greater substance and stability. Three more BIMSTEC summits have been held (in Myanmar in 2014, Nepal in 2018, and Sri Lanka in 2022). A BIMSTEC secretariat was established in Dhaka in 2014. This gives Bangladesh important stakes in the success of BIMSTEC. In 2022, two important decisions were taken: BIMSTEC adopted a charter (ratified in 2024); and the areas of cooperation were narrowed down from an unwieldy fourteen to seven, with a different BIMSTEC member acting as the lead in a particular sector. The seven areas of cooperation are trade, investment and development (Bangladesh); environment and climate change (Bhutan); security and energy (India); agriculture and food security (Myanmar); people-to-people contact (Nepal); science, technology and innovation (Sri Lanka); and connectivity (Thailand). However, there is the danger that, with Myanmar beset by serious internal turmoil, BIMSTEC could stagnate once again.

South Asian cooperation will take off only when all its constituent countries regard their primary identity as South Asian, and if the focus of regional cooperation is on areas where the common interests of the member countries outweigh their differences. Environmental challenges, control of communicable diseases and pandemics, dealing with terrorism, countering drug smuggling and tackling the trafficking of women and children are potential areas of cooperation requiring urgent attention. One critical area is the harnessing of the region's water resources. Given the common geography, there is a vital need for much greater cooperation in harnessing and managing water resources. To be fair, South Asia has already done much better than similarly placed countries elsewhere in the world. With Pakistan, India has signed the Indus Waters Treaty (1960) and with Bangladesh, the Ganga Waters Treaty (1996) and the Kushiyara Water Sharing Agreement (2022). However, South Asian countries have insufficiently internalized the idea that their very survival in the long term depends on ensuring that the rivers that flow into the subcontinent from Tibet—not just the major rivers like the Indus, Sutlej, Karnali/Ghaghra and the Brahmaputra, but smaller ones too—are not obstructed in any way. Middle riparian India bears the brunt of any untoward happenings in Tibet (as happened when the Sutlej flooded large parts of Himachal Pradesh in 2000, and as the Parechu river threatened to in 2004), but any depletion of water flows into India will ultimately affect lower riparians Pakistan and Bangladesh too. This is a real danger, since China is actively building dams on, and even has plans to divert, rivers rising in Tibet and flowing into the Indian subcontinent. Any irresponsible Chinese activity in Tibet could accelerate the shrinking of Tibetan glaciers and change the climate that sustains hundreds of million people living in South Asia. Chinese activities that induce climate change in South Asia would definitely be considered a hostile act by all South Asian countries. Climate change could threaten the very existence of a low-lying country like Bangladesh or a small island country like the Maldives. Thus, all South Asian countries have a legitimate interest in having a dialogue with China on this point. India does have agreements with China for exchange of hydrological data, but these are not working to India's satisfaction. It would be desirable if India, Pakistan and Bangladesh could jointly broach this subject with China. They could also consult with countries like Russia, Kazakhstan, Cambodia, Laos, Vietnam and Myanmar that face similar problems vis-à-vis China. However, for the moment, that is a goal too far, since China's policies in South Asia are designed to drive a wedge between India and its South Asian neighbours.

If South Asia were a united and vibrant region, it could easily extend its reach and spread its influence to the Persian Gulf, Central Asia and South-east Asia—all regions where, historically, Indian influence has been preponderant. It is only because South Asia itself has been divided that India has lost its natural influence in these regions and other powers have stepped in. For example, all South Asian nations, particularly India, Pakistan and Bangladesh, have common interests and vital stakes in the Persian Gulf region. More than half a billion South Asian Muslims have close emotional and spiritual bonds to the holy places of Islam in the region, like Mecca, Medina, Najaf and Karbala. Millions of exploited workers from South Asia, together with the rich expatriates, constitute a very large proportion of the population of the Persian Gulf kingdoms and sheikhdoms and are critical to their functioning and prosperity. All South Asian countries have overwhelming energy dependency on the Persian Gulf region. Similarly, if Pakistan can somehow be persuaded to change its traditional mindset, it can work with India and Afghanistan in re-establishing South Asia's traditionally strong but now considerably weakened contacts with Central Asia. To India's east, the optimal success of India's Act East Policy requires, at the very least, Bangladesh's cooperation.

Whatever the proponents of 'Akhand Bharat' might think, it is unrealistic to imagine that the Indian subcontinent will ever be reunited. Nor is this necessary or even desirable. However, dramatic developments do sometimes occur completely unexpectedly, as seen in Europe. While retaining their respective political sovereignties, European countries have set aside their deep-seated historical animosities to come together in an unprecedentedly peaceful and cooperative relationship. It is doubtful if the soldiers who fought in World War II could have imagined in their wildest dreams that their great-grandchildren would be born in a Europe without borders and with a single currency. It took Europeans thirty-five years from the signing of the Treaty of Rome in 1957 that set up the European Economic Community to set up a European Union by the Treaty of Maastricht in 1992. Of course, the European project is now facing an uncertain future after Britain's exit from the European Union (Brexit) and as divergent strategic and economic perspectives of the twenty-seven members of the EU and their internecine rivalries are becoming visible. Is it too much to dream that one day the artificial South Asian political order established following the Partition of undivided India will be undone and that there could be open borders and free movement of people, goods and capital among South Asian countries? It may come about, but perhaps only when the younger generations of South Asians, which do not carry bitter memories of old feuds and antagonisms, begin to wield political power.

Chapter 3

Pakistan and Afghanistan

Pakistan's Troubled Identity

Pakistan is India's most difficult neighbour and cannot be dealt with like its other South Asian neighbours for a number of reasons—its mindset; its strategic significance for outside powers; its military, nuclear and missile capabilities; and its territorial dispute with India over Kashmir. The most important difference between Pakistan and India's other neighbours is that for both countries the relationship is as much a domestic as a foreign policy issue, even if politicians are reluctant to admit this. Pakistan's raison d'être, simply put, is that the Muslims of India cannot live and prosper in a single state dominated by Hindus. India obviously feels differently, and this gives rise to Pakistan's political compulsion to prove otherwise. Hence the centrality in India's political discourse of so-called 'secularism'—a concept that arose in medieval Europe against the history of church-state conflict, but which, transplanted on an alien Indian soil, has acquired a totally different meaning that has much to do with politics and little with religion. In India, where faith and religion are a central and integral element in the lives of most people, the state needs to treat all religions even-handedly. It has to be active in educating the people in the essential tenets of all religions and not be indifferent to religion. It is because secularism has become a political football that there is so much sensitivity in India in the matter of religious divisions rather than in the far more deep-rooted and pernicious caste divisions that all political parties are unfortunately encouraging and exploiting.

It complicates matters when Pakistan arrogates to itself the role of being the protector of the rights and welfare of Indian Muslims while persecuting the dwindling numbers of Hindus and Sikhs in Pakistan.

Seven and a half decades after its independence, Pakistan continues to search for a durable and credible identity other than its being 'not Indian'. Pakistan's rulers constantly strive to show how the country is equal to, if not better than, India in all respects. The complex psychology of the Pakistani ruling elite, dominated by the military, is seen in a small but telling illustration: some of Pakistan's missiles are, curiously, named after various foreign invaders who ravaged India, including the territory of present-day Pakistan, centuries ago! In particular, even after more than five decades, the Indian role in the creation of Bangladesh continues to rankle, with the Pakistani military in search of 'revenge' for its humiliating defeat in 1971. The mindset of the ruling elite is a cocktail of arrogance and brashness, at times bordering on cockiness, which has of late become even more potent with the addition of a measure of fundamentalism. This has led to a policy of unremitting hostility towards India, which periodically breaks out into conflict. The Pakistani ruling elite's perception of their country's place in the region and the world has led to Pakistan pursuing policies that have held back economic and social development and progress, not only in its own country but also in South Asia as a whole. The deleterious consequences of Pakistan's approach have been the creation of artificial barriers with India, the expending of tremendous resources, time and energy to sustaining Indo-Pakistan tension, and confrontation and wars that have vitiated the overall atmosphere in South Asia. Regrettably, outside powers have, for their own reasons, encouraged and abetted Pakistan by providing it the money, arms and technology to sustain its aggressive and confrontationist policies towards India.

India's policy towards Pakistan has oscillated like a pendulum. The two countries have fought military battles on the ground in South Asia, diplomatic battles throughout the world and cricket battles on playing fields. Diplomatic, transport and other links between the two have been disrupted from time to time. At the same time, Indian prime ministers like Rajiv Gandhi, Inder Kumar Gujral, Atal Bihari Vajpayee and Manmohan Singh frequently gave in to romanticized sentimentalism about Pakistan. Other prime ministers too have been gullible and lenient towards Pakistan. After the 1947-48 war in Kashmir, Nehru took the matter to the UN Security Council, where India has faced endless troubles. After the 1965 conflict, Lal Bahadur Shastri agreed to an uneasy peace brokered in Tashkent in 1966. Even after India's decisive victory in the 1971 war, a trusting Indira Gandhi let Pakistan off the hook by signing the 1972 Shimla Agreement that, among other things, put off a final settlement of Jammu and Kashmir. In 2002, after fully mobilizing the Indian armed forces, Vajpayee held back from attacking Pakistan. Even after the horrific terror attacks in Mumbai in 2008, in which the state of Pakistan definitely had a hand, Manmohan Singh did nothing by way of retaliation against Pakistan.

While India's intention in all these cases was probably not to aggravate the situation, its reasonableness has invariably been misinterpreted as a sign of weakness and has only served to reinforce the traditional Pakistani military stereotype of India as a flabby, ineffective giant. Given such misconceptions, it is not surprising that most of the outstanding problems between the two countries remain unresolved. There are no quick fixes; the most realistic hope is that the two countries can manage the problems. India should be patient.

Recent Trends

After both India and Pakistan became declared nuclear powers in 1998, the nuclear factor made the prospect of war between the two countries more dangerous than that of traditional war, such as the wars of 1965 and 1971. This emboldened Pakistan to engage in risky provocations. Its response to Prime Minister Vajpayee's bus journey to Lahore was its Kargil misadventure in the summer of 1999. The failed Agra summit of 2001 led to the attack on India's Parliament a few months later, as a result of which India and Pakistan almost went to war in 2002. It is also true that both in 1999 and 2002, international pressure played a role in preventing the situation from escalating. Prime

Minister Vajpayee did not give up his quest for peaceful relations with Pakistan, and his persistence did eventually yield results. In 2003, both countries agreed to a ceasefire along the Line of Control. Following an agreement between General Musharraf and Prime Minister Vajpayee in January 2004, wherein Musharraf agreed that he would not permit any territory under Pakistan's control to be used to support terrorism, the suspended regular composite dialogue headed at the Foreign Secretary level, supplemented by a high-level political dialogue, was resumed in 2004. The Joint Commission was revived in 2005. Road, rail and air connectivity between the two countries significantly improved. In response to Musharraf's search for 'out-of-the-box' solutions to the Kashmir problem, backchannel confidential discussions between India and Pakistan were initiated. At the popular level, traditional public hostility in Pakistan towards India dissipated. All sections of Pakistani society—journalists, academics, artistes and businessmen—displayed enthusiasm and self-confidence in wanting normal and more intensive ties with India. No longer were cricket matches between India and Pakistan regarded as surrogate military battles. Some glimmers of change in the Pakistani mindset were also visible. Attempts were made to trace the roots of Pakistan not to the two-nation theory but to the economic and religious insecurity of the Muslims in pre-Independence India, and to rediscover the secular elements in Jinnah's heritage. Against a background of unremitting hostility, war and absence of dialogue for long periods, these were encouraging signs.

The thaw did not last long. Pakistan's political turmoil in 2007 disrupted the peace process and the backchannel discussions on Kashmir. Musharraf was ousted and the Pakistan army came under pressure, but it was only biding its time and was unwilling to give up its old ways. Reality checks came in in July 2008 with the bombing of the Indian embassy in Kabul, a series of terrorist attacks in various Indian cities, the breakdown of the military ceasefire along the Line of Control and, finally, the horrific terrorist attacks in Mumbai in November 2008. Not unexpectedly, Pakistan has not been cooperating in the 26/11 investigations. While this increased India's distrust of Pakistan, contacts and dialogue with Pakistan continued. When Nawaz

Sharif became prime minister, there were hopeful signs that there could be normal trade relations. On coming to power in May 2014, Prime Minister Modi invited Nawaz Sharif (and other South Asian leaders) to the inauguration of his government. The two leaders also had a couple of meetings in Ufa and Paris in 2015. Unfortunately, Pakistan's response to Prime Minister Modi's gesture of making a stopover in Lahore in December 2015 to greet Nawaz Sharif on his birthday was an attack at an airbase in Pathankot.

Since then, bilateral relations have steadily deteriorated as Pakistan continued to foment terrorism against India, stir up trouble in Kashmir, rake up the Kashmir issue at international forums, patronize and finance the Hurriyat in Kashmir, and support Khalistani groups. India's patience, already wearing thin, ran out after a Pakistani attack on an Indian army camp in Uri in September 2016. India responded to this provocation with a surgical strike in Pakistan-occupied Kashmir. In February 2019, following an attack on a convoy of security forces in Pulwama, India launched an air strike against targets in Balakot in Pakistan. India also withdrew Pakistan's Most Favoured Nation status, which it had been granting so far on a non-reciprocal basis, and hiked customs duty on imports from Pakistan to 200 per cent.[1] Less than six months later, in August 2019, India made inoperative Article 370 of the Indian Constitution, which grants special status to Jammu and Kashmir. Pakistan's response was to withdraw its high commissioner from India, cut off transport, communication and postal links, and suspend trade and cultural relations with India. There have been some backchannel contacts with Pakistan, but the only outcome has been a February 2021 understanding on maintaining a ceasefire along the LOC.

In general, since 2019 India appears content to continue with the current low level of relations with Pakistan. Other than routine diplomatic interactions, India and Pakistan have been holding technical discussions on water sharing, as provided for under the Indus Water Treaty. They also concluded an agreement on the opening of a land corridor to the holy shrine of the Sikhs in Kartarpur in Pakistan. Periodic discussions on release of fishermen and civil prisoners have also been held. However political-level contacts are absent, other than formal interactions within the framework of multilateral forums like the SCO. Meanwhile, India has stepped up pressure on Pakistan internationally to curb its engagement with and support to terrorist activities against India. India has learnt to live with, and can cope with, Pakistan-sponsored terrorism. No longer does India believe that persuasion and incentives will bring about a change in Pakistan's attitude. India seems to have decided that it will just have to be patient till there is a fundamental change in Pakistan. There is no ground for any optimism that this is likely to happen any time soon. Once again, the Pakistan army has allegedly manipulated the outcome of the 2024 election to install a pliable regime in office.[2] Meanwhile, India has other priorities to which it needs to devote greater time and attention.

It is in Pakistan that some pressure is building to have a normal relationship with India. A recent indicator of this was Prime Minister Shahbaz Sharif's admission in a January 2023 interview that wars with India have only brought misery, poverty and unemployment to Pakistan, and that Pakistan wants talks and peace with India.[3] Of course, there is the unrealistic precondition that talks cannot take place unless India undoes the abrogation of Article 370, which is an impossibility after the Supreme Court verdict holding it a legally valid act. What explains this seeming shift in mood, insincere though it may be? Pakistan is in deep economic trouble and is facing serious internal threats from jihadist groups like the Tehrik-e-Taliban Pakistan (TTP). With Pakistan's western front—NWFP, the tribal belt and Afghanistan—today posing the greatest threat to the security of the Pakistani state, it makes sense for Pakistan to want to reduce tensions with India. At the diplomatic level, Pakistan is no longer able to generate much sympathy for its traditional viewpoint on Kashmir. Instead, what defines Pakistan's image in the world is its role as a global centre of terrorism and Islamic fundamentalism (its role in providing shelter to Osama bin Laden and support to the Taliban is no longer disputed), as well as of nuclear proliferation. There is increasing realization among the Pakistani public too that India has left Pakistan far behind, and that hostility towards India has only hurt Pakistan. For all the exertions of Pakistan over the last seven and a half decades, India has decisively forged ahead of

Pakistan, whether it is in terms of economic growth, the maturity of its political institutions, or its engagement with the rest of the world. The earlier desperate attempts by Pakistan to equate itself with India have turned out to be futile and hollow, and have harmed it more than they have India. The Pakistan army's image among the Pakistani people has also taken a beating, though people do recognize that it is perhaps the only institution in Pakistan that works. At the same time, people in Pakistan today are less convinced about an imagined threat from India, which has traditionally provided the justification for the Pakistan army's privileges and perks, and more concerned about the Pakistan army's abuse of power and rapacious loot of the resources of the state.

A fundamental problem in dealing with Pakistan is that today there are multiple centres of power in the country. The most important among them is the army, which is adept and experienced in manipulating the politicians and now prefers to exercise power from behind the scenes. Traditionally, it has been a disciplined force where the army chief calls the shots. But every new army chief determines his own policy and does not necessarily continue the policies of his predecessor. Moreover, of late there are signs of factions emerging in the army. Then there are the politicians, who are generally seen as corrupt and self-serving. Thus, Imran Khan was forced out of office but he enjoys tremendous popularity among the people in Punjab and cannot be ignored. A third centre of power is the judiciary, which played an important role in Musharraf's ouster. Finally, there are outside powers like China and the US, who seek to remote-control Pakistan so that it follows policies that suit them.

The Jammu and Kashmir Issue

Over the decades, numerous efforts have been made to resolve the festering sore of the status of Jammu and Kashmir (J&K). Notwithstanding its public position that J&K is an integral part of India, in practice India has repeatedly signalled its readiness for a compromise. For example, India signed a ceasefire agreement in 1949; engaged in discussions with Pakistan in the mid-1950s for a possible partition of the state; withdrew from territories it had occupied during the 1965 war; left open the question of the final settlement of J&K in the 1972 Shimla Agreement; and almost agreed to withdraw from the Siachen Glacier. Its latest effort in this direction was the intensive backchannel dialogue with Gen. Musharraf between 2005 and 2007 to try to produce a mutually acceptable compromise solution. The backchannel talks were held in great secrecy and few details were made available to the public at the time. Now, it has been revealed that some of the elements of a possible solution were: no territorial changes; 'soft' borders; greater autonomy and self-governance in both parts of J&K; a cross-Line of Control consultative mechanism; and demilitarization of the state at a pace that would be determined by the decline in cross-border terrorism. These also came to naught, since subsequent army chiefs and civilian leaders disowned the backchannel talks. In any case, there is good reason to be sceptical of the desirability and viability of backchannel talks. While a backchannel dialogue may suit a military dictatorship, the disadvantage is that this does not create the ground for inputs in the form of public and political opinions and reactions on such an emotive and vexed issue, whose solution would have to be widely accepted in both countries. In an open, democratic polity like India, any major foreign policy initiative has to enjoy a broad political consensus if it is to succeed.

In 2019, following its re-election, the present Indian government under Prime Minister Modi came to the conclusion that it was futile to try and reach any agreement on J&K with Pakistan. Pakistan, it reasoned, is riding a tiger that it cannot dismount. Thus, in the first week of August 2019, the Indian government took a momentous decision to restructure the Indian state of J&K, which had so far enjoyed special status under Article 370 and 35A of the Indian Constitution. The decision was overwhelmingly endorsed by Parliament but evoked a frenzied and hysterical response from Pakistan.

Constitutionally and legally, J&K is an integral part of India. J&K acceded to India in October 1947, on the same conditions as the other princely states. However, Pakistan refused to accept this decision, and its unremitting effort since has been to somehow grab

J&K. In 1947, its troops, disguised as tribesmen, had invaded Kashmir. They were repulsed, but Pakistan managed to retain its occupation of Gilgit-Baltistan and a sliver of the territory of J&K. India took up Pakistan's aggression with the UN, which passed a couple of resolutions. Significantly, these did not question the legality of J&K's accession to India. While calling for a ceasefire, they called on Pakistan to withdraw its troops, permitted India to keep some troops in the state to maintain law and order and, once these steps had been taken, envisaged a plebiscite to decide the future of J&K. Since these preconditions were never met, no plebiscite could be held. Meanwhile, the process of integration of J&K with India continued apace. Article 370 was introduced as a temporary measure because of the unsettled conditions in the state. In 1965, Pakistan again invaded Kashmir. In 1999, it sought to capture the Kargil heights, a move that if successful would have jeopardized the road link to Ladakh from Kashmir. Both attempts failed.

For decades India has tried to deal with Pakistan patiently and in a spirit of compromise, but to no avail. In contravention of the 1972 Shimla Agreement, reinforced by the 1999 Lahore Declaration, which envisaged peaceful bilateral settlement of differences, Pakistan has continued to pursue hostile, dangerous and destructive policies in J&K. After careful deliberation, the government came to the conclusion that there was no chance of any viable solution to the problem of J&K through an agreement with Pakistan. Nor was the status quo tenable. India's security concerns had deepened. China had made deep inroads into Gilgit-Baltistan and was building a strategic corridor, the China-Pakistan Economic Corridor (CPEC), between East Turkestan and Pakistan. New Delhi was deeply distrustful of the long-term, and sinister, motives of the Kashmiri separatist groups and suspicious of even the so-called mainstream Kashmir political parties. India could not continue to pander to separatist sentiments in Kashmir. True, there was the human suffering of the people of the divided state of J&K, but this was not more, in fact, it was far less than that of divided communities in other parts of the subcontinent such as Bengal and Punjab, the continuing human suffering of the Muhajirs (Muslims who had migrated from India) in Pakistan and their kin in India, or the divided communities in the border areas of Rajasthan. Both from a security and political perspective, it was impractical of think of 'soft' borders between J&K and Pakistan-occupied Jammu and Kashmir (POJK) while the rest of the India-Pakistan border remained fenced. Another thing to bear in mind is that whereas in India, because of the protection afforded by Article 370 of the Indian Constitution, the demographic profile of J&K has remained unchanged since 1947, this is not so in POJK, where large-scale immigration of settlers from Pakistani Punjab has taken place. Finally, the pre-1947 princely state of J&K was an administrative rather than a coherent political entity. It has at least five distinct regions—viz. Jammu, Kashmir Valley, Ladakh, Pakistan-occupied Kashmir and Gilgit-Baltistan. There was no reason for India to show greater concern about keeping the pre-Independence character and boundaries of J&K than of other Indian states. After all, Punjab, Uttar Pradesh, Bihar, Assam, Madhya Pradesh, Andhra Pradesh and other Indian states have been reorganized for political and administrative exigencies.

Historically and culturally too, J&K has always been an integral part of India. Amarnath (in Kashmir) and Vaishno Devi (in Jammu) are important Hindu pilgrimage destinations. In Kashmir, Srinagar is the site of a shrine of Adi Shankaracharya, the revered Indian monk and philosopher, and the Martand temple, India's oldest sun temple. The original inhabitants of Kashmir, who have been resident there for millennia, are the Hindu Kashmiri Pandits. With the advent of Islam, many became Muslims but, interestingly, some retained their original surnames. Sadly, in 1990, virtually the entire population of the remaining Hindus in Kashmir was forcibly driven out. Many were brutally massacred. That marked the end of Kashmir's fabled syncretic culture (Kashmiriyat). Since then, the people of Kashmir have had to live with Pakistan-abetted terrorism and separatism, necessitating the presence of Indian security forces.

Why did the Indian government take this step? Clearly, the situation in J&K was not satisfactory. The policies followed over the previous seven decades had failed to normalize the situation and fully integrate J&K with the rest of India. Moreover, abolishing Article 370 has always been a core item on the BJP's political agenda. There were many inequities and injustices committed under the cover of Article 370. Kashmir Muslim politicians indulged in electoral gerrymandering to ensure that they would always dominate the politics of J&K. The Jammu and Ladakh regions were given step-motherly treatment. The generous assistance that J&K got from New Delhi was mostly siphoned off to benefit family and friends of the ruling political class. Unlike in the rest of India, there were no job reservations for lower-caste and tribal communities in Kashmir. Among other things, people were denied the benefits of progressive legislation that forbids child marriage and guarantees the right to education. When Partition took place in 1947, refugees who streamed into J&K from the neighbouring regions (now part of Pakistan) were not given state citizenship rights, which meant no access to land, education or voting rights in the local elections. Kashmiri women who married outside J&K lost their inheritance rights. Regrettably, a sense of entitlement and unaccountability got ingrained among the Kashmiri ruling elite even as Pakistan stoked terrorism and separatism, and signs of growing and dangerous radicalism became visible. Anti-national activities, like desecration of the Indian flag, pelting of stones at security forces, and talking about creating an Islamic caliphate in Kashmir could not have been allowed to carry on indefinitely.

For the moment, there are still some curbs in J&K on movement and communications, intended to foil continuing Pakistani-directed attempts to stir trouble. Thankfully, the situation is rapidly improving. People across India have supported the government's decision to revoke Article 370. Jammu and Ladakh are functioning normally, and even in Kashmir only a handful of districts is subject to restrictions. Tourism is booming. Hard work and imaginative policies are needed to gain the confidence of all sections and ensure all-round development. The old state of J&K has been separated into two, with the regions of Jammu and Kashmir as one entity and Ladakh and Kargil as another. Both are currently Union Territories controlled by the Central government in New Delhi. Hopefully, as promised, statehood will be soon restored to J&K and a new, responsible leadership will emerge in the state. Ladakh will remain a Union Territory. Of course, problems haven't gone away. There are sporadic terrorist attacks in J&K, but their frequency is much reduced. Tensions and differences remain between the Buddhist-majority Ladakh and Muslim-majority Kargil regions in the Union Territory of Ladakh. Ladakhis want to have a representative government and constitutional guarantees that their culture and traditions will be preserved. One hopes that with greater integration with the rest of India, J&K and Ladakh will attract investments that will promote, among other things, tourism, agro-industries and manufacturing, thereby bringing much-needed security, peace and prosperity to the local people. From India's point of view, Kashmir is no longer on the agenda for discussion with Pakistan, except the question of vacation of the POJK territory by Pakistan.

Leverages against Pakistan

What can India do to exert pressure on Pakistan? For many years now, India seems to have ruled out a military solution to its problems with Pakistan. After having threatened to go to war against Pakistan in 2002, India had to demobilize its troops after a few months. Perhaps the nuclear 'balance of terror' was at work. The international community, led by the United States, did its utmost to avert war between the two nuclear-armed adversaries. However, under Prime Minister Modi, India is willing to take greater risks, as it has showed with its surgical strikes and the Balakot operation. Nor have India's periodic 'leaps of faith' (Indus Waters Treaty, Shimla, Lahore, Agra) with military or military-dominated regimes in Pakistan worked. There is little hope for a lasting deal with a Pakistani military regime. The possibility of a more normal relationship between India and Pakistan would increase if somehow a lasting, genuinely democratic political structure were to emerge in Pakistan.

India's levers against Pakistan are limited. One lever is the flow of Indus waters from India into Pakistan. This is a card that India has started to carefully play. Many scholars and historians have been of the view that more than anything else, it is the desire to control the waters of the Indus and its tributaries that flow from J&K that lies at the root of Pakistan's obsession with grabbing Kashmir. Water may become a future source of conflict between India and Pakistan. While the water availability situation in the Indian states bordering Pakistan is grave, it is much more serious for Pakistan. Unfortunately, the lever of the Indus waters was signed away in a one-sided agreement struck in 1960. India cannot abrogate it legally, and were it to try to do so, it would probably come under severe pressure from the international community. There is also the question of what India's abrogation of such a treaty would mean for India's relations with China, which controls the sources of three major Indian rivers—the Sutlej, the Brahmaputra and the Karnali/Ghaghra—flowing into India. Therefore, India has taken a subtle, nuanced and incremental approach on the Indus Waters Treaty rather than look at it as a black-and-white situation calling for either abrogation of the treaty or acceptance of the current situation.

Under the Indus Waters Treaty, although India is entitled to fully utilize the waters of the three eastern rivers—namely, the Sutlej, Beas and Ravi—a substantial quantity of water from these rivers continues to flow into Pakistan, which Pakistan is not entitled to use. This is because India has not completed the various planned projects on the eastern rivers, such as the Indira Gandhi Canal, the Sutlej-Yamuna Link Canal and the Thein Dam. Since Indian states pursue their own narrow interests, it has been difficult to convince the concerned Indian states that they should put aside their differences and not let Pakistan use these waters. In the last few years, some schemes and projects have been devised to enable India to use more of the waters of the eastern rivers. The potential benefits to India are significant. Thus, the Indira Gandhi Canal could be extended further south into Rajasthan and Gujarat. Provision of more water to Gujarat could well make Gujarat a granary like Punjab and Haryana. Of course, this does entail substantial sums of money, but the sums are relatively insignificant—and effective—compared with the large sums that India continues to spend on military measures against Pakistan. One problem is that there will always be seepage, and it is impossible for India to completely block the flow of the eastern rivers into Pakistan. However, if India can manage to actually reduce the existing flow of the eastern rivers into Pakistan by even as little as 10 per cent or 20 per cent, it would create the conditions for organized opposition by the powerful farmers' lobby in Pakistan against the military regime. It would also be an important psychological move that should do much to convince the Pakistani military establishment that India is not a toothless tiger. Since India is entitled to fully utilize the waters of the eastern rivers within the framework of the Indus Waters Treaty, Pakistan has no legal case for raising objections.

The second prong of India's strategy involves the western rivers viz. Indus, Chenab and Jhelum. India is entitled to utilize the waters of the western rivers for storage of water up to 3.6 million-acre feet. Pakistan has been routinely objecting to any projects by India on the western rivers. Earlier, it was the Baglihar dam to which Pakistan objected, but the matter was eventually decided in India's favour by a neutral expert. In 2018, after long delays, India inaugurated the Kishenganga Hydroelectric Project in J&K. India has also started work on the Ratle Hydroelectric Power Project. Under the Indus Waters Treaty, there is a graded approach for resolution of disagreements between India and Pakistan. At the lowest level, there is a Permanent Indus Commission with a representative each from India and Pakistan to resolve questions arising from the interpretation or implementation of the treaty. If this body is unable to resolve an issue, the matter is treated as a difference to be resolved by a neutral expert appointed by the World Bank. If the case cannot be resolved by the neutral expert, it is treated as a dispute that is to be resolved by arbitration at the Permanent Court of Arbitrage in The Hague. However, Pakistan has escalated matters by seeking to initiate arbitration proceedings on the Kishenganga and Ratle projects rather than refer the matter to a neutral expert as proposed by India. Changing its 2016 position on this matter, the World Bank in 2022 initiated parallel processes for referring the matter both to a neutral expert and allowing the matter to go for arbitration. It appears that it did this because it wanted to avoid a situation where the Indus Waters Treaty could be jettisoned, even though it acknowledged that its role is limited and procedural, and that there are practical and legal risks in carrying out the two processes concurrently.

India has objected to this course of action, pointing out that having two dispute resolution processes simultaneously is not in accordance with the treaty provisions and that it is not for the World Bank to interpret the treaty. Thus, in January 2023, India had formally asked Pakistan for a review and modification of the Indus Waters Treaty. India is not participating in the arbitration proceedings. It has put revision of the Indus Waters Treaty as an issue for discussion with Pakistan even as other elements of the India-Pakistan dialogue remain suspended. More than semantics or verbal duelling, it is only action on the ground taken by India on the eastern rivers—and full utilization of the waters of the western Rivers permitted under the Indus Waters Treaty—that will create the necessary pressure on Pakistan. This is a long-term strategy that will take five to ten years to put in place. Unlike in the past, over the last few years, India has been actively working to better utilize its rights under the Indus Waters Treaty. In order to ensure that the various projects are completed urgently, a task force has been set up to monitor progress. These are steps that set the stage for a possible abrogation of the Indus Waters Treaty, should such a decision be taken any time in the future.

India's possible arguments for a revision of the treaty could go something along the following lines: The India-Pakistan Indus Waters Treaty is a unique treaty of water-sharing in the world where the upper riparian has been so generous towards the lower riparian. India did this consciously at great sacrifice to the welfare of its, in the interest of better overall relations with Pakistan and a settlement of the Kashmir question. It was expected that this would reassure Pakistan about possible disruptions in the waters of the rivers flowing into Pakistan from J&K and thereby facilitate a lasting solution to the Kashmir dispute. Unfortunately, despite India's generosity, Pakistan has not reciprocated, and, on the contrary, it has followed a deliberate policy of destabilizing India and hurting India economically. It has not honoured its solemn commitments such as the Shimla Agreement, a generous agreement given by a militarily victorious power to a vanquished power in the hope of a long-term peaceful, stable and cooperative relationship between India and Pakistan. Pakistan's sponsorship of terrorism directed against India is not only against the letter and spirit of its various bilateral commitments to India and the principles of the UN and international law, but it also constitutes a breach of faith and trust and an overtly hostile and bellicose act tantamount to a declaration of war. Secondly, India's own water needs in J&K have grown. The people of J&K and their elected representatives have been asking for the right to utilize the waters of the rivers flowing through J&K into Pakistan. India is very keen that there should be accelerated economic development of J&K. India is confident that the rulers of Pakistan, who profess concern for the welfare of the people of J&K, would not oppose any steps that India takes to promote it.

Looking to the Future

Taking a long-term view, India must not give up hope that a time will come when Pakistan will realize that if the two countries work together, South Asia could become a formidable force in the world. India-Pakistan confrontation is only helping outside powers. However, it suits China, Pakistan's closest ally, to have India-Pakistan antagonism continue. Gandhi's speech at his prayer meeting on 4 January 1948 may turn out to be prophetic. He said:

> Mistakes were made on both sides. Of this I have no doubt. But this does not mean that we should persist in those mistakes. For in the end we shall only destroy ourselves in a war and the whole of the sub-continent will pass into the hands of some third power. That will be the worst imaginable fate for us. I shudder to think of it.[4]

While China's attitude remains intractable, it is commendable that of late, India has had considerable success in changing the attitude of the United States and Saudi Arabia, which have traditionally been Pakistan's other principal foreign supporters.

Will wiser heads eventually prevail in Pakistan? Whether India and Pakistan are fated to live forever in a state of confrontation and hostility depends in large measure on whether there will ever be an end to military rule in Pakistan. As long as Pakistan is dominated by the military, it is highly unlikely that it will give up its compulsive hostility to India. Normal relations with India would remove the Indian threat perception that provides justification for the Pakistan army's continued rule, either directly or from behind the scenes. The people of Pakistan have to be more vocal and aggressive in questioning Pakistan's need for a huge military budget and enormous military perks. Meanwhile, India will have to deal with whoever wields effective power in Pakistan without giving legitimacy and support to the Pakistani military, which continues to foment terrorist activity directed against India and has made only tactical adjustments to its overall strategy of weakening and hurting India. Large sections among the people of Pakistan have no antipathy towards India. Indian visitors to Pakistan generally encounter warmth and hospitality from ordinary Pakistanis. At the same time, it will not be easy to eradicate the deeply rooted anti-India narrative that prevails in the official propaganda and education system of Pakistan. Getting Pakistan to envisage normal rather than adversarial relations with India will be a long and arduous task.

As of now, there is little reason to feel optimistic about Pakistan. Pakistan, governed by a selfish ruling class that is unmindful of the welfare of the masses, is bankrupt and in the middle of both a political and security crisis. Besides, the continued all-around Punjabi domination in Pakistan has led to growing resentment and alienation among the people of other states, who feel that the non-Punjabis are regarded and treated as second-class citizens. From a security perspective, Pakistan's biggest challenge will be Afghanistan. Pakistan has always feared Pashtun nationalism, which has deep roots. No regime in Afghanistan since 1949, when a Loya Jirga rescinded all earlier agreements between Afghanistan and the British in India, has accepted the validity of the Durand Line as the Pakistan-Afghanistan border, neither on paper nor on the ground. Earlier, Pakistan was able to successfully manipulate the Taliban. Today the Taliban regime that has come to power in Afghanistan is more self-confident and less reliant on Pakistan. It has even given shelter and support to radical groups like the Tehrik-e-Taliban Pakistan (TTP), which is seeking to overthrow the Pakistani regime. Of late, the Baluch people too have been organizing violent protests, including some terrorist activities, against the exploitative Chinese presence and activities in Baluchistan.

India's Interests in Afghanistan

Afghanistan and India lost geographical contiguity following India's Partition. As the base from which, over the centuries, foreign invaders launched attacks into India, Afghanistan was always vital for India's security. Successive rulers of northern India have sought to exercise control over the Pashtun belt in eastern and southern Afghanistan, whose history and culture is closely linked to that of Punjab. In practical terms, notwithstanding the Durand Line Agreement of 1919 that demarcated the respective spheres of influence of the Afghan kings and the British empire, undivided India extended up to the Hindu Kush. After 1947, Afghanistan and India naturally drew closer together because of their shared inimical relationship with Pakistan. The two countries had a close, friendly and cooperative relationship, especially people-to-people ties, till the Taliban took over Afghanistan in the 1990s. Under Taliban rule, an Islamic state was established in Afghanistan, and the Sikhs and Hindus living in Afghanistan were persecuted. India had to close down its embassy and all other consular establishments in Afghanistan. During the period of Taliban rule, India worked closely with the anti-Taliban Northern Alliance and with Iran to try and oust the Taliban, but without much success. It was only when the United States unleashed the so-called 'war on terror' against Afghanistan after 9/11 that the Taliban regime could be removed.

After the Taliban were overthrown in 2001, India re-established its presence in the major provinces of Afghanistan, with consulates general in Jalalabad, Kandahar, Herat and Mazar-e-Sharif. For the next couple of decades India concentrated on providing Afghanistan generous assistance for development projects in diverse sectors, including large infrastructure projects like the Zaranj-Delaram Road in southwest Afghanistan, which connects Afghanistan's girdle road to Zahidan in Iran. Other major projects undertaken by India are the power transmission line between Pul-e-Khumri and Kabul, reconstruction of the Salma Dam power-cum-irrigation project, and construction of a new Parliament building. India also assisted Afghanistan in human resource development and capacity building, gave the country humanitarian assistance, undertook high-impact community development projects, facilitated institution building and enhanced trade and investment though air and land connectivity. As a result of its development assistance programme, India enjoyed a high level of public confidence and support among the Afghan people.

Although its security is deeply affected by what happens in Afghanistan, the United States kept India out of meaningful discussions on Afghanistan's security, except as part of the Afghanistan and Turkey-sponsored Heart of Asia-Istanbul Process involving Afghanistan's immediate and extended neighbours. India's consistent political preference was for an Afghan-led broad-based government in Afghanistan, but it could do little to influence the political choices of the major players—the United States and Pakistan. This was a deliberate US policy, no doubt encouraged by Pakistan, whose cooperation was vital for the United States to sustain its military presence in Afghanistan. In the initial years after the Taliban was ousted, bilateral India-Afghan military cooperation was absent. This changed subsequently, with the signing of the Agreement on Strategic Partnership in 2011. India began to share its experience in counter-insurgency with Afghanistan and also to train Afghan pilots and help in the maintenance of Afghanistan's fleet of helicopters, but studiously refrained from sending its soldiers to Afghanistan.

The United States did a commendable job in unseating the Taliban from power but, unsurprisingly, as had happened with many other powers in the past, it got bogged down in Afghanistan. Two decades of the United States' so-called 'Global War on Terror' only aggravated the problems the war was intended to resolve. The al-Qaeda could not be controlled, much less eliminated, notwithstanding the targeted assassination of Osama bin Laden in 2011 by the US in Pakistan. Nor could the US eradicate the Taliban's hold and influence in Afghanistan. Narcotics trade was booming during the period of US occupation of Afghanistan. US anger and frustration rose as Pakistan was unable or unwilling, probably both, to cooperate with US satisfaction in tackling the terrorist menace. Despite having pumped in enormous sums of money and huge military resources into Afghanistan, the US military forces and the NATO-led and supported International Security Assistance Force (ISAF) could not achieve a decisive military victory. The prolonged presence of foreign troops in Afghanistan only gave a sharper edge to the nationalism of the fiercely independent Afghan people, without changing their lives for the better. The West's push to artificially recreate a Pashtun-dominated Afghanistan was a strategically erroneous decision: the defeat of the Taliban in 2001 represented the military defeat of the Pashtuns at the hands of the non-Pashtun ethnic groups represented by the Northern Alliance, assisted of course by the US military. Both logic and prudence dictated that the non-Pashtuns, who had contributed to the overthrow of the Taliban regime, should not have been deprived of a share in power, much less marginalized. Moreover, the United States could have achieved more success in rooting out terrorism if it had leant hard on Pakistan to wholeheartedly cooperate in this exercise by stopping the flow of weapons to Afghanistan, closing down the training camps on its soil and curbing trafficking of narcotics.

Twenty years of India's patient engagement with Afghanistan went out of the window with the hasty and unseemly withdrawal of US troops from Afghanistan in August 2021 and the return of the Taliban to power. India's immediate priority was the evacuation of Indian nationals in Afghanistan and provision of humanitarian assistance. India also feared that the return of Taliban rule in Afghanistan could lead to attacks in Kashmir. Like most other countries, India has not recognized the Taliban government in Afghanistan. In 2022, it established a non-diplomatic presence, ('technical mission') in

Afghanistan to handle trade and economic matters. In March 2024, in what amounts to a tacit recognition of the Taliban government in Kabul, an official delegation from the Ministry of External Affairs led by the joint secretary dealing with Afghanistan visited Kabul for talks with Afghan foreign minister Muttaqi. It appears that India has come to the conclusion that Afghanistan is far too important for India to ignore and that there is no alternative to dealing with the Taliban regime, which is in effective control of the country. At the same time India has to keep engaged with the people of Afghanistan, who have considerable goodwill for India. India has continued to provide food, medical and humanitarian assistance to the people of Afghanistan. An air corridor with Afghanistan has been operative since 2022. India has also hosted and provided training facilities to an Afghan cricket team that performed remarkably well in the ICC World Cup cricket tournament in India in 2023 and has done much to raise the morale of the Afghan people. However, India has been very strict about giving visas to Afghans. This has hurt Afghan students and those training under the Indian Technical and Economic Cooperation (ITEC) courses in India. India's reasoning seems to be that many Afghans have passports of other countries too, including Pakistan, and many undesirable elements could enter India using this loophole. Hopefully, some solution will be found following the recent official-level meetings in Kabul.

While India would very much like that Afghanistan evolves into a sovereign, stable and united country, free from outside influence, Pakistan's obsession to control Afghanistan would make that very difficult. Before the US waged war against Afghanistan in 2001, the ruling Taliban regime in Afghanistan was being manipulated by Pakistan. As long as there is an antagonistic India-Pakistan relationship, India does not want Afghanistan to come under Pakistan's exclusive sphere of influence. India is leery not just of Pakistan's influence in Afghanistan. Throughout history, India did not want that Afghanistan should be under the control of outside powers because of the fear that they could, as others have in the past, use it as a platform to attack India. It seems that the United States would have liked to stay on in Afghanistan for the long term, not just out of concern over the activities of the al-Qaeda, but even more because of Afghanistan's strategic location at the crossroads of South, Central and West Asia. India is also concerned about growing Chinese influence in Afghanistan.

Tackling the Root Causes

Unless the root causes that have created the present situation are understood and tackled, Afghanistan will never become stable. Despite the warring tribal and ethnic diversities and rivalries, Afghanistan has an identity—as the strategic space between India, Iran and the Central Asian deserts and steppes beyond the Amu Darya river. Because of its strategic location, Afghanistan was often incorporated into the territories of the surrounding states for the sake of these states' own security rather than because Afghanistan by itself was a tempting target. Strong empires in India and Iran, like the Mughal and Safavid, competed in Afghanistan; when they weakened, the Afghans asserted themselves and invaded these countries. Tsarist Russia's push to the south in the nineteenth century brought another player into the equation. Throughout history, Afghanistan has survived because of its geographical location, which made it an indispensable overland trading link between India and the rest of the world. But Afghanistan as a state with its present political boundaries is a relatively recent phenomenon.

The Talibanization of Afghanistan is a result of the policies of the United States, Pakistan and Saudi Arabia over the years. Afghanistan is floundering and has fallen into a morass of instability, insecurity and poverty because the roots of its economic life have been sapped by Pakistan's policy of restricting its deep-rooted economic, cultural and people-to-people contacts with India. Now, as in the past, Afghans look principally to India's large and rich market for sustaining their livelihood. Afghanistan on its own does not have the resources that can enable it to be function as even semi-independent, economically. If the traditional links of the Pashtun-populated eastern and southern regions of Afghanistan with India could be restored, a radical transformation in Afghanistan is possible. Afghanistan could be an important source of hydropower and minerals for India. It can also earn large sums of money as a tourist destination and as a transit zone for Central Asian gas and oil transportation to India as well as for trade between India and countries to the west, like Iran, Turkey, the Central Asian republics, Russia and even Europe.

The Pakistan Factor in Afghanistan

The problem is that Pakistan does not want this to happen. It wants to ensure that Afghanistan remains Pakistan's economic and strategic backyard. Afghanistan's problems cannot be resolved without Pakistan's cooperation. At the same time, given the traditional hostility and suspicion between Afghanistan and Pakistan, and Pakistan's policy of wanting to keep Afghanistan under its thumb, neither the Afghans nor Indians nor the rest of the world want to let Pakistan have a free hand in Afghanistan. From India's perspective, there have been only temporary gains in the present situation insofar as Pakistan is now forced to pay more attention to security problems on its western frontier, which relieves some pressure on India. But in the long term, a Pakistan in turmoil is not desirable either, as it is the buffer that protects the whole of the Indian subcontinent from the turbulent lands to its west. Now that foreign troops have left Afghanistan, common sense dictates that Pakistan and India should jointly deal with a possible security threat to the subcontinent that could emanate from an Afghanistan in chaos, or controlled by an outside power. There is also the threat that Islamic fundamentalism poses to social harmony and stability in both countries.

As Pakistan grapples with mounting security problems on its Afghanistan frontier, it remains to be seen whether it becomes more amenable to accepting the reality that its essential interests in Afghanistan coincide in many respects with India's, and that India has many capabilities that could be very useful in Afghanistan. Pakistan will first have to get out of its outdated mindset of 'strategic depth,' which envisages the dispersal of Pakistan's airfields in Afghanistan outside the range of the Indian military's offensive capabilities. This is not a relevant consideration today when both sides have missiles and drones. If India and Pakistan were to cooperate on Afghanistan, the prospects of an early return to stability in Afghanistan would improve. The first thing that Pakistan must be persuaded to do is to give India free transit access to and from Afghanistan.

The undertaking of this cooperation within a regional framework could assuage Pakistan's fears about India's presence in Afghanistan. In any case, Afghanistan's other neighbours, like Iran, Turkmenistan, Tajikistan and Uzbekistan, have a legitimate interest in Afghanistan and will have to be involved in the quest to bring peace and stability to Afghanistan. Nor can Russia be left out. A century ago, Russia had a decisive role to play in settling with British India the status of Afghanistan. Thirty-five years ago, it was the Soviet invasion of Afghanistan that set off the chain of events that led to Afghanistan's current turmoil. China too will have to be involved. Ideally, Afghanistan's neighbours and other powers with a legitimate interest in Afghanistan's affairs should explore the possibility of Afghanistan remaining a neutral nation. That would benefit everyone while not posing a threat to anyone. India has much to gain were Afghanistan and Pakistan to be economically re-integrated into South Asia. Perhaps that is the only way that the intractable problem of the Durand Line can be resolved.

Chapter 4

Bangladesh and Myanmar

Bangladesh: A Special Neighbour

Bangladesh is not just another neighbour of India. For India, Bangladesh will always remain very special for many reasons. Geography dictates that the destinies of both nations are, and will always remain, inextricably intertwined. If India's map is likened to a human figure, with Jammu & Kashmir as the head and the North-east region as an outstretched arm, then Bangladesh is the joint that connects the North-east region with the rest of India. It plays as vital a role in India as does a joint in a human body. Its geographical location and relative size vis-à-vis India make Bangladesh feel that it is landlocked, specifically 'India-locked'! Similarly, India's North-east region too regards itself as being 'Bangladesh-locked'. From the perspective of India's North-east, Bangladesh is India's most important neighbour, one that it simply cannot afford to ignore.

As a neighbouring country, Bangladesh creates for India many problems that are common between neighbouring states elsewhere in the world but which apply uniquely in the case of India and Bangladesh in South Asia. To illustrate: Sri Lanka and the Maldives, being islands, inevitably have much less intense cross-border movement by sea with India than do states that share land borders with India; Bhutan and Nepal have open borders with India; with Pakistan the cross-border movement of people to and from India is minimal and very tightly regulated. Bangladesh, however, is India's most populous neighbour with which India shares the longest (more than 4000 kilometres) and a very porous land border. There is large-scale and regular cross-border movement of people, more from Bangladesh to India. India is dependent on Bangladesh to a much higher degree than on any other neighbour, in matters like harnessing water resources, tackling illegal migration and combating terrorism. In the sub-region of east and North-east India, the relative power of Bangladesh and India is well matched.

Bangladesh is also India's largest trading partner in South Asia—not counting informal trade, which is estimated to be several times higher than the official trade. Interdependence between India and Bangladesh is high. Even though this is logical, given their geographical proximity, its potential has still not been fully exploited. Even today, Bangladesh depends on India for many of its requirements, including cotton yarn to produce readymade garments that constitute Bangladesh's largest export and limestone from Meghalaya for its cement plants. For the North-east region, particularly Tripura, Bangladesh is the nearest and most cost-effective source of goods and products, since high transportation costs often make goods and products manufactured outside the North-east region uncompetitive there. It is in recognition of this reality of interdependence that the 1947 agreement setting up the General Agreement on Tariffs and Trade (GATT), the precursor to the WTO, had a special provision (Article 24.11) for India and (undivided) Pakistan, which read as follows:

> Taking into account the exceptional circumstances arising out of the establishment of India and Pakistan as independent States and recognising the fact that they have long constituted an economic unit, the contracting parties agree that the provisions of this Agreement shall not prevent the two countries from entering into special arrangements with respect to the trade between them, pending the establishment of their mutual trade relations on a definitive basis.[1]

Unfortunately, until quite recently, India and Bangladesh could not manage to build even normal trade relations, let alone special arrangements.

The Bangladeshi Psyche

In trying to understand Bangladesh, one has to take into account the complexity of the psyche of the Bangladeshi people. It has elements of irrationality and schizophrenia as Bangladeshis struggle to reconcile their multiple identities. As Bengalis, the people of Bangladesh take great pride in their identity and see themselves as inheritors of the rich and vibrant Bengali history, culture and traditions. But they are also the inheritors of an equally strong Islamic identity, which has sharpened during the last century. Under British rule, the Muslims in Bengal did not prosper as much as the Hindus who constituted the land-owning and better-educated section of Bengali society. Hindus also managed to adapt much better and faster to British rule. The resentment and grouses of the Muslims of Bengal got a fillip with the Partition of Bengal in 1905, which accentuated their sense of separateness from the Bengali Hindus and increased mistrust between the two communities. Even though it was annulled six years later, the Partition of Bengal laid the foundation for the Partition of India along communal lines four and a half decades later. India may never have been partitioned but for the popular support that the Muslim League got in Bengal in the 1945–46 elections and the 'Direct Action Day' riots in Bengal that triggered off countrywide communal violence. Asserting their Islamic identity, the Muslims of Bengal played a vital role in the creation of Pakistan in 1947. A quarter of a century later, asserting their Bengali identity, they destroyed the Pakistan they had been instrumental in creating.

The new state of Bangladesh created by Sheikh Mujibur Rahman was a secular one. After his assassination, the military leaders who ruled Bangladesh, Zia-ur-Rahman and Hossain Mohammad Ershad, once again gave primacy to the Islamic identity and converted the country from a secular to an Islamic one. Culturally, the people were officially transformed from Bengalis into Bangladeshis. This turnaround is explained by the fact that while they were part of a united Pakistan, the Bangladeshi (then East Pakistani) ruling elite, especially the military, shared many interests with the West Pakistani ruling elite. Despite the bloody repression of East Pakistan by West Pakistan in 1971, these old links and common attitudes have not gone away. There remain many influential pro-Pakistani elements in Bangladesh, who are happy to cooperate with Bangladesh's estranged sibling and one-time tormentor, Pakistan. But at the popular level the cultural and linguistic tug towards India's West Bengal remains strong among Bangladeshis. Bangladesh asserts its cultural identity vis-à-vis Pakistan, and its religious identity vis-à-vis India. It considers itself culturally and intellectually superior, and is culturally more advanced than Pakistan but knows that in terms of hard power it is inferior to it. It has the complexities and insecurities of a small country vis-à-vis India, but tends to behave like a bully towards the North-east region, which it considers as its *lebensraum*. A Bangladeshi in his seventies has been an Indian, a Pakistani and now a Bangladeshi. In this way, the mindset of the Pakistani has not left at least many sections of the Bangladeshi ruling elite, and this has added to the already complex personality of the Bangladeshi. The elite has its vested interests in playing up Bangladesh's Islamic identity. The role of the Islamist groups was more brazen during the rule of the Bangladesh National Party (BNP), but their influence remains considerable even under the rule of Sheikh Hasina and the avowedly secular Awami League (AL). India remains concerned about continuing attacks on the Hindu community living in Bangladesh and the seizure of their property. Over the decades, this has led to a steady decline in the Hindu population of Bangladesh.

Bangladesh is painfully aware of India's considerable and enduring influence on Bangladesh, but its elite feels that Bangladesh doesn't get its due share of respect from India as an independent, sovereign country. Bangladesh, with its large population and impressive social indicators, aspires to become a more consequential power in the world. As India's military operations in 1971 showed, Bangladesh cannot defend itself militarily against India. Geographically surrounded by India, Bangladesh feels vulnerable and realizes that it needs India's goodwill and support. For many decades, till quite recently, it masked its insecurities through various stratagems. For a long time it refused to openly acknowledge India's role in its creation and raised the bogey of threat from India, forgetting that the Indian military once (in 1971) did occupy Bangladesh but left Bangladesh with its territorial integrity scrupulously intact. It sought leverage over India by being obstructionist and uncooperative in providing it transit to its North-east region, and by providing shelter and support to Indian separatist and militant groups. As is the case in general with comparatively smaller countries that have a much larger neighbour, Bangladesh feels more secure if India's presence in Bangladesh is weaker and that of outside powers stronger.

The most important of the outside powers is China, which is Bangladesh's largest trading partner, a major source of development assistance and by far the most important supplier of defence equipment and training, including submarines. China figures prominently in Bangladesh's security calculations, which inevitably exclusively revolve around India. For decades, India was the enemy in Bangladesh's military planning and thinking. Fortunately, of late, Bangladesh has become cautious about getting entangled in China's strategic plans and has so far resisted its persistent efforts to get a stronger presence in Mongla and Chittagong Ports. In 2016, China managed to get Bangladesh on board its Belt and Road Initiative (BRI), principally by pushing the Bangladesh-China-India-Myanmar (BCIM) initiative as part of the BRI, but Bangladesh is now more cautious about the BCIM in view of India's distinct lack of enthusiasm for the grouping. Perhaps, Bangladesh has drawn lessons from the debt trap Sri Lanka found itself in with China. While it is encouraging that Bangladesh today is much more mindful of India's legitimate security concerns, India will have to be watchful of unremitting Chinese pressure on the leadership of Bangladesh to give it a greater presence in the country. A regular, frank dialogue between India and Bangladesh, both at the government level and between the think-tanks of the two countries, is essential. Whether this sensitivity to India's security interests will outlast Sheikh Hasina's rule remains to be seen. The United States, with its numerous pressure points on Bangladesh, has also been working to prevent Bangladesh from getting close to China, but its open desire to effect a regime change in Bangladesh that will bring the BNP and the Islamists to power is not in India's interest.

A Period of Neglect and Indifference

India's relations with Bangladesh have gone through many ups and downs since 1947. Till 1971, Bangladesh was a part of Pakistan, with whom India's relationship during that period was confrontational and competitive. In the years immediately following Bangladesh's independence, bilateral relations were cordial and close. However, during the military rule in Bangladesh for a decade and a half following the assassination of the founder of Bangladesh and its first president Sheikh Mujibur Rahman in 1975, the two countries could not develop the kind of relationship that should have existed between them, despite many complementarities, people-to-people contacts, trade and mutual dependence. Bangladeshi leaders tried to avoid any meaningful discussion on matters of interest to India. Bangladesh studiously avoided any mention of India's role in its struggle for independence. Meetings on issues that required frequent interaction were put off for months, sometimes years, and when held produced predictably routine outcomes. Unsurprisingly, bread-and-butter issues like border management and water resources did not make much headway. Transit matters were not even discussed.

Since 1991, the two main political parties—the Bangladesh National Party (BNP) led by Khaleda Zia (1991–96 and 2001–06) and the Awami League (AL) led by Sheikh Hasina (1996–2001) were alternately in power for the next fifteen years. In general, India has been more comfortable with the Awami League than the BNP since the BNP and the Bangladesh army have close links with Pakistan's ISI and the Islamist parties whose agenda is anti-Indian. When the Awami League was in power, there was some movement in bilateral relations, including the signing of the Ganga Waters Treaty. However, under BNP rule, especially during its second term from 2001 to 2006, India's relations with Bangladesh remained very strained. Bangladesh brazenly harboured and actively connived with Indian criminal, separatist and violent groups to try to destabilize India's North-east region and foment terrorist activities across India. This was exposed by the 2004 Chittagong arms haul. It was also a period of debilitating political violence and instability within Bangladesh. The political process was derailed by the January 2007 constitutional coup that put off elections for two years and forced Bangladesh's two principal parties, the Awami League and the Bangladesh National Party, off the political stage. As in the past, a caretaker government was formed to hold elections, but this time it remained in power for two years, with real power being exercised by the Bangladesh armed forces from behind the scenes. The Awami League handsomely won the 2008 elections and was re-elected in 2014 and 2018, while the BNP progressively became much weaker. Sheikh Hasina, leading an Awami League that now seems to be heavily infiltrated by pro-Pakistan and pro-China elements, secured an unprecedented fourth term in office in the 2024 elections.

Changes since 2009

There has been a distinct change for the better in India-Bangladesh relations since Sheikh Hasina came to power in 2009. There is now a much more cordial and cooperative atmosphere in India-Bangladesh relations. The credit for this should go principally to Sheikh Hasina. Internally, she took major steps, such as rewriting history books to reflect the truth about the Bangladesh Liberation War (including India's role in it), reinstating secularism in the Constitution of Bangladesh, and setting up a tribunal to investigate war crimes committed during Bangladesh's Liberation War. Those who were found guilty were punished, many by the death penalty. Sheikh Hasina has wisely and sincerely realized that an improvement in Bangladesh's ties with India is in their own interest. It required considerable courage for her to effect this change in attitude in the face of frequent charges by her political opponents accusing her of selling out Bangladesh's interests to India. Bangladesh's approach to India is now rational and reasonably predictable. The key factor that changed the India-Bangladesh relationship is Bangladesh's willingness to be mindful of and responsive to India's security concerns. It has assured India that its soil won't be used for any activity inimical to India's security interests.

Unlike in the past, Bangladesh today acknowledges India's role in its freedom struggle and has suitably honoured Indian soldiers who made a valuable contribution to Bangladesh's independence. Regular high-level military exchanges are now taking place between the two countries. Some other steps that have been taken are: the Bangladesh armed forces have been brought under civilian control and oversight; changes in the teaching and training curriculum have been made; war games are no longer exclusively focused on India. These steps are welcome as there is a need to change the Bangladesh army's mindset about India, but only time will show whether the mindset of the military has actually changed.

Bangladesh's attitude to its territory being used by Indians for transit has also changed. No longer is Bangladesh reticent about giving transit facilities between the North-east region and the rest of India. The new buzzword is 'connectivity' rather than the politically controversial term 'transit'. Thus, India now has use of the Chittagong and Mongla ports for transit, transshipment via the Ashuganj river port, which has facilitated cargo shipments to Tripura, new ports of call on inland waterways, new coastal shipping routes and even an India-Bangladesh river cruise. There is much better rail connectivity now with the Agartala-Akhaura rail link. The number and routes of passenger trains and bus services between India and Bangladesh have gone up sharply. The opening of multiple border haats has facilitated cross-border trade. New integrated customs check posts at Petrapole and Agartala enable smoother movement of goods and people by road between the two countries. As a result, people-to-people exchanges have boomed, with more than 2 million Bangladeshis officially visiting India every year for tourism, shopping, medical treatment, etc. Many more are believed to be crossing the border informally. Conversely, Indians also constitute the largest number of foreign visitors to Bangladesh. Each country has opened new consular establishments in the other—in Agartala and Guwahati by Bangladesh, and in Khulna and Sylhet by India.

India has heartily welcomed Bangladesh's change of attitude. It has responded by giving Bangladesh full, duty-free and quota-free access to the Indian market, and by removing the restrictions on Bangladesh's access to and from Nepal and Bhutan, whether it relates to trade or transit, or power exchange. It has made a conscious effort to be sensitive to Bangladesh's touchiness and has given it generous assistance through credit lines in many sectors, particularly infrastructure, for development purposes. India unhesitatingly accepted the international arbitration decision that favoured Bangladesh on the delineation of India's maritime boundary with Bangladesh, a gesture that was widely appreciated in Bangladesh. The long-pending Land Boundary Agreement with Bangladesh has also been signed, bringing to a close the problems of undemarcated land boundary segments, exchange of enclaves and settlement of adverse possessions. It is heartening that finally there is a more coherent strategic perspective in India's approach to Bangladesh and that adequate attention is being paid to this critical and complex relationship. Decision-makers in India have given up their earlier prejudiced and somewhat disdainful opinion on Bangladesh. Hope and cautious optimism have replaced the earlier attitude of exasperation and neglect.

The challenge is to ensure that this change in Bangladesh's attitude will outlive regime changes there and make the achievements of the last decade and a half sustained and irreversible. Many in Bangladesh are critical of Sheikh Hasina's policies towards India. They feel that Bangladesh has given away too much to India without getting enough in return. Many observers had been of the view that with Sheikh already in power for fifteen years and a growing anti-incumbency sentiment against her, she may find re-election a more difficult task in the 2024 elections. Ignoring US pressure and the demand of the BNP that she step down and a neutral government be reinstituted to conduct the elections, Sheikh Hasina handsomely won the 2024 elections, which were boycotted by the BNP even though its strategy of boycotting the 2014 elections had not brought it any benefit. The BNP, together with its storm trooper ally, the Jamaat-e-Islami Bangladesh, do retain significant public support, even though the latter has been deregistered as a political party. India is more comfortable with an Awami League-led government since its earlier experience of dealing with BNP-Jamaat-e-Islami governments in Bangladesh had not been a happy one.

Of course, all of Bangladesh's differences with India, many quite serious, have not gone away. Issues of border management, water resources, trade, transit and economic cooperation remain sensitive political matters in Bangladesh. Some latent and long-term security threats to India from Bangladesh persist. India has to be wary of Pakistan and China using Bangladesh as an avenue to undertake disruptive and violent anti-Indian operations. This is because the border between India and Bangladesh is highly porous, and over the years a soft, somewhat shadowy border zone, inhabited by religious fanatics, terrorists, smugglers, gunrunners, drug dealers, traffickers and other assorted criminals, many with international linkages, has come up. Some Bangladeshi workers returning from the Gulf countries have been radicalized and are spreading fundamentalist sentiments within Bangladesh society. Such elements from Bangladesh have infiltrated India and are spreading their influence in West Bengal. The Central government is concerned that the West Bengal government is encouraging illegal migration of Muslims from Bangladesh into India for use as a vote bank. The situation is particularly serious in the West Bengal districts bordering Bangladesh. A similar situation has improved in Assam, where the Central and state governments are cooperating in checking this menace. In the past, India's political leaders too have failed to put the national interest above their immediate and narrow political and personal interests. For the sake of vote-bank politics, governments at the Centre and in the states wilfully ignored for many years the systematic influx of illegal migrants from Bangladesh into India.

Over the years, India-Bangladesh relations have suffered because West Bengal, by far the largest Indian state bordering Bangladesh, has been at odds with the Central government in New Delhi. For more than five decades, political parties opposed to the ruling party or coalition in the Central government have ruled West Bengal. This has also held up an agreement on the sharing of the waters of the Teesta, on which Bangladesh has been very keen. An agreement was almost concluded in 2011, but New Delhi was unable to persuade the West Bengal chief minister to agree to the deal. Over the years, the water sharing issue has become more complicated. Reliable data is not available on how much water from the Teesta is actually available for sharing because of a decline in the availability of water in the river and Sikkim claiming its share in it. Another looming problem is the Ganga Waters Treaty, which expires in 2026. Given the decline in the flow of water in the Ganga over the last three decades and Bangladesh's complaints that it does not get its due share of water during the dry season, renewing the agreement or signing a new one is not going to be an easy task, even without the additional complication of getting the agreement of the West Bengal government to any deal. What is needed is a river basin management approach, but political posturing on both sides has made water sharing an emotional issue and has precluded a rational approach.

Bangladesh and North-East Region

Development of the North-east region is a very important political, economic and social issue for India, and also a formidable foreign policy challenge. The North-east region, sandwiched between Bangladesh, Tibet and Myanmar, shares 98 per cent of its borders with these three countries. Its natural, shortest and easiest access to the rest of India is across Bangladesh. The region can really develop only if it has opportunities for trading with the rest of India, as well as with the rest of the world. These are complementary, not exclusive, goals. Increased trade and connectivity can improve the lives of the inhabitants of the North-east region. However, raising the level of trade for this region with the outside world is not that easy. It requires a coherent and sustained political strategy of many parts. It is very encouraging that since 2014. The Central government in New Delhi has accorded high priority to development of the North-east region. This has given the BJP considerable political influence in the North-eastern states, which now have a louder voice that is heard more attentively in New Delhi.[2]

Now that Bangladesh has given all-round transport facilities to India—land, rail and river connectivity, including the use of Chittagong and Mongla Ports for transit—one can expect this region to rapidly develop and flourish. Over time, it should be possible for the eastern and North-eastern regions of the subcontinent, which are comparatively less prosperous than the rest of the subcontinent, to narrow the gap. In pre-Independence India, the eastern regions of India constituted an integrated political, economic and cultural space. As the pioneering region of India's industrialization, it was perhaps the country's richest and most prosperous region. Sadly, where Kolkata and Dhaka were once flourishing commercial and economic centres of the Indian subcontinent, today they have fallen far behind many other regions of the subcontinent. This is primarily the result of the region's uncoordinated development. This region can regain its earlier competitiveness and prosperity if India and Bangladesh remain sincerely committed and determined to take advantage of their numerous similarities, complementarities and synergies in their economy, culture, history, language and society in order to unlock this region's enormous natural wealth and human resources. Perhaps then this region can once again play a leading role in national life—in politics, economic development and intellectual debate.

India is extremely wary of the North-east region developing ties with Tibet, as this has many political and security implications because China, which controls Tibet, claims Arunachal Pradesh as its territory. Nor does India want its North-east region to be sucked into China's economic vortex. Thus, India is opposed to converting the Track-II so-called 'Kunming Initiative' or the BCIM, which brings together Bangladesh, China's Yunnan Province, India and Myanmar, into an official-level body. Given the mounting internal political problems and unrest in Myanmar, there are limits to the extent to which the North-east region can develop by taking advantage of its geographical contiguity with Myanmar. Thus, Bangladesh remains critical for the development of the North-east region.

Myanmar: An Underrated Neighbour

Myanmar (formerly Burma) is a somewhat underrated neighbour of India, even though it remains important for India from several perspectives. There are close historical, ethnic, cultural and economic links between the North-east region and Myanmar. As the border between India and Myanmar is not under the full control of the Central authorities of either India or Myanmar, it is a fairly porous one and people can move across it quite freely. This also enables insurgent groups operating in India to seek sanctuary in Myanmar. Thus, Myanmar's cooperation is critical for the maintenance of peace and security in India's North-east region. Then there is the economic importance of Myanmar for the North-east region since Bangladesh and Myanmar are the only outlets for the region. Myanmar is also the unavoidable geographical link for greater overland connectivity between India's North-east region and South-east Asia.

India's Myanmar policy is also driven by the China factor. Should Myanmar get irreversibly locked in China's tight economic and strategic embrace, it would pose serious security dangers to India. By establishing a substantial presence west of the Ayeyarwaddy (Irrawady) river and on the Rakhine (Arakan) coast, China has considerably neutralized India's strategic preponderance in the Bay of Bengal. In north Myanmar, China has de facto control over Myanmar's Kachin state bordering India's state of Arunachal Pradesh. These Chinese moves have to be actively countered; otherwise, over time, China could bring Arunachal Pradesh into its economic orbit and militarily outflank India there via Myanmar. Growing Chinese influence in regions of Myanmar that border India would enable China to step up its support to rebel and insurgent groups in India's North-east region. China already has a strong foothold in Bangladesh. A China-sponsored link-up between Myanmar and Bangladesh would bring China right to India's doorstep and complete its encirclement of India from the east. Fortunately, there is growing concern and suspicion within Myanmar itself about China's growing influence. Myanmar is keen to have a much closer relationship with India, which is seen as the only viable alternative to balance China's steadily increasing encroachments into it, especially in the states of Kachin and Shan, as well as on the Rakhine coast where India recently opened a consulate in Sittwe.

Historical Perspective

India and Myanmar share a complex and delicate relationship arising out of the history of their interactions during the nineteenth and twentieth centuries. Although Burma had a benign view of India and a close cultural affinity with it in the pre-colonial era, things changed during British colonial rule. In the nineteenth century, large numbers of Indians were part of the British colonial troops that fought the three Anglo-Burmese wars, which resulted in the annexation of Burma to the British empire in 1886. These troops were later used by the British to garrison the country. As India and Burma were both part of the British empire, the British made Burma a province of British India, which it remained till 1937 when it became a separate colony. In the first four decades of the twentieth century, the British encouraged large-scale emigration of Indians to Burma, with the result that just before the World War II the population of Indians in Burma was about 2 million. A large percentage of them were migrants from what is now Bangladeshi territory to the Arakan coast (the so-called Rohingyas), while the traders, moneylenders, agriculturists and professionals were concentrated in Yangon, Mandalay and the Irrawaddy valley. Indians dominated Burma's civil service and police force and controlled a significant share of Burma's trade and industry. Indians also served as intermediaries between the British colonists and the local Burmese population. The role that the Indians played in suppressing Burma—as administrators and policemen—and their continuing dominant position in Burma's economy, as landlords, workers, proprietors and moneylenders, gave rise to a strong nationalist sentiment in Burma against the Indian community, which translated into a widespread, popular anti-Indian sentiment.

Nevertheless, when Burma and India became independent within a few months of each other, state-to-state relations were good because of the excellent personal equations between Jawaharlal Nehru and Burma's leaders, both the nationalist hero General Aung San, and Burma's first prime minister U Nu. In 1951, the two countries signed a Treaty of Friendship. India gave considerable military and economic assistance to Burma in its early years of independence. Problems surfaced when a military coup took place in Burma in 1962 and U Nu and other Burmese leaders took refuge in India. Properties owned by Indians were taken over and a significant number of people of Indian origin left Burma for India. However, a very large number of Indians stayed back in Burma too. Many of them remain stateless to this day. For three decades thereafter, India had minimal contact with Burma. India's support to the democratic movement during the pro-democracy uprising in 1988 plunged bilateral relations to a new low.

It is only over the last three decades or so that India has begun to give Myanmar the importance it deserves in its foreign policy priorities. Till the early 1990s, India's overall Myanmar policy was unduly focused on support for Aung San Suu Kyi (ASSK), who has a strong India connection (her mother was ambassador to India, and she herself had studied in India and was later given the Jawaharlal Nehru Award for International Understanding). As this left India out in the cold while China made deep inroads into Myanmar, India's Myanmar policy was wisely reviewed in 1992 and India began to engage with Myanmar's military regime. Since then, India has been following a pragmatic policy towards Myanmar. It toned down its rhetoric over ASSK and dealt with the military junta in Yangon even as it lent its gentle support to the democratization process in Myanmar.

Bilateral Relations in the Twenty-First Century

For about two decades since 2000, India significantly stepped up its level of engagement with Myanmar. There was a steady exchange of high-level visits, including at senior military levels, between the two countries. India signalled to Myanmar that it would deal with whoever was in power and had no intentions of promoting democracy in Myanmar. Thus, when the military loosened its grip on Myanmar in 2010 and a kind of partial democracy was introduced, India maintained its earlier policy. Although Aung San Suu Kyi's party, the National League for Democracy (NLD), boycotted the 2010 elections, she nevertheless enjoyed widespread grassroots support. The 2015 elections gave the NLD an overwhelming majority, but the military would not let ASSK become the president, the most powerful political post, and she had to be content with the post of 'state counsellor', functioning like a prime minister exercising much less formal political power. In that position, she tried to expand her power, much to the dismay and anxiety of the military. When the NLD again comfortably won the 2020 elections, the military could take it no longer and they staged a military coup in February 2021. ASSK was arrested and multiple charges were levied against her. Through all these political vicissitudes, India has taken care to deal with all sides—the military, which continued to exercise considerable power behind the scenes, with the military-supported governments of Thein Sein and Win Myint, as well as with Aung San Suu Kyi and her party. Similarly, it has taken the February 2021 military coup in its stride and continues to pragmatically deal with the new political realities in Myanmar. Initially, India expressed its concern at the coup and called for cessation of violence, upholding of the rule of law and release of political detainees. Since then there has been a shift in India's stand. While refraining from joining the anti-Myanmar chorus of the West, India now does voice its grave concern at the ongoing security and humanitarian situation, which has direct implications for India, and has called for resolution of issues through dialogue and Myanmar's return to democracy at the earliest. By supporting Myanmar's 'transition to a federal democracy', India appears to be cautiously moving towards nudging the military regime in Myanmar to enter into some kind of power-sharing arrangement with the National Unity Government (NUG), a Myanmar government-in-exile formed by a group of elected legislators who were ousted in the February 2021 coup, as well as with the rebel groups who have taken control of some key regions along Myanmar's borders with India and China.

In this way, over the last three decades or so, relations between India and Myanmar have steadily improved. Parliamentary exchanges and visits between chief ministers of the Indian states bordering Myanmar with their counterparts across the border were encouraged. In general, India is focusing on its humanitarian assistance, development partnership and capacity-building programmes. On the security side, Myanmar's record of cooperation with India in tackling insurgent groups operating on both sides of the border and in curbing illegal migration has been mixed. Nevertheless, India has stepped up its defence cooperation, including supply of military hardware and training, with Myanmar's army and navy. India gifted a submarine to Myanmar, a first for that country. India's development and technical assistance to Myanmar was significantly stepped up. India has also invested in major infrastructure projects in Myanmar, including in the transportation and energy sectors, which it needs to protect. Direct shipping and air routes were established between the two countries. Of late, Myanmar is India's only neighbour that has a surplus trade balance with India, principally because of the large quantities of agricultural produce and pulses that it exports to India. People-to-people contacts were encouraged, including by leveraging the enormous cultural and spiritual influence that India, as the land of Lord Buddha, exercises on both the rulers and the ordinary people of Myanmar.

However, serious constraints remain. Restrictive trade and currency regulations have limited the volume of cross-border trade to a fraction of its potential. The existing sole border trading town of Moreh in Manipur is no longer enough. More border posts in the North-east region need to be developed connecting Mizoram, Manipur, Nagaland and Arunachal Pradesh with Myanmar. This should be combined with the development of infrastructure. A couple of decades ago, India built a border road from Tamu in Manipur to Kalemyo and Kalewa in Myanmar, and there are plans for building cross-border road links from Mizoram to Myanmar. Unfortunately, roads and bridges on both sides of the border are in bad shape, and a lot more needs to be done. There have been many plans on the anvil for at least two decades. Thus, there is an agreement on developing a multi-modal (river and road) link between Mizoram and Myanmar's Sittwe port along the Kaladan River that flows from Mizoram into Myanmar. Another is a trilateral highway between India and Thailand via Myanmar. There has also been talk of a rail link from India to Myanmar. Sadly, all these projects have so far made slow progress, in part because of the coronavirus pandemic, the security situation in Myanmar after the 2021 military coup and the overall focus of the authorities in Myanmar on the country's internal issues. One hopes these projects can take off at an early date as better transportation links will make Indian products more competitive in Myanmar.

Refugees in India

For years, India continued to host many dissident Myanmar democrats and accepted a reasonably large number of Myanmar refugees. Of late, as internal troubles have mounted in Myanmar, India has tightened restrictions on refugees from it. India, which is not a signatory to either the 1951 Convention Related to the Status of Refugees nor the 1967 Protocol Relating to the Status of Refugees 1967, has taken the line that it is not obliged to accept refugees. India is concerned that accepting refugees could compromise its internal security and change the demography of the areas where the refugees settle down. The first category of refugees consists of those coming to Mizoram, and to a lesser extent to Manipur, from the neighbouring Chin State of Myanmar. Their numbers are in the tens of thousands. Although the official line is that the refugees should be identified and deported, in practice the Mizoram authorities, conscious that the refugees share a cultural and ethnic identity, and often family ties, with the Mizos, has been allowing them to take shelter in the state. Many are in makeshift camps, while some are staying with relatives and friends.

The second category of refugees from Myanmar consists of the Rohingya Muslims resident in Rakhine State, who have for decades faced discrimination and persecution, including denial of citizenship rights. As a consequence of widespread attacks and violence against them in a military campaign from 2017 onwards, hundreds of thousands of them have fled to neighbouring countries, especially Bangladesh, and anywhere between 20,000 and 40,000 slipped into India. Bangladesh has been seeking India's help to persuade the authorities in Myanmar to take back the refugees. India's response has been to provide relief assistance to the refugees living in the camps in Bangladesh. Thanks to the patronage and support they got from some political parties in India, a large number of them settled down in different parts of India. The presence of Rohingyas in India has become a sensitive domestic political issue. Fearing that there could be radicalized elements, criminals and third-country agents among them, India is not at all keen to host them, and they are being treated as illegal foreigners. India has been trying to evict them, but it has not pushed the Myanmar authorities on this point since it needs Myanmar's cooperation to tackle cross-border insurgencies and illegal activities. India has, however, been providing assistance for housing and other development projects in Rakhine State for refugees who might be returning to Myanmar.

Even though India is on the right track, it needs to keep a vigilant eye to ensure that its interests in Myanmar are not compromised. It must develop and maintain a viable and coherent strategy that weaves together the interests of the various stakeholders within India. For a long time Myanmar could not get the serious and sustained attention of decision-makers in New Delhi since the bordering North-eastern states of India are political lightweights that are often ignored, and their complexities little understood by an indifferent political class and bureaucracy ensconced in geographically distant New Delhi. Fortunately, this has changed after the present government came into power in 2014.

In Myanmar, the political scene has become increasingly complicated. It is a divided society and polity. The military has been unable to establish its authority throughout the country. The NUG government-in-exile poses a political challenge. Ethnic armed organizations, militias and guerrilla outfits have proliferated. Decades-old ethnic rivalries remain alive. Recent successes by rebel groups in taking control of large sections of the area adjoining the India-Myanmar border have led to a new surge of people, including some soldiers from the Myanmar army, seeking shelter in India. Insurgent groups in India have been misusing the open border to carry out attacks on the Indian side and escape into Myanmar. There has been a rise in the flow of illegal migrants as well as in the smuggling of narcotics and gold into India. As a result of these developments, in February 2024, India suspended the 2018 Free Movement Regime with Myanmar (which permits local residents residing within 16 kilometres on either side of the border to move freely across the border without visas) and announced that it intends to construct a border fence between its territory and Myanmar. On the political side, it is doubtful if the military, having released the democratic genie in 2010, will be able to put it back in the bottle. Continuing turmoil in Myanmar is not in India's interest, as this could spill over into neighbouring regions of India where the existing political and security situation is already quite delicate. Policymakers will need to give focused, high-level attention and priority to the North-east, and to Myanmar within the framework of a comprehensive policy for dealing with its North-east region, Bangladesh and Myanmar.

Chapter 5

Sri Lanka and the Maldives

Sri Lanka's Ethnic Divide

For many decades, India's relations with Sri Lanka were in large measure determined by Sri Lanka's sharp ethnic divide since Sri Lanka's independence in February 1948 and the unresolved conflict that engulfed the country for a quarter of a century. India has a deep interest in Sri Lanka's internal politics as Sinhala-majority Sri Lanka has a substantial Tamil population with close emotional, cultural and historical links to Tamils in India. There is considerable public sympathy within Tamil Nadu for the cause of the Sri Lankan Tamils, something that no government in New Delhi can ignore, even more so when the Central government is a coalition which includes influential regional Tamil parties. Although the Tamils and the Sinhalas had been living peacefully on the same island for centuries, colonial Britain's policy of openly favouring the minority Tamils in administrative jobs created resentment among the majority Sinhalas, creating a backlash that swung the pendulum to the other extreme after Sri Lanka gained independence. A series of steps taken by Sinhala leaders since the start of the government-driven policy to convert Buddhist-majority Sri Lanka into a Sinhala-Buddhist nation, including grant of special status (foremost place) for Buddhism under the 1978 Constitution, made the Tamils living in Sri Lanka feel like second-class citizens.

The Tamil population in Sri Lanka consists of two distinct elements. The first is the much larger group of Sri Lankan Tamils who have lived for centuries in the areas of traditional Tamil habitation in northern and eastern Sri Lanka. A subset of the Sri Lankan Tamils is the Muslim Tamils, who have gradually acquired a separate cultural and political identity. The second is a smaller group of Indian Tamils taken by the British colonialists from India as indentured labour to work on tea and rubber plantations in the Sri Lanka highlands and as construction workers. The original intention was that they would be only temporary residents of Sri Lanka, but over time they developed roots and settled down there and demanded equal rights with the local population. Any real or perceived discrimination against either category of Tamils has an understandable fallout in India.

The problem started immediately after Sri Lanka's independence when, as a result of the provisions of the Citizenship Acts of 1948 and 1949, a majority of the Indian Tamils were disenfranchized. They became stateless and Sri Lanka sought their repatriation to India. While Jawaharlal Nehru was cautious in accepting the Sri Lankan demand and agreed to accept as Indian citizens only those Tamils in Sri Lanka who qualified for citizenship under the provisions of the Indian Constitution, prime ministers Lal Bahadur Shastri and Indira Gandhi signed bilateral agreements in this regard with the Sri Lanka government in 1964 and 1974 respectively. These agreements acknowledged that the Indian Tamils were the joint responsibility of both Sri Lanka and India, and provided for the repatriation of a fixed number of Indian Tamils to India, and for a fixed number to be given Sri Lankan citizenship. While India's gesture did remove an irritant in India-Sri Lanka relations, it did not resolve the problem as there were many shortcomings in the agreements, particularly the dilemma of how to deal with the natural increase in numbers. India's approach may well have created more long-term problems through the message it sent out, both to the Sri Lanka government as well as to the Sri Lankan Tamils. On the one hand, it reinforced Sinhala chauvinist sentiment about the Tamils (both Indian and Sri Lankan) not really belonging to Sri Lanka and being India's responsibility. On the other hand, it conveyed to the Sri Lankan Tamils that they could count on popular sentiment in Tamil Nadu to manipulate India's position in their favour. In 1982, the Indian government revoked the 1964 and 1974 agreements. This gave rise to fear among the Indian Tamils that a large number of them who did not wish to be repatriated to India could once again become stateless in Sri Lanka. Fortunately, this potential problem was removed by a legislation passed by Sri Lanka in 1988.

India's 1971 operations in Bangladesh further strengthened the conviction of many Sri Lankan Tamil leaders that India would intervene in Sri Lanka to 'liberate' Tamils, on the lines of what it had done in Bangladesh. The policy that India under Indira Gandhi followed in the early 1980s in supporting Sri Lankan Tamil parties and Tamil militant groups certainly seemed to point in this direction. However, the 1983 anti-Tamil riots in Sri Lanka, which led to a brutal crackdown on Tamils and the exodus of large numbers of Tamil refugees to India, spurred India under Rajiv Gandhi to be more active in pushing the Sri Lanka government to find a solution that would satisfy the Sri Lankan Tamils. Most notable was India's initiative in arranging talks between the Sri Lanka government and the various Tamil groups and parties, including the Liberation Tigers of Tamil Eelam (LTTE), in Thimphu and elsewhere in 1985–86. Regrettably, but unsurprisingly, these talks failed and the Sri Lanka civil war continued for over two and a half decades.

The Tamil factor is a very important one in shaping India's policy towards Sri Lanka as well as in influencing Sri Lankan perceptions of India. India does not want a separate Tamil state to come up in Sri Lanka, as this would have the potential of stoking Tamil separatism within India. Faced with many secessionist movements within the country, India can hardly encourage the breakup of another country. India wants Sri Lanka to be stable and united. Moreover, any independent Tamil state in Sri Lanka is likely to become dependent on outside powers for its survival. Meanwhile, a large number of the Sri Lankan Tamil refugees who came to India during the period of the civil war in Sri Lanka are reluctant to go back. On the Sri Lankan side, the Sinhala ruling elite has traditionally been deeply suspicious of India, which it sees as a supporter of the Tamils. One hopes that this perception will change over time. Under the present government, India is playing a more active role in Sri Lanka, guided by its overall national interests rather than just Tamil Nadu politics. India needs to build links with all communities in Sri Lanka, and of late it has indeed been making a conscious effort to reach out to the Sinhala ruling elite. One does not know how long this entrenched Sinhala oligarchy will manage to retain its grip on power in the face of its growing unpopularity among younger people. Perhaps, the political winds in Sri Lanka would blow in India's favour if the island nation were to become a genuine democracy. That is for the people of Sri Lanka to decide. Having burnt its fingers with its IPKF intervention, India would wisely not want to wade into the choppy and dangerous waters of Sri Lanka's domestic politics.

India's Security Concerns and the LTTE War

A second Indian concern is that there should not be any inimical foreign presence in this strategically located neighbouring country, as that could pose a direct threat to the various nuclear, space and defence establishments concentrated in peninsular India. During his visit to Sri Lanka in 2017, Prime Minister Modi made it a point to emphasize that the security of the two countries, whether on land or in the waters of the Indian Ocean, is indivisible. India's approach creates understandable sensitivities within Sri Lanka.

As the civil war raged in Sri Lanka in the early and mid-1980s, India was also increasingly concerned about Sri Lanka's growing military ties with Pakistan and China, and its perceived strategic proximity to the West, especially after the United States was given permission to set up a powerful Voice of America station in Sri Lanka (which India suspected of being a cover for electronic snooping on India) and a Singapore-based US company was given the leasing rights for oil storage tanks in the strategic harbour of Trincomalee. India sought to resolve its security concerns and the ethnic problem in Sri Lanka by resorting to strong-arm tactics in 1987. It dramatically airlifted relief supplies to Jaffna in northern Sri Lanka in June 1987 to break the Sri Lankan military's siege of the city. A month later, in July 1987, the India-Sri Lanka Accord was signed, paving the way for deployment of the Indian Peace Keeping Force (IPKF) in Sri Lanka to enforce the accord. India's concerns about the Voice of America radio station, about keeping out foreign military personnel and experts from the Sri Lankan army, and about keeping foreign companies out of Trincomalee were also addressed in confidential letters exchanged at the time of the signing of the India-Sri Lanka accord. The Sri Lankan government passed the 13th Amendment to the Sri Lankan Constitution, which provided for provincial autonomy to a united Tamil-majority North-eastern province. However, India's strategy failed because the LTTE and the Sri Lankan government continued to distrust each other, and neither trusted India too. Unsurprisingly, this accord foundered in the light of double-crossing in which all sides were engaged. India, which had been arming and supporting the LTTE, was now attempting to disarm it, even as the organization continued to enjoy considerable support and funding from Tamil Nadu. Similarly, the Sri Lankan government, which had been fighting the LTTE and had invited the Indian military to help it do so, started secretly supplying weapons to the LTTE to fight the Indian army. The truce that followed the induction of the IPKF turned out to be temporary. The 13th Amendment was not implemented, the Sri Lankan Army did not withdraw to the barracks and the LTTE did not disarm. Obviously, this bizarre situation was unsustainable and resulted in the hasty and unceremonious withdrawal of the IPKF in 1990. An enraged LTTE retaliated against India by assassinating former prime minister Rajiv Gandhi in 1991.

Having badly burnt its fingers in the military and diplomatic fiasco over induction of the IPKF in Sri Lanka, India stayed away from getting directly involved in the Sri Lankan conflict. Despite many entreaties by successive Sri Lankan governments and Tamil parties to play a more active role in ending the conflict and helping them work out a negotiated settlement, India merely kept a close and watchful eye on developments in Sri Lanka. Even if it wanted to, India was not in a position to play a direct role in trying to resolve the Sri Lanka ethnic conflict. Politically, India's hands were tied as a result of Rajiv Gandhi's assassination, since this precluded any contact with the LTTE. Nor could India openly give military assistance to the Sri Lankan government, which explains India's reluctance to sign the Defence Cooperation Agreement proposed by the Sri Lankan government, or to undertake high-profile defence projects and activities in Sri Lanka. India, thereby, left the field free for other powers like Norway, Japan, EU, China, Pakistan and the United States to be much more active and influential in Sri Lanka than India would have liked, not just in steering talks between the Sri Lanka government and the LTTE but also in the military and economic fields. India's cautious approach led to an undesirable drift in India's Sri Lanka policy. Fortunately, after Rajiv Gandhi's assassination, public opinion in Tamil Nadu turned away from the LTTE, even though the LTTE did manage to influence the political debate in Tamil Nadu. India quietly undertook military cooperation with Sri Lanka in the form of exchange of visits, training, sharing of intelligence, joint naval exercises and supply of non-lethal military equipment. It is heartening that despite their experience with the IPKF, Sri Lankans today do not consider the Indian armed forces as a threat. Conscious of the influence of Tamil Nadu politicians on India's Sri Lanka policy and of Tamil popular opinion regarding the LTTE, the Sri Lankan government keeps its ear close to the ground to monitor popular and political sentiment in Tamil Nadu.

The conflict in Sri Lanka raged for over two and a half decades. Pressure on the LTTE from the international community mounted after the so-called 'Global War on Terror' was launched post-9/11. Following the curbs imposed on the LTTE's functioning and fundraising in Western and other countries, the organization beat a tactical retreat. It agreed to a ceasefire in February 2002 and began talks with the Sri Lanka government. Hopes that the Ceasefire Agreement of 2002 and the subsequent rounds of talks under the aegis of the Norwegian mediators (with the approval of India) would lead to an agreement faded after Mahinda Rajapaksa became President in November 2005. In January 2008, the Sri Lankan government formally abrogated the Ceasefire Agreement and the International Sri Lanka Monitoring Mission set up in 2002 under an agreement between Sri Lanka and Norway to monitor the ceasefire folded up. It was evident that neither the Sri Lankan government nor the LTTE was sincere about seeking a political solution to the conflict. Each was convinced that it could militarily triumph over the other, even though a decisive military victory had eluded both sides for more than a quarter of a century. The Sri Lankan government was intent on dealing with the LTTE from a position of strength, while the LTTE's determination to seek a military solution was strengthened after it lost its control of the Eastern Province.

Eventually, in 2009, the LTTE, after having been defeated in the Eastern Province, was defeated in the north too. India was not directly involved in this operation that, perhaps not coincidentally, took place while it was busy with general elections. Behind the scenes, however, there was intense consultation between India and the Sri Lankan government. India also shared valuable intelligence with the Sri Lankan armed forces and interdicted LTTE supply lines. However, this military victory did not resolve the basic issues before Sri Lanka. With the end of the civil war, the immediate priority was to bring some order and normality to the war-affected zones in the north and east of the country. India played a lead role in this by undertaking a massive programme of demining, relief and rehabilitation, involving the rebuilding of railways and roads, housing construction and medical assistance.

The Post-2009 Political Situation

One would have thought that after the remarkable achievement of defeating the LTTE there would be an enlightened and united Sinhala leadership that would earnestly seek to work for the welfare of all people and communities in Sri Lanka. India repeatedly urged Sri Lanka to make a new beginning to find a permanent political solution to address the legitimate aspirations of the Tamil community and other minorities within the framework of a united Sri Lanka. This did not happen. Sinhala-Buddhist chauvinism remains strong. A wide Tamil-Sinhala divide persists. There has been no sincere attempt to find an inclusive political solution involving a credible devolution package that could satisfy the genuine grievances of the Tamils in Sri Lanka. The blame for this lies principally with the Sri Lankan leaders who have been in power after the defeat of the LTTE. The Rajapaksa clan, now in a triumphal mood after the party's comfortable victory in the 2010

Presidential and Parliamentary elections, further tightened its grip over Sri Lankan politics. Although Mahinda Rajapaksa was defeated in the 2015 elections, the Rajapaksa family, exploiting public dissatisfaction with the Sirisena-led coalition and riding on a huge popularity wave among the Sinhala-Buddhists, regained power in the 2019 elections. All sections of the Sinhala ruling elite have unabashedly followed pro-Sinhala policies.

As for the Tamils, they remain a divided lot without any effective leadership. Given the resolute opposition of the Sinhalas and the Muslims to the Tamil demands for powers over land, police and merger of the Eastern and Northern Provinces, the chances of success for the Tamils remain bleak. India's periodic calls for implementation of the 13th Amendment have fallen on deaf ears. To signal its unhappiness, as well as to put pressure on Sri Lanka to investigate human rights violations during the war against the LTTE, India voted in favour of UN Human Rights Council resolutions critical of Sri Lanka in 2012 and 2013, though it abstained on resolutions in 2014 and 2022 that called for an international investigation. The Tamil issue may be quiescent for the moment, but it has not gone away. As there is simmering discontent among the Tamils, it cannot be ruled out that Tamil extremism, fuelled by moral and material support from the Tamil diaspora, could revive.

The China Factor

As is the case with India's other neighbours, China of late has been very active in spreading its influence in Sri Lanka. Sri Lanka's strategic location in the middle of the Indian Ocean makes it a kingpin in China's Belt and Road Initiative. For Sri Lanka, China is a useful partner to balance India's influence, especially when China has deep pockets to make large-scale investments in the country without asking too many awkward questions or imposing stringent conditionalities. Starting with the 1952 rubber-rice barter deal under which Sri Lanka exported its rubber to China in return for Chinese rice, China has steadily extended its cooperation with Sri Lanka, becoming an investor in infrastructure projects, a supplier of defence equipment, a major trading partner and an important source of tourism. China's influence rapidly expanded under the Rajapaksa family rule of Sri Lanka when relations were upgraded to a Strategic Cooperative Partnership and Sri Lanka joined China's Belt and Road Initiative. Sri Lanka freely took large loans from China on rapacious terms, backed by Sri Lanka's sovereign guarantee, for economically unviable vanity projects, involving kickbacks for the Rajapaksa clan. The flagship Chinese projects in the country are the Hambantota Port and Colombo International Financial City. In addition, China managed to get the East Colombo Port Project, which had been promised to India and Japan. When Sri Lanka was unable to repay the loan, it took for the Hambantota port, China converted the debt into equity and forced Sri Lanka to hand over Hambantota Port to it on a ninety-nine-year lease. Recently, China has announced its intention to create a logistics hub in Colombo Port and to set up an oil refinery at Hambantota.

China's considerable presence and influence in Sri Lanka is a reality that cannot be wished away. From time to time, Sri Lanka has been acquiescing in China's activities on its soil that are seen by India as adversely affecting India's security. The visit of a Chinese submarine to Colombo Port in 2014 deeply upset India, as did the visit of the dual-purpose Chinese naval ship Yuan Wang 5 to Hambantota Port in 2022. It is perhaps not coincidental that immediately after the visit of the Chinese ship, India issued a travel advisory leading to a drop in the numbers of Indian tourists visiting Sri Lanka. Under continued Chinese pressure, and ignoring India's advice, Sri Lanka again granted permission to a Chinese research vessel, Shi Yan 6, to dock in Colombo in October 2023, on the condition that it would be only for replenishment of fuel and provisions and not for conducting any research activity. In January 2024, when China approached Sri Lanka with another request, Sri Lanka, amidst Indian concerns,[1] imposed a one-year moratorium on foreign vessels conducting research in Sri Lanka's territorial waters. India is particularly sensitive to Chinese attempts to establish a foothold in northern Sri Lanka. In recent years, India has managed to spike a Chinese housing project for war-affected areas in Sri Lanka, as well as a hybrid wind and solar energy project in three islets off the coast of the Jaffna peninsula. As more such Sri Lankan flirtations with China cannot be ruled out, India will have to remain alert and lay down red lines that Sri Lanka should not be allowed to cross.

Economic and People-to-People Ties

As India struggled to find a way to regain a central role in the resolution of Sri Lanka's ethnic conflict, the rapid growth of trade, economic and people-to-people ties between India and Sri Lanka over the last couple of decades augurs well for the long-term future of India-Sri Lanka relations. The Sinhala ruling elite, even while trying to distance itself from India, realizes that India's growing economy and proximity is an opportunity for Sri Lanka. Sri Lanka was the first country to sign a Free Trade Agreement with India in 1998, which became operational in 2000. The modest positive results of this agreement in promoting Sri Lanka's exports and attracting Indian and foreign investment prompted Sri Lanka to propose a Comprehensive Economic Partnership Agreement, but that initiative has not taken off. Thereafter, negotiations were held to conclude a new framework, the Economic and Technology Cooperation Agreement (ETCA). That too hasn't worked out so far, in part because of disruptions caused over the last few years by the Covid-19 pandemic, followed by the political turmoil and economic crisis that hit Sri Lanka in 2022. Even without these agreements, India has become Sri Lanka's largest trade partner. In addition to many projects in Sri Lanka under India's credit lines, many private Indian companies have investments in Sri Lanka, including in the West Container Terminal of Colombo Port. The strategically located Trincomalee Oil Tank Farm, which figures in the 1987 India-Sri Lanka Accord, is finally under India's effective control. A few tanks have been taken on long lease by Lanka Indian Oil Corporation, a wholly owned subsidiary of Indian Oil Corporation in Sri Lanka, and another sixty-one tanks have been given to a new company jointly owned by Indian Oil and Ceylon Petroleum. India is also looking to develop other projects in and around Trincomalee.

Connectivity between India and Sri Lanka has improved. There are now ferry services between Indian and Sri Lankan ports, and there is a proposal for a Chennai-Colombo corridor. Liberalization of air services has led to a sharp rise in the number of Indian tourists visiting Sri Lanka, and India is today Sri Lanka's largest source of foreign tourists. Steps have been taken to develop a Buddhist tourism circuit spanning India and Sri Lanka. There has some talk of establishing a land bridge between India and Sri Lanka, as opposed to the Sethusamundaran canal project which certain vested interests in India have been pushing. Although India's long-term interest should be in establishing a land bridge connecting India and Sri Lanka, as has been done by many countries around the world that have analogous geographical locations, this is not likely to come about easily as there are many sensitive political and security issues involved.

One issue that has defied resolution is that of Indian fishermen in Sri Lankan waters. In 1974 and 1976, two maritime boundary agreements were concluded with Sri Lanka. One important concession made by India was the ceding of Kachchateevu, a small barren island in the Palk Bay, to Sri Lanka. With this, the traditional fishing rights of Indian fishermen in these waters were given up legally. In practice, however, Indian fishermen continued to fish in these waters, which are rich in marine life, including by use of bottom trawlers. As this puts the Sri Lanka fishermen at a disadvantage, the Sri Lankan coast guard and navy periodically detain Indian fishermen and confiscate their boats. The problem was kept under control during the period of the Sri Lankan civil war, as LTTE-controlled northern Sri Lanka was a war zone and relatively few fishermen ventured out. After the end of the civil war, this complex issue, which involves livelihood and humanitarian concerns on both sides, has resurfaced quite prominently, and remains unresolved.

There have been some encouraging developments for India since 2022, when Sri Lanka was afflicted by a grave economic crisis, brought on by the China debt trap that Sri Lanka fell into as well as the grave mismanagement of the economy during its rule by the Rajapaksa clan. Deep tax cuts and a ban on use of chemical fertilizers adversely impacted rice and tea production. The Easter bombings in 2019, followed by the coronavirus pandemic, badly affected tourism, on which Sri Lanka is heavily dependent. Add to this widespread corruption and cronyism, and it is no surprise that by 2022 Sri Lanka found itself in a parlous economic situation. Widespread violence and political disturbances throughout Sri Lanka forced the Rajapaksa family out of power, and Ranil Wickremesinghe, a compromise and politically weak candidate dependent on the Rajapaksa clan for his survival, took over as President. This provided India with the opportunity to regain considerable lost ground in Sri Lanka. While China did nothing to help Sri Lanka, India swiftly stepped in with substantial loans, grants, currency swap arrangements and deferment of payment of liabilities to help Sri Lanka stabilize its economy. India's financial assistance package amounted to $3.8 billion.[2] India also took the lead in getting the IMF and the Paris Club to restructure Sri Lanka's debt. These steps have been appreciated by the Sri Lankan government. They have created a much better atmosphere in India-Sri Lanka relations and helped to mitigate the long-standing strong and widespread anti-India feelings among the Sinhalas arising out of India's perceived 'big brother' attitude and pro-Tamil leanings.

While Pakistan and Bangladesh have complexes vis-à-vis India because of the circumstances of their creation, and Nepal and Bhutan feel vulnerable because of their small size and landlocked status, Sri Lanka is quite different from India's other neighbours. Although Sri Lanka as a much smaller neighbour of India's does suffer from insecurities, India is less of a bogeyman for it than it is for other neighbours of India. Rich in resources and strategically located in the middle of the Indian Ocean, Sri Lanka has reason to be self-confident. Even though its history, culture and ethnicity are closed linked to India, it sees itself, with good reason, as much an Indian Ocean country as a South Asian one. Its history and culture are linked to, but sufficiently independent of, mainland India's. Memories of Indian kingdoms invading and occupying Sri Lanka make Sri Lanka wary of too close ties with India. Its location in the middle of the Indian Ocean makes it a convenient and efficient shipping hub for trade between the eastern and western shores of the ocean. It is also an attractive tourist destination. Its people have a longer life expectancy and are better educated and more prosperous than other South Asians. Sadly, Sri Lanka's hubris has been its undoing. Instead of being a thriving and prosperous country, Sri Lanka became the most militarized state in South Asia, torn by an active ethnic conflict that raged for over a quarter of a century. It remains to be seen if Sri Lanka has learnt the right lessons from its flawed policies of the last few decades.

The Maldives: A Unique Neighbour

With a population of just a little over half a million, living on atolls and islands spread out over a territory of about 90,000 square kilometres, the Maldives is unique among India's neighbours. Its population is a mixture of Tamil, Malabar, Sinhala, Arab and African blood and is today 100 per cent Sunni Muslim. Islam is the official religion, and open practice of any other religion is prohibited. The Portuguese, the Dutch and the British had occupied it successively. The Maldives remained a British protectorate till 1953. Even after it gained independence in 1965, British influence lingered on, including British use of an air base at Gan till 1976. Political uncertainty and instability continued till Maumoon Abdul Gayoom took over as President in 1978, a position he continued to hold for the next three decades.

Among India's neighbours, the Maldives is the least connected to, and least integrated with, India. The coastal Indian states have very little knowledge about the Maldives, and vice versa. India established its mission at the level of chargé d'affaires only in 1972, upgrading it to ambassador level in 1980. Yet India, (along with Sri Lanka, the Maldives' only other neighbour) matters hugely to the Maldives. In 1988, Indian military intervention foiled a coup attempt in the Maldives. Notwithstanding their occasional anti-India rhetoric, all Maldivian Presidents (except Muizzu) and other leading political personalities of the Maldives have made it a point to regularly visit India as they instinctively understand that the Maldives cannot survive without India's support, and that in times of crisis India is a net security provider. India helps to sustain the Maldivian economy in many ways. It is a popular destination for medical tourists and students from the Maldives, and provides all the construction material and a significant share of personnel to build, maintain and service the numerous high-end luxury tourist resorts that are the mainstay of the economy. While earlier the Maldives was not a very popular destination for Indian tourists, during the Covid-19 pandemic, tourists from India accounted for nearly half of foreign tourists in the Maldives. Many Indian doctors, nurses, technicians and teachers also work in the Maldives. India has been helping the Maldives with grants and loans for infrastructure and development projects like hospitals, technical education institutes, housing, human resource development, as well as disaster relief whenever required, as during the 2004 tsunami, the 2014 water crisis and the 2020 global pandemic. All these factors would seem to make it desirable for the Maldives to maintain a close and friendly relationship with India.

Evolution of Ties since 2008

As long as President Gayoom was in power, India-Maldives relations were on an even keel. With the amendment of the Constitution in 2008, many political parties mushroomed in the Maldives, and India became a factor in its internal politics. India-Maldives relations hit a dangerous low in the period from 2012 to 2018 during the Presidencies of Waheed and Yameen. President Yameen was invited, together with other leaders of India's neighbours, for Prime Minister Modi's swearing-in ceremony in May 2014. In a signal to Yameen, Prime Minister Modi noted that the two countries had a shared recognition that the security interests of both countries are interlinked, and remarked that each side would continue to be sensitive to the concerns of the other. Yameen, however, came under the strong influence of China, which used its deep pockets and unprincipled approach to influence Maldivian politics and decision-making and draw it away from India. By visiting the Maldives in 2014, Chinese President Xi Jinping sent an unambiguous signal about the importance of the Maldives in China's strategic perspective, primarily arising out of its favourable geographical location—along the principal sea lines of communication (SLOCs) of the northern Indian Ocean—and its proximity to India and the US base in Diego Garcia. Thus, Yameen signed on to China's Maritime Silk Road project, granted generous terms to China for infrastructure projects, stealthily signed a Free Trade Agreement with China, permitted Chinese warships to dock in Male, and sought to make China a member of SAARC. Even as it signed on to numerous Chinese projects financed by usurious Chinese loans and became dangerously indebted to China, Yameen cancelled a 2010 contract given to an Indian company to upgrade and manage the airport at Male. In fact, at one point, when the political crisis in the Maldives was particularly deep, official Chinese media brazenly warned that if India were to send troops to the Maldives, China would take action to stop it!

India watched the unfolding developments in the Maldives very attentively. It did not close any doors to any political party or grouping in the Maldives. At a press conference in May 2018, India's former external affairs minister, Sushma Swaraj, noted that despite the Maldives putting 'India first' in its foreign policy, there had been slight ups and down in its relations with India under all governments earlier too. But India's relationship with the Maldives was not broken, and cannot break, because it is India's neighbour. Relations, she said, were not bad and had stabilized. Nevertheless, the very next month, the Maldives asked India to withdraw two helicopters gifted to it by India and did not approve its own request for a Dornier maritime patrol aircraft from India. Indians were being denied work visas for the Maldives. Fortunately for India, Yameen and his party were defeated in the 2018 Presidential elections, and the 2019 Parliamentary elections brought to power the opposition Maldivian Democratic Party. Prime Minister Modi, who had to cancel his 2015 visit to the Maldives because of the political crisis there, made it a point to participate in the inauguration ceremony of President Ibrahim Mohammed Solih in November 2018, and followed it up with a state visit in June 2019. During Solih's tenure, bilateral relations between India and the Maldives steadily strengthened, and the Maldives maintained its 'India First' policy. India significantly stepped up its financial and technical assistance to the Maldives. Many new infrastructure projects came up or are in the pipeline. The most important of these is the Greater Male Connectivity Project, the largest infrastructure project in the Maldives, and various projects in Addu City, the second largest urban conglomeration in the Maldives located in the southernmost atoll of the Maldives archipelago. India would like to open an Indian consulate in Addu City, but so far the Maldives has not given its approval to this. India would do well to focus on efficient project implementation, an area where India has traditionally been weak.

India's Security Interests

India has important security interests in the Maldives. Fortunately, with the signing of the Maritime Boundary Treaty in 1976, India has no maritime boundary disputes with the Maldives. India's role as a net security provider to the Maldives was starkly brought out when Indian armed forces intervened to help put down a coup against the President in 1988 but withdrew its troops immediately thereafter. The range of Indian activities in the Maldives is broad—high-level visits, a defence cooperation dialogue, ship visits, naval exercises, humanitarian assistance and disaster relief, maritime domain awareness, search missions, air surveillance, medical evacuations, training, and so forth. India has been very flexible and accommodating towards Maldivian sensitivities in meeting the Maldivian requirements of defence training and equipment, including vessels and vehicles. Till 2022, the Maldives and India, together with Sri Lanka, regularly participated in the Colombo Security Conclave, a body set up in 2011 to look at maritime safety and security, counter terrorism and radicalism, combat trafficking and transnational organized crime, as well as promote cybersecurity, protect critical infrastructure and technology, and render humanitarian assistance and disaster relief. Mauritius joined it in 2022. Bangladesh and the Seychelles are observers in this body. Another security concern for India is that even though the Maldives has a very high per-capita income, there are plenty of unemployed young people who have become easy prey for drug traffickers and promoters of fundamentalist ideologies as the country loosened its authoritarian strings and ushered in democratic rule. On a per-capita basis, Maldives had the highest recruits into the ranks of ISIS.[3]

While India's relations with the Maldives steadily grew during the five years of Solih's tenure as President, relations have got complicated following the victory of the Yameen-supported People's National Congress candidate Mohamed Muizzu, who campaigned on an 'India Out' slogan in the 2023 Presidential elections and a pledge not to allow any foreign military personnel to be stationed in the Maldives. In this context, the stationing in the Maldives of two advanced light helicopters and a Dornier aircraft that have been gifted to the Maldives, together with military and technical crews to operate them, has become a very sensitive domestic political issue there. Although these aircraft are intended to facilitate medical evacuations from remote islands and to patrol the extensive Exclusive Economic Zone (EEZ) of the Maldives, there is widespread suspicion among a section of Maldivian politicians about the true intention behind these deployments. With the Maldives insisting that India withdraw all its military personnel servicing and maintaining these aircraft and helicopters, the two countries have negotiated, and implemented, an agreement that these personnel will be replaced by civilians. On the other hand, the Maldives has sharply stepped up its ties with China, which it considers as a close ally and development partner. It granted permission for a Chinese 'research vessel' to visit the country in February 2024 and signed an agreement with China in March 2024 that envisages it providing free-of-charge military assistance to the Maldives, including military training and supply of non-lethal military equipment. Details about the agreement are not available. China, for its part, has been making gratuitous comments about 'firmly opposing external interference' in the internal affairs of the Maldives and 'supporting the Maldives in safeguarding its national sovereignty, independence and national dignity'.[4] The Maldives has also imported drones from Turkey, whose reach could extend up to Indian territories in the Lakshadweep islands. These developments understandably arouse great concern in India. As there is a distinct possibility that China could be looking to eventually set up a base in the Maldives, India has swiftly countered this possibility by setting up a naval base (INS Jatayu) in the Minicoy Island of the Lakshadweep archipelago, about 100 nautical miles from the nearest island of the Maldives.

There are other clear disturbing signals that the Maldives wants to loosen its links with India. India's hope that the new leadership of the Maldives would move beyond electoral rhetoric and refrain from jeopardizing a relationship that has been vital for the survival, stability and prosperity of the Maldives has been belied. Unlike earlier Maldivian Presidents, who visited India first after assuming office, Muizzu made his first trip to Turkey, followed by a visit to China. Moreover, the Maldives pointedly did not participate in the Colombo Security Conclave in 2023 but instead sent its Vice President to an Indian Ocean Forum set up by China. It decided not to renew an agreement with India for hydrographic surveys that expired in June 2024. It has also announced that it wants to reduce its dependence on India for medical treatment, supply of food, medicines and other essentials and is looking to countries like Turkey, Thailand, Sri Lanka and the United Arab Emirates to replace India.[5] After three Maldivian junior ministers made gratuitous and insulting remarks about India and Prime Minister Modi, there has been a spontaneous 'Boycott Maldives' campaign by Indian travel agents, tourists, trader bodies and film-makers, resulting in a sharp decline in Indian tourists visiting the Maldives, which has begun to hurt the Maldivian economy.

India will have to remain vigilant and alert to ensure that the Maldives does not become a security threat to it. While Muizzu's policies have raised some alarm within the Maldives itself, the results of the parliamentary elections in the Maldives in April 2024 gave an overwhelming majority to Muizzu's party, clearly indicating that, at least for now, Muizzu's policies enjoy popular support. This does not augur well for India, which is in a wait-and-watch mood. It has not disrupted the supply of essential commodities to the Maldives under a 1981 trade agreement and continues to give generous development assistance to the country. The present situation is somewhat delicate for India. Even as it has to be careful not to be seen as interfering in the domestic affairs of the Maldives, it has made it clear that it will not sit back passively if the policies followed by President Muizzu are inimical to India's security. External Affairs Minister Jaishankar made the point to the visiting Maldives foreign minister to India in May 2024 that it is in the common interest of both sides 'to reach an understanding on how best we take the relationship forward' and that relations between the two countries are based on 'mutual interests and reciprocal sensitivity'.[6]

Chapter 6

Nepal and Bhutan

Nepal: A Critically Important Neighbour

Relations with Nepal have a vitally important domestic as well as foreign policy dimension for India. Many factors make India's relationship with Nepal critical. These include the extensive people-to-people, religious, cultural and economic links between the two countries, the traditionally open border and the resultant security problems for India, the free Indian currency convertibility in Nepal, the presence of Nepali Gorkhas in the Indian army, the millions of Nepalis living and working in India, and the major rivers that flow from Nepal to India. All these elements arise out of the fact that the hill kingdom of Nepal, like other Himalayan kingdoms, has extensive ties with the bordering regions of India. The mid-hills and the swampy jungles and lowland regions in the south of Nepal (called the Terai), in particular, are deeply connected to the neighbouring Indian regions. Buddha was born in Lumbini, and Sita in Janakpur, both of which are in Nepal today. The Nepalis living in the mid-hill regions seamlessly moved into Darjeeling, Sikkim, Bhutan and Assam. Today's Nepal is the creation of Prithvi Narayan Shah, whose conquests in the eighteenth-century unified Nepal and created a vast empire that included present-day Uttarakhand and Himachal Pradesh and extended to the Sutlej River. Following the Anglo-Nepali War, the Treaty of Sagauli was signed in 1816 between British India and Nepal, as a result of which the British recognized Nepal's independence but forced it to cede considerable territory to them, including all lands west of the Kali River, east of the Mechi River and parts of the Terai.

Nepal is a classic case of the principle that the closer a country's ties with another, the greater its insecurity with respect to that country. Thus, Nepal has posed a formidable challenge to Indian diplomacy since the mid-twentieth century. India-Nepal relations are regulated by the bilateral Treaty of Peace and Friendship of 1950, whereby the two countries agreed to grant each other's citizens national treatment in all matters, including in the matter of taking up jobs, doing business and owning property. This was ensured through an open border and the free circulation of Indian currency in Nepal. Actually, the Treaty merely formalized the existing ground situation. As it closely mirrored the 1923 Nepal-Britain Treaty, the 1950 India-Nepal Treaty did not materially change the extant situation. Nor was there any viable alternative before either side. In the absence of any natural geographical boundaries, it would have been virtually impossible, and financially ruinous, to close or even regulate the traditionally open India-Nepal border. The benefits of the treaty were obviously more for Nepal, whose citizens could take advantage of India's large and diversified economy and higher level of development. Nepali migration into India has also acted as a safety valve for Nepal. The reciprocal facilities that Indians were entitled to get in Nepal (as envisaged by the confidential letters exchanged) were not available in practice, though some Indians, principally Marwari traders, managed to take advantage of the provisions to set up very profitable trading and other businesses in Nepal. Otherwise, Indians living and working in Nepal have been unable to buy property in Nepal or get long-term employment visas.

Security Issues

It is the security provisions of the treaty that are noteworthy and have become controversial. The 1950 India-Nepal Treaty was signed against the backdrop of the impending Chinese invasion of Tibet after the communists came to power in China in 1949. As India considered Nepal to be part of its security perimeter, it was keen to ensure that its security interests remained protected in a new treaty with Nepal. Under the treaty, Nepal agreed to depend on India for its security. Through a confidential exchange of letters, the two sides agreed that in case of any threat to the security of the other by a foreign aggressor, the two governments would consult with each other and devise effective countermeasures. Nepal agreed that it would not import arms, ammunition and other military equipment without India's consent. As part of the follow-up measures to the 1950 treaty, Nepal and India agreed that there would be joint manning of posts on the Nepal-Tibet border, and an Indian Military Mission was set up in Nepal. India's payback to the Rana regime was its tacit agreement to protect it against the democratic winds that had begun blowing in Nepal too under the influence of the political ferment in India in the closing years of the British Raj.

Over the decades, India has accepted, sometimes tacitly, sometimes reluctantly, Nepal's many deviations from the 1950 treaty, both in letter and spirit, and has progressively given more generous terms of both trade and transit to Nepal. From time to time, Nepal has been asking for a revision of the 1950 treaty. Although India has on more than one occasion publicly conveyed its willingness to have a fresh treaty, Nepal has hesitated from following it up meaningfully. Even the Maoists, who have been calling for the scrapping of the 1950 treaty and for closing the open border between India and Nepal, are now more cautious and measured in their remarks. The general thrust of their position is that while Nepal would like a new treaty with India, the two sides should sit together and review their relationship with an open mind. On the border between the two countries, the Nepali position is that they would like it regulated better. From time to time, Nepal has also been talking of stopping the recruitment of Gorkhas into the Indian Army, a sensitive, complex and delicate issue. Very recently, after India moved to recruit all its soldiers through the Agnipath scheme, it made it clear that despite Nepal's objections, Nepalis too would be recruited only under this scheme. One doesn't know what the eventual outcome of this standoff will be, but for the moment Nepal has suspended recruitment of Nepali soldiers into the Indian army, a decision that does not seem to bother India, which has large numbers of able young men keen to join the army.

India's principal grouse with Nepal is that the latter has not shown sufficient sensitivity to India's genuine security concerns arising out of its open border with India. Dramatically highlighted by the hijacking of the Indian Airlines flight from Kathmandu to Delhi in December 1999, these concerns have remained a persistent headache for India for many decades. Nepal has become a useful and important centre for intelligence and subversive operations for foreign powers as well as for non-state actors against India. The open border and weak political and state structures in Nepal make it easy for foreign powers to infiltrate spies into the country, pump in forged currency, engage in arms and drug trafficking, encourage fundamentalist religious groups and activities, and conduct terrorist activities. The presence and activities of foreign powers in Nepal, especially China, are almost exclusively linked to the overall policy of these countries towards India.

China Factor

Over the last seven or so decades, Nepal has skilfully managed to carve out a larger political space for itself vis-à-vis India by leveraging, among other things, its geographical contiguity with Tibet. No longer does India have the kind of overwhelming presence and influence it once did in Nepal. It has to share it considerably with China, which has started taking greater interest in Nepal affairs for two reasons: one, to put pressure on India, for whom Nepal is extremely important and sensitive; two, to ensure that Nepal clamps down on Tibetan refugees and their activities on its soil. China has been particularly active since 2008, when there was a widespread, serious revolt and violence in Tibet. Nepal's monarchs, particularly King Mahendra and his successor King Birendra, encouraged China's involvement in Nepal as a means to check the overwhelming Indian influence in and pressures on Nepal. This is a general policy that the Nepali ruling elite of all hues has followed, the difference being only one of degree. Most problematic for India have been the leftist parties and the Maoists. After the leftist parties began to enjoy political power, particularly during the period when K.P. Sharma Oli was the prime minister, China has been openly using its deep pockets to influence decision-making in Nepal. It is now actively and brazenly interfering in Nepal's domestic politics and has managed to penetrate both the economy and the security system of Nepal.

Earlier, keeping in mind India's sensitivities, Nepal was careful not to let China be involved in projects in the Terai, close to the Indian border. This is now routinely ignored by Nepal. Many Chinese projects using Chinese manpower, as well as so-called Confucius Institutes, which are projected as cultural centres but are widely regarded as listening posts, have come up in the Terai. Nepal has joined China's Belt and Road initiative. China has proposed a railway line from Tibet to Kathmandu and Lumbini, but Nepal, worried about falling into the Chinese debt trap as Pakistan and Sri Lanka have, is insisting that such a project should be supported by a grant, not a loan. From an Indian perspective, any such project would be particularly dangerous, not only for the easy access that it would give China to the heart of Nepal, but also because the Chinese manpower that would come for the construction of the project may stay back and merge with the local population.

Nevertheless, there are limits to China's influence in Nepal. China's shutting down of the Nepal-Tibet border for nearly three years during the coronavirus pandemic was a reality check for the Nepalis. Nepali politicians do understand that they will have to be watchful of China and are unlikely to enter into any alliance with China against India. The ground realities of Nepal's relations with India dictate that Nepal cannot be equidistant between India and China, much less openly favour China while snubbing India. Despite occasional reckless rhetoric emanating from Kathmandu, the leftist parties realize the dangers of following policies that needlessly antagonize India. No sensible leader of Nepal would want to upset an ongoing arrangement that is clearly beneficial to Nepal. When he first came to power in 2008, Prime Minister 'Prachanda' unprecedentedly made his first overseas visit to China, on the pretext of attending the closing ceremony of the Olympic Games. By contrast, more recently, after becoming prime minister in 2022, Prachanda made it a point to ensure that his first overseas trip was to India in 2023, even though it was slightly delayed because of his preoccupation with handling domestic political issues. Predictably, the Opposition parties in Nepal have characterized Prachanda's 2023 visit to India as a sell-out.

The 'Ugly' Indian

India has to take considerable blame for the tensions between Nepal and India. In earlier decades, India did make many mistakes. In general, India took Nepal too much for granted. Under Prime Minister Nehru, India's approach towards Nepal was imperious, dismissive and neglectful. Nepal's foreign policy was heavily controlled by India. Indian envoys to Nepal, particularly in the 1950s and 1960s, often tended to behave like viceroys. The Indian government and public need to show greater sensitivity to Nepali pride and uniqueness. Nepal is the only South Asian country that not only successfully fought off the British and escaped becoming a part of the British empire in India, but also has a tradition of expansionism and a self-perception of being the traditional 'superpower' of the Himalayas. Large sections of the Indian public, even the political class, have never quite understood, much less appreciated, the independent and sovereign nature of Nepal. Instead, Nepal is regarded like another Indian state, even though it is vaguely seen as being somewhat different. Too little effort has been made in trying to understand the complexities of Nepal and the complexes of Nepal's ruling elite.

Landlocked Nepal's umbilical and all-round dependency on India, combined with its fiercely independent and proud consciousness of its separateness from India, have understandably made anti-Indianism the foundation of Nepali nationalism. A widespread feeling that India gives priority to projects that serve India's security and developmental needs rather than Nepal's arouses animosity and distrust of India in Nepal. On the ground, India's slipshod implementation of projects on the Kosi and Gandak rivers in Nepal in the 1960s created the suspicion that India had somehow cheated Nepal. This has given rise to negative feelings about India among wide sections of the Nepali public and has acted as a hindrance to cooperation in other projects involving Nepal's water resources. It does not help India's image in Nepal that the Indian states that border it are among the relatively less developed states, where border posts for customs and phyto-sanitary checks are in poor condition. Fortunately, over the last few years, a couple of modern integrated check posts have been set up at the main border crossings, and more are planned. The fact that the Indians across the border that cuts through the Terai region are the kith and kin of the Madhesis who have not been given a meaningful share in Nepal's power structure has tended to create a perverse, if wholly misplaced, superciliousness towards India on the part of the ruling Nepali elite.

Nepalis deeply resent India's decisive influence in Nepal's internal political affairs over the decades. Examples of this in the early years are: The refuge granted to King Tribhuvan and the subsequent restoration of the monarchy in 1951; the degree of support and facilities in India that Nepal's democratic movements and parties have received at various times for undertaking their political activities in Nepal; and India's economic squeeze on Nepal in 1989–90, which led to the institution of the multiparty system in Nepal. The irony is that all political parties in Nepal also actively seek to involve India in Nepal's domestic politics! Nepal's political parties too have sometimes dabbled in Indian politics, but these adventures have proved costly, as B.P. Koirala and the Nepali Congress found when they incurred the wrath of Indira Gandhi for supporting the Jayaprakash Narayan movement in the mid-1970s, which formed the backdrop to the notorious declaration of Emergency in India in 1975.

After Nepal entered a decisive new phase in its political life in 1990, when the political parties united to convert it into a constitutional monarchy, one would have thought that both India and Nepal, conscious of their mutual dependence and the deep-rooted nature of their multifaceted relations, would welcome this opportunity to make a fresh start in bilateral relations, unencumbered by past prejudices and attitudes of the monarchy and the earlier ruling elite under the so-called Panchayat system introduced in 1961 that concentrated all power in the hands of the monarch. This did not happen. Nepal was in a state of political instability during the decade of the 1990s as the Nepali Congress, the Communist Party of Nepal and the monarchy jostled for power. When a section of the Communist Party broke away and formed another group (Maoists), which launched an insurgency in a bid to seize power, the situation worsened. The royal massacre of June 2001 resulted in the death of all members of the royal family except the king's younger brother Gyanendra, who ascended the throne. Gyanendra steadily gathered more power in his hands and marginalized the political parties. Worried about the Maoists' links with and suspected support to their Indian counterparts and other insurgent groups, India kept harping on the twin pillars of constitutional monarchy and multiparty democracy as the key to political stability in Nepal.

End of the Monarchy

By 2005, however, India's policy had changed. The trigger was the arrest of leaders of political parties and the declaration of a state of emergency by King Gyanendra. India condemned this decision and also suspended military supplies to Nepal. Now India's objective was to bring together the mainstream political parties and the Maoists. Possibly, this was because of the growing influence of the Communist Party of India (Marxist) on the new government, combined with the personal assessment of the Nepal situation by a new foreign secretary whose immediate previous assignment had been as ambassador to Nepal. Over the next few months, India facilitated, and was an implicit guarantor of, a historic 12-point agreement between the Maoists and a seven-party alliance signed in Delhi in November 2005. This was an important turning point in Nepal's politics; it triggered a popular anti-monarchy movement (Jan Andolan) in April 2006, as a result of which the king restored Parliament and agreed to give up power, culminating in the formal abolition of the monarchy in 2008.

Even though the monarchy had become unpopular by early 2006, it was nevertheless the symbol of Nepal's sovereignty and identity and the glue of its unity. Ignoring this vital factor, India hastily gave in to pressure from the street for abolition of the monarchy. There was the strange spectacle of Prime Minister Manmohan Singh, who was then in Berlin, reiterating the principle of multiparty democracy and constitutional monarchy while his foreign secretary in Delhi was telling a press conference that India firmly supported the democratic forces in Nepal and would accept whatever the people wanted! With surging mass protests on the streets and the army reportedly unwilling to fire at its own people, perhaps it was too late to save the monarchy. But India's antipathy towards the monarchy had been visible for more than a year. India did not sufficiently engage with the king to dissuade him from his autocratic ways. Circumstances also played a role. King Gyanendra's scheduled visit to India in December 2004 was cancelled at the last minute because India's political leaders were preoccupied with the demise of former prime minister P.V. Narasimha Rao on the very morning that King Gyanendra was to come. Even worse, the Indian leaders found no time to find another early convenient date for King Gyanendra's visit for the next several weeks! Such was the low priority accorded to a vital neighbour. That is how Nepal, from being a Hindu monarchy for over two and a half centuries, became a secular republic. It is ironic that whereas in 1951, India had helped to end the Rana rule and restore the monarchy in Nepal, fifty-five years later it played an active role in its abolition.

Unfortunately, the abolition of the monarchy has brought political instability to Nepal. The immediate post-monarchy euphoria rapidly evaporated as rivalries among political forces and parties came to the fore. Thanks to interminable infighting and deep-seated rivalries among the myopic, selfish and power-hungry political parties, Nepal remains deeply divided politically. One has seen aimless meandering of the political processes in Nepal over the last fifteen years, with the prime minister's post a revolving door for politicians from the Nepali Congress, the communists and the Maoists. With some difficulty, elections were held in 2008 for a Constituent Assembly, but it failed in its task. Elections had to be called again for a second Constituent Assembly and Parliament in 2013.

The Madheshi Issue

One of the biggest issues has been the desire of the Madheshis, the inhabitants of the Terai region, to get their due share of political power, to which there is strong resistance from the entrenched power elite of the hill regions and Kathmandu Valley. Madheshi grievances are many. They demand, among other things, delimitation of provinces and constituencies; representation in constitutional bodies and in the bureaucracy, army and police; and removal of discrimination against foreign women married to Nepalis. India did not handle this matter in good time and with the requisite attention. Thus, after the Constituent Assembly had hastily adopted the Constitution without any debate or discussion in September 2015, the Indian Foreign Secretary made a last-minute dash to Nepal to persuade Kathmandu to accommodate Madheshi demands. India advised all sides and the political leadership of Nepal to show the necessary flexibility and maturity to ensure that the Constitution to be adopted should have broad-based acceptability. This well-intentioned but clumsy and futile intervention expectedly failed. Worse, it wiped out the goodwill generated following Prime Minister Modi's two visits to Nepal in 2014 and the assistance it had given when Nepal was struck by an earthquake in April 2015. The new Constitution left the Madheshis dissatisfied. As a pressure tactic, in 2015, the Madheshis disrupted supply lines for critical commodities from India, a step that was viewed by the Nepali elite as having been encouraged and facilitated by India. This gave rise to very strong and widespread anti-India sentiments in Nepal, which have lingered on. A miffed India pointedly only 'noted' but did not welcome the new Constitution. Prime Minister Modi, in his congratulatory message to the new prime minister, K.P. Sharma Oli, hoped that he would carry all sections of society along so that there's peace and stability in Nepal—a tall order under the circumstances.

India's New Approach

In the coming years, Nepal will continue to pose a formidable challenge to Indian diplomacy. There is a need to craft a new paradigm for bilateral relations with Nepal that takes care of mutual concerns and sensitivities. The long-term stakes for India in Nepal are huge. As by far the larger neighbour, India realizes that it has to make some unilateral economic concessions and pander to the psychological sensitivities and insecurities of Nepal, even though the Nepali elite, with its sense of entitlement, has never appreciated the measures taken by India for Nepal's development and security. India also has to focus in particular on the youth in Nepal. India has stepped up its development assistance, particularly infrastructure-related, to Nepal. Consciously orienting its cooperation with Nepal in keeping with Nepal's priorities, India is rapidly developing cross-border rail links, roads, bridges, power transmission lines and oil pipelines. In a welcome change from the past, Nepal is now open to India's involvement in setting up hydropower projects in Nepal, which has had to accept India's conditionality that it would not buy power from projects financed by third countries. Currently Nepal exports a modest amount of power to India, and is planning to export electricity to Bangladesh too. In addition to the two ongoing projects (Arun-III and Arun-IV), a long-term Power Trade Agreement envisaging power generation in Nepal up to 10,000 MW over the next ten years was concluded during Prime Minister Prachanda's visit to India in June 2023. It would involve, among other things, revival of the giant multipurpose Pancheshwar project, which has been languishing for nearly three decades since the signing of the Mahakali Treaty in 1996. There is also an agreement for export of power from Nepal to Bangladesh via India. India needs upper riparian Nepal's cooperation for harnessing the waters of the many rivers flowing from Nepal to India that sustain the livelihood of hundreds of millions of Indians living in the plains. This would be more for irrigation, flood control and preservation of the environment than for power generation. In this connection, there are plans to take forward the Sapta Kosi High Dam multipurpose project. Whereas in the past India tended to use transit facilities as a tool to put pressure on Nepal, India's approach is now more generous. Thus, under the revised Transit Treaty of 2023, India has greatly expanded the transit facilities available to Nepal. In addition to the ports of Haldia and Visakhapatnam, India has given Nepal access to Mundra Port in Gujarat and Dhamra Port in Odisha. Nepal can also use India's inland waterways for transit.

On the political side, some fundamental changes have come about in Nepal over the last three decades or so. The domination of the Rana elite in Nepal's economy, politics and the military has greatly reduced. Although the Nepali monarchy is no more, there remains a small, but growing, sentiment for its restroration. The Nepali Congress, traditionally the most influential and pro-India political force in Nepal, has had to cede considerable political space to the leftist parties. On the other end of the spectrum is the Communist Party of Nepal (Unified Marxist-Leninist). Its leader, K.P. Sharma Oli, is pro-China, though he is careful to periodically make the right noises about relations with India. The Maoists, led by Prachanda, are an interesting case study. Political outcasts for close to a decade, feared and hounded by both the Nepali and Indian establishments, they are now in mainstream politics. Interestingly, Prachanda is now trying to shed his revolutionary image. Thus, he donned the traditional Nepali dress of *daura-suruwal* and made it a point to visit and pray at Hindu temples during his visit to India in 2023, possibly to burnish his credentials with the Modi government in India or to pander to popular sentiment in Nepal, or both. The fear of the Maoists that they may be called to account for the mayhem and killings they engineered for over a decade has perhaps led them to seek a non-confrontational, even cooperative, attitude towards India, whose help they may need at international human rights forums. There are other, smaller political parties who can tilt the balance of power in Nepal's hotly contested and competitive politics. Paharis, the inhabitants of the hill areas who have dominated Nepali politics for decades, have been forced to share power, howsoever little, with the Madheshis and the tribal communities in Nepal (Janjatis). Some progress has been made on addressing Madheshi grievances. On the eve of Prime Minister Prachanda's visit to India in 2023, Nepal passed legislation enabling grant of citizenship and guaranteed political rights to women foreigners married to Nepalis. However, immediately on Prachanda's return to Nepal, the country's Supreme Court put a stay on the legislation. All this shows that while the Madheshi problem may be quiescent for the moment, it hasn't gone away.

Despite Nepal having considerably diversified its foreign relations and contacts, India remains hugely important for it. Its so-called 'China card' has its limitations. Its open border with India is critical for Nepal's survival. India's national treatment of Nepal's citizens has enabled

Nepal to send large numbers of its unemployed to India (about 8 million Nepali citizens live and work in India), thereby relieving social tensions and pressures within Nepal itself. The pensions and salaries paid to soldiers who have served or serve in the Indian Army sustain lakhs of families. India accounts for 30 per cent of Nepal's foreign tourists and one-third of foreign direct investments in Nepal. Nepal's currency link to the Indian rupee provides it monetary stability. The recent agreements that have been entered into to integrate the two countries' systems for digital financial connectivity should help to mitigate the difficulties that ordinary people—students, pilgrims, tourists, medical patients—in both countries face in making inter-country currency payments and transfers.

India has to try to ensure that Nepal's political structure is an inclusive one that takes cares of the interests of all sections of the society, without which Nepal can hardly remain united, peaceful and stable. Drawing lessons from its experience with East Pakistan in 1971, India has a legitimate worry that instability in Nepal could spread to neighbouring regions of its own territory. India cannot compromise on its core security concerns that arise from the open border regime between India and Nepal. Nepal has to be made to appreciate that an open border regime works successfully only when the countries have shared security perspectives. For its part, India will have to live with the vicissitudes of Nepali politics. As India's economy is rapidly developing and the prospects for India's continued economic growth are promising, Nepal should endeavour to leverage its special ties with India to benefit from the country's economic rise. Sadly, the Nepali elite's attitude towards India doesn't inspire much confidence. Nepali politicians are unpredictable and mindset of the Nepali elite a real problem. For example, one regrettable step Oli has taken (possibly instigated by China) is to claim—and formalize through amendments to the Constitution as well as depictions on currency notes and official maps—that the main stream of the Kali river in its upper reaches (which defines the India-Nepal border) lies further to the west. By laying a spurious claim to territory that has traditionally been and remains under India's control, Nepal has created an artificial territorial dispute with India. India needs to exercise patience with Nepal. Nepal will require India's constant attention and vigilant watch at the highest political levels.

Bhutan: A Cautious Opening

Bhutan, like Nepal, was never part of the British Indian empire, nor did the British seek to make it so. Bhutan's importance to Britain lay in its being a desirable buffer, and later a useful intermediary, with Tibet. Britain was happy to leave Bhutan on its own so long as it played that role and agreed to give up its influence in the region of the Dooars, the gateway to Assam. Bhutan remained isolated, culturally and politically unaffected by the impact of British rule in India. India did not seek to change the relationship it inherited from the British. The 1949 India-Bhutan Friendship Treaty was modelled on the 1910 Treaty between Britain and Bhutan, under which Bhutan agreed to be guided by Britain in its foreign relations and Britain agreed not to interfere in Bhutan's internal affairs. It also contained security clauses similar to those later negotiated between India and Nepal in 1950, but without any side letters, thereby leaving some ambiguity as to whether India had the obligation to defend Bhutan. Nevertheless, in the light of the Chinese army's entry into Tibet in 1950, Bhutan was happy to hear Nehru's assertions about the Himalayas being India's security frontier. It was not until Jawaharlal Nehru's arduous journey by yak and pony to Bhutan in 1958 that Bhutan began to gradually and cautiously come out of its self-imposed isolation. The Chinese takeover of Tibet in 1959 greatly worried the Bhutanese, who sealed their border with Tibet, hitherto their principal trading partner and the power from which security threats to Bhutan had traditionally emanated. Consequently, a wary Bhutan cautiously agreed to develop closer ties with India, as India had been urging upon Bhutan for some time. Sikkim's merger into India in 1975 worried Bhutan, as did the migration of ethnic Nepalis to Bhutan.

While India has been involved in Bhutan's socio-economic development since the early 1960s, it was only in 1968 that India and Bhutan established formal diplomatic relations. This was followed by a 1972 Agreement on Trade, Commerce and Transit (last renewed in 2016) that establishes a free trade regime between India and Bhutan and provides Bhutan duty-free transit facilities. More than 80 per cent of Bhutan's trade is now with India. The restrictions that India imposes on export of foodstuffs do not apply to Bhutan. India embarked on an extensive programme for Bhutan's development, almost entirely financing it for the first decade. The programme included construction of roads and power stations, technical assistance in the fields of agriculture, health and education, and training of personnel in diverse fields such as administration, judiciary, police, academia and entrepreneurship. India has also recently agreed to extend rail connectivity to Bhutan and to upgrade border infrastructure, which will promote trade and travel.

India has invested heavily in Bhutan's infrastructure. One-third of India's foreign aid goes to Bhutan, of which about two-thirds is as grant. India accounts for about half of Bhutan's foreign direct investment and 80 per cent of the grant support that Bhutan gets from all sources. Power generation is the main sector for Indian investments. Four major hydroelectric plants—Chukha (336 MW), Kurichhu (60MW), Tala (1020 MW) and Mangdechhu (720 MW)—have already come up. Work is ongoing on two more projects—Punatsangchhu-I (1200 MW) and Punatsangchhu-II (1020 MW). There is an ambitious plan to develop more hydropower projects up to a capacity of 10 GW, but there are constraints—geological difficulties, non-availability of local workers, Bhutan's insistence on only government-to-government projects and pricing of the power sold to India. During the lean season, India also exports a small quantity of power to Bhutan. The money that Bhutan earns from sale of surplus electricity to India accounts for about 40 per cent of Bhutan's export revenue. This has given Bhutan a relatively high per-capita income in South Asia and enabled it to reduce its budgetary dependence on India.

An 'Exemplary' Relationship

From India's point of view, the relationship with Bhutan is a model one. Both sides describe it as exemplary. India has handled relations with Bhutan with diligent attention and sensitivity, taking care to develop relations with it at a pace with which Bhutan is comfortable, and being conscious of not doing anything to smother its independent personality. Over the years, India has helped Bhutan become a member of various international organizations, including the UN, and has not raised objections to Bhutan getting development assistance from multilateral and bilateral aid donors. Bhutan has also become a member of SAARC and BIMSTEC. Earlier, Bhutan had a bilateral diplomatic mission only in India, but it has gradually opened resident diplomatic missions in neighbouring Bangladesh and Thailand, as well as in Kuwait (for workers in the Gulf), Australia (for students) and the European Union. It also has missions in the UN offices in New York and Geneva. China has been conspicuously excluded, both because of India's sensitivities and also because Bhutan has a deliberate policy of eschewing diplomatic relations with the permanent members of the Security Council or other big powers, as it does not want to get entangled in their rivalries. Despite its persistent efforts, China has not managed to entice Bhutan to join its Belt and Road Initiative. Only India, Bangladesh and Kuwait have resident diplomatic missions in Bhutan, though the UN and some other foreign development agencies do have their offices in Thimphu.

There is close cooperation between India and Bhutan in the defence and security fields. Since 1962, India has maintained an Indian Military Training Team (IMTRAT) in Bhutan, which has trained the Royal Bhutan Army. India looks after Bhutan's defence, with Bhutan in turn undertaking not to do anything that may pose a danger to India. In keeping with the changing times, India and Bhutan mutually agreed to update the 1949 Treaty with the 2007 India-Bhutan Friendship Treaty, which explicitly recognizes Bhutan's sovereignty and no longer formally requires Bhutan to be guided by India in foreign policy, though in practice Bhutan has found it expedient to closely consult with India. The treaty takes care of India's essential security interests. It envisages close cooperation between India and Bhutan on issues relating to their national interests and commits both sides to not allow use of its territory for activities harmful to the national security and interests of the other. The earlier treaty's provisions regarding free trade and movement of people remain in force.

China's attempt to occupy the strategic Doklam plateau in 2017 was foiled with Indian assistance. However, China has fortified its ground positions in the area and is continuing to pressure Bhutan. Although Bhutan has been conducting its own border negotiations with China since 1984, it closely consults with India in this regard. So far, China has not succeeded in persuading Bhutan to cede Doklam to it in return for China giving up its claims to some areas in north Bhutan. There are, however, reasons to be concerned. In October 2023, Bhutan's foreign minister visited China, and his public statements gave rise to speculation that Bhutan may succumb to Chinese pressure on Doklam and even establish diplomatic relations with China. If that were to happen, Bhutan would be going down a dangerous and slippery slope. Perhaps that is why the King of Bhutan paid a visit to India shortly thereafter, presumably to reassure India that Bhutan would do nothing that would adversely affect India's security and have an overall negative fallout on the India-Bhutan relationship. Wanting to leave nothing to chance, Prime Minister Modi took time off from his election campaigning to pay a return visit to Bhutan in March 2024, in the course of which he had discussions not only with the King of Bhutan and the new prime minister of Bhutan but also with the former king of Bhutan (the present king's father) who remains influential in Bhutan's policy-making circles.

Bhutan has also cooperated with India in clearing out the bases of ULFA and Bodo groups from its territory in 2003–04, as it believed that these groups posed a security threat to both itself and India. Behind Bhutan's move was its fundamental principle of preserving its distinctive culture and identity and not encouraging any groups that have their own political agenda or social structure that could create controversy, discord or conflict in the nation.

The Refugee Issue

One issue that could have but has not been allowed to become an irritant in India-Bhutan relations is the question of the Lhotsampas, or persons of Nepali origin, euphemistically termed as Southern

Bhutanese by Bhutan, who came as labourers to work in the dense tropical forests of Bhutan's foothills over the last century or so and settled down in southern Bhutan. As their numbers increased, Bhutan got worried that they would change Bhutan's demographic structure and thereby dilute its national identity. Accordingly, some time ago it decided not to give Bhutanese citizenship to those who had migrated to Bhutan after 1958. In the early 1990s, Bhutan evicted about 1,00,000 people of Nepali origin, forcing them to live in refugee camps in Nepal. In recent years, Bhutan has been apprehensive that extremist elements like the Maoists/Naxalites may have infiltrated the refugee camps in Nepal, and that if Bhutan were to take in such people they would be a disruptive element in its society and polity. India, unwilling to offend either Nepal or Bhutan, continued to maintain, somewhat unrealistically and ostrich-like, that this was a bilateral matter between Nepal and Bhutan, conveniently ignoring the fact that these people had taken refuge in India but were forcibly dumped into Nepal by India. This was a strange reaction from a government that otherwise legally absorbs millions of Nepalese and turns a blind eye to the millions of illegal Bangladeshi migrants that have entered India, has accepted Afghan and Tibetan refugees, including Tibetans who first took refuge in Bhutan in 1959 and were later accepted within India.

India's attitude gave an opportunity to outside powers to insert themselves into the affairs of South Asia, showing up India's inability to solve problems in its backyard even when it involved two countries with which it claims special relationships. Finally, it is the Western countries that came to the rescue of the hapless refugees. The United States agreed to accept the bulk (about 60,000) of the refugees, and a few other Western countries like Australia, New Zealand, Denmark, Netherlands, Norway and Canada have taken in another 20,000 or so. India's approach was a regrettable signal that it is the United States, rather than India, that can solve South Asia's problems. No doubt this will unduly encourage India's neighbours to seek the help of outside powers rather than turn to India to resolve issues. Nor does India appear to have looked at the long-term security implications of a large number of persons of South Asian origin, indebted and grateful to the countries which gave them refuge, being used to further the agendas of these countries in South Asia. As for Bhutan itself, repatriation of the refugees will not solve the underlying problem of how to make the persons of Nepali origin feel that they are equal citizens of Bhutan.

Looking to the Future

Bhutan remains one of the most closed countries to the outside world. Having repelled on multiple occasions attacks from Tibet as well as occasional forays by the Dooars from the south, Bhutan is justifiably proud of its sovereignty and independence. It has made great efforts to retain its distinct identity. However, it has had to adjust its perspective and policies to a fast-changing world and advancements in technology. The King remains the most revered and popular figure, who keeps in touch with the people in the course of his extensive travels across the country. Sensing the winds of change globally, in 2008 the King gave, as 'a gift to the nation', a new Constitution that makes Bhutan a democratic, constitutional monarchy with some trappings of democracy. The King retains control of key institutions and powers such as control over the armed forces, the right to gift land and grant citizenship, and the right to be kept informed of affairs of the state, including international relations. Many holders of constitutional posts remain loyal to the King. Thus, it is important for India to maintain close and frequent contact with the King, even as it necessarily has to deal with the democratically elected representatives of the people. Keeping in mind the changes that have come about in Bhutan over the last couple of decades or so, India has to engage imaginatively and tactfully with a more urbanized intelligentsia that is more critical of India, as well as an aspirational younger generation greatly influenced by social media, and which no longer views India as a destination of choice for education. A lower profile of IMTRAT in Bhutan is also much needed. Trust, mutual respect and sensitivity are essential for ensuring that India-Bhutan relations remain undisturbed.

Chapter 7

Tibet and China

Historical Trajectory of Relations

For long time, there was, in India, a narrative that China is a neighbour with which India had a peaceful, trouble-free relationship for millennia till the 1962 conflict. This is a misreading of the nature of India's relations with China. The reality is that India and China have never been neighbours and their historical interaction has been minimal, whether by way of trade, people-to-people contacts or even conflict. The reason is simple: India and China did not share a common border till the Chinese takeover of Tibet in 1950. Whatever trade took place involved various intermediaries and staging posts in Central Asia or South-east Asia for overland and maritime trade respectively. The most meaningful contacts between India and China involved culture and religion. Buddhism was India's most significant export to China, Xuan Zang and Fa Hien being the best-known among the Chinese monks and travellers who visited India and took back to China large numbers of Indian religious texts for translation. Other than that, there was mutual ignorance between China and India. Despite China's pretensions to be the 'Middle Kingdom' or the civilized centre of the world, traditional popular Chinese perceptions of India bordered on the reverential. When Indian Ambassador K.M. Panikkar presented his credentials to Mao Zedong, the latter opened the conversation following the credentials ceremony by saying that in China, there was an old belief that if a man had lived a good life, he would be reborn in India. Chinese perceptions of India changed when India was under

British colonial rule, when opium from India was introduced in China and Indian soldiers were used to suppress the Boxer Rebellion (1899–1901) as well as for policing work in Hong Kong and China.

A new chapter opened in the middle of the twentieth century when India became independent in 1947 and the communists took over China in 1949. Prime Minister Nehru had a romanticized view of India's relations with China. He thought that as newly independent and large developing countries, India and China should, and would, work together for peace, growth and prosperity in Asia. When China invaded and took over Tibet in 1950, Nehru ignored the advice of his senior colleagues like Sardar Patel, who said this would have negative consequences for India's security. India unilaterally gave up its presence in Tibet and signed the 1954 Panchsheel Agreement with China, which laid down five principles—mutual respect for each other's territorial integrity and sovereignty; mutual non-aggression; mutual non-interference; equality and mutual benefit; and peaceful coexistence—as the framework not only for relations between the two countries but also for their relations with all other countries. Unfortunately, while recognizing Tibet as an autonomous region of China, India did not push China to agree on delineation of the India-Tibet border and was taken in by Chinese assertions that this could be done at a later time. Meanwhile, Nehru unilaterally incorporated the Aksai Chin region in India's official maps. In retrospect, it is clear that China's policy towards India in the 1950s was formulated with the objective of its securing control of Tibet. China lulled India into complacency with its mendacious *'bhai-bhai'* and *Panchsheel* rhetoric, and got India to vacate its presence in Tibet and East Turkestan as well as to recognize Tibet as a region of China in the 1954 India-China Trade Agreement. It cleverly put off settlement of the India-Tibet border alignment so that it could quietly go ahead with the construction of the East Turkestan-Tibet highway passing through Aksai Chin, which was critical for China to consolidate its hold on Tibet. When this came to light, India-China relations got acrimonious, sharply deteriorating from 1958 onwards. India and China fought a border war in 1962, which brought a chill in relations and a mutual downgrading of diplomatic representation. It was only in 1976 that ambassador-level diplomatic relations were restored.

The next landmark in bilateral relations was the visit of Prime Minister Rajiv Gandhi to China in 1988, the first by an Indian prime minister to China since Nehru's visit in 1954. India agreed to decouple the border question from the overall relationship, which steadily improved over the next decade and a half or so. Popular opinion in India about China also began to change. China was increasingly seen as a rapidly growing and influential world power, and an essentially benign neighbour from which India could learn much. At least, that was the perception of the younger generation of Indians that did not have unpleasant memories of earlier decades when China was viewed with enormous suspicion and hostility. The border also remained peaceful. In 1993, during Prime Minister Narasimha Rao's visit, the two countries signed an agreement to maintain peace and tranquillity along the Line of Actual Control. Three years later, during Chinese President Jiang Zemin's visit in 1996, an agreement on confidence-building measures in the border areas was signed. Relations took a dip after Pokharan-II, but once China had come to terms with India becoming a nuclear weapons power in 1998, bilateral ties regained momentum. Over the next few years, frequent high-level visits and meetings took place, both in the capitals of the two countries as well as on the margins of multilateral and regional gatherings. India and China developed a regular pattern of exchanges and visits in diverse fields, including among senior officers of the armed forces. Military confidence-building measures, including low-level joint military exercises, were initiated.

Measures were initiated in 2001 to exchange maps that would clarify the Line of Actual Control, but this initiative petered out quickly. In 2004, when India and China agreed to search for a political solution to the border dispute, India decided not to pursue the matter of continuing the exchange of maps of the Western, Middle and Eastern Sectors, a practice that was stopped by the Chinese for no plausible reason in 2002 after India had presented its map of the Western Sector. In 2003, during Prime Minister Vajpayee's visit, China implicitly recognized Sikkim as a part of India, and the traditional trade route between India and Tibet via the Nathu-la pass in Sikkim was re-opened in 2006. It was also decided that border talks would be held through special representatives of the leaders to find an early political solution to the boundary question, based on agreed political parameters and guiding principles rather than only the legal and historical claims of the two sides. During Chinese prime minister Wen Jiabao's visit to India in April 2005, the two countries curiously agreed to have a strategic and cooperative partnership! Early political settlement of the boundary question was seen as a shared strategic objective. While this gave justifiable ground for optimism about an early breakthrough on the border issue, this was not to be, and the talks between the special representatives have meandered aimlessly for two decades.

On the other hand, bilateral trade and tourism have sharply increased over the last couple of decades or so. China has become India's largest trading partner, although the economic relationship is not without its problems. India is concerned over its ballooning trade deficit and pattern of trade with China. India exports mostly raw materials and commodities, and China mostly manufactured products. As China is a non-market economy with opaque pricing mechanisms and hidden subsidies, Chinese companies are suspected of dumping, and of resorting to non-tariff barriers and other unfair trade practices. Considering that many Chinese companies are suspected to have intelligence links, India remains wary of Chinese companies investing in sensitive sectors and regions in India. India has taken various measures to restrict Chinese investments in sensitive areas, banned many Chinese apps, and is taking steps to reduce its import dependence on China and diversify its trade. Success in this has been modest so far, since a lot of global manufacturing capacity is located in China and alternative sources at competitive prices are not easy to find.

The Border Dispute

Unfortunately, the rapidly developing overall bilateral relationship began to unravel from about 2006 onwards. Initially, the Chinese claims on Arunachal Pradesh were the trigger. The deliberately strong, blunt and repeated public reiteration of the Chinese claim on the Indian state of Arunachal Pradesh through remarks by high-level Chinese officials, the renaming of places in Arunachal Pradesh, the issuing of stapled visas to residents of Arunachal Pradesh (and also Jammu and Kashmir) and the publication of maps showing the state as part of China upset India and triggered a widespread wave of public indignation across the country. While the official Chinese position has been that the whole of Arunachal Pradesh belongs to China, for many years China did not press this claim forcefully, and it was given out by well-informed sources that in any border settlement, China's real interest was in getting control of Tawang, not the whole of Arunachal Pradesh. It was not long before China turned up the heat on its borders with India. The standoff in the Depsang area of Ladakh-Aksai Chin in 2013 was the first instance of Chinese muscle-flexing. When Prime Minister Modi assumed office in May 2014, he tried to seriously explore the possibility of a cooperative relationship with China. However, Chinese intrusions into Chumar in Ladakh in September 2014, even as Chinese President Xi Jinping was in India, made it clear that China did not intend to give up its policy of keeping India under pressure on the border. A severe crisis came in the summer of 2017 over Doklam near the India-Bhutan-Tibet tri-junction. Fortunately, India held its nerve, did not give in to Chinese bullying and intimidation, and managed to prevent Bhutan from drifting into China's orbit. This was only a temporary reprieve for India. China has continued to build up its military infrastructure and increase its permanent troop deployment in the Doklam area. India remained engaged with China at the highest levels, hopeful that there could be progress in resolving the border dispute if there was an understanding at the political level. Prime Minister Modi had discussions with President Xi Jinping on many occasions, including at informal summits at Wuhan (2018) and Mamallapuram (2019).

All these efforts came to naught. In June 2020, there were serious border clashes in the Pangong Tso and Galwan sectors in Ladakh resulting in the deaths of soldiers on both sides. This was a tipping point in India's approach to China. India viewed China's actions as a breach of the 1993 and 1996 agreements. While the Indian counter-offensive and negotiations have resulted in disengagement in the Pangong Tso sector, the dispute over the Galwan and Depsang sectors remains unresolved despite many rounds of talks. Meanwhile, both sides have deployed hundreds of thousands of troops on the border and have sharply speeded up border infrastructure construction to prepare for what is likely to be a prolonged and tense confrontation. India has taken a firm position that there cannot be a return to normal India-China relations unless there is a peaceful border. As a result of China's recent actions over Arunachal Pradesh and incursions into Ladakh, the latent Indian distrust of China, always well entrenched among the security agencies, has now extended to think tanks, academia and the general public. It has given India the reality check that despite China being one of its largest trading partners, India's relationship with it is essentially a political and strategic one, arising from the fact that both are neighbours with an unresolved boundary dispute and a live border.

China's recent aggressive actions and postures make it clear that it is in no hurry to conclude a boundary settlement with India and that its long-term intentions towards India are hostile. Before Galwan, India's approach to the border issue and to overall relations with China was somewhat muddled. A sense of history was missing in its approach towards China. All this has changed now. Post-Galwan, the Indian leadership is quite clear that in the long term India's relations with China are likely to remain hostile, at best adversarial. This skirmish has completely eroded India's trust in China. There has been no substantive engagement at the highest political level for four years.

As India cannot afford to risk losing whatever disputed areas it already holds, it has no alternative but to patiently wait till its own economic strength and standing in the region and the world is comparable to that of China, or hope that China's position weakens. Like China, India too should not show undue anxiety to settle the boundary question. India can keep China engaged and let the border talks continue. But India has changed its tactics. India has stepped up its vigilance on the border and remains firm and confident that it can handle Chinese border provocations. In a welcome and long overdue step, India has started to build up its logistics and infrastructure in the border areas, including the reopening of closed airstrips and the building of new ones in both Ladakh and Arunachal Pradesh. Work has been speeded up and more funds have been allocated for this purpose. In addition, the areas that are opened up by roads must also be settled with people, otherwise China could continue to nibble at them. Although unsettled frontiers do remain a source of tension, chances are that after the Galwan incident there may not be armed clashes in the near future, as such a course of action carries considerable risks. Any adventurism will no doubt be effectively tackled at the military level by the Indian army, now much better prepared than in 1962. For China, the greater danger is that this would reinforce anti-China sentiment among its other neighbours who are also targets of its irredentist territorial claims. Even more dangerous would be the possibility that were such a move to go wrong, internal discontent and disturbances could be triggered within China.

India would be wise to develop leverages vis-à-vis China on the border issue. India must not show any signs that it is willing to compromise its principled position on its territorial integrity. China has not given up any of its claims; rather, it has hardened its position on Arunachal Pradesh and Ladakh, and has questioned the legitimacy of India's decision to scrap Article 370. It is good that India has recently reiterated its claim to the Shaksgam valley of Pakistan-occupied Kashmir, which was transferred from Pakistan to China in 1963. It must persist in reasserting its concern over the Karakoram Highway linking Pakistan-occupied Kashmir with East Turkestan, which is now being upgraded into the China-Pakistan Economic Corridor (CPEC). As part of its negotiating strategy, India must extend its claim lines into Tibet, beyond what it may eventually agree upon in a final settlement. It should put in a claim to Kailash and Mansarovar. If China can lay claim to Tawang in Arunachal Pradesh on the grounds of its cultural, historical and spiritual links with Tibet, the case for India's claim to Kailash-Mansarovar region on similar reasoning is more substantive. After all, hundreds of millions of Hindus consider this the abode of Lord Shiva. Fortunately, India's current leadership is convinced of the need to stand up to China to protect India's vital interests. China would also be well advised not to misjudge India's strength and resolve. Over the last few years the boundary question has become more complicated and an early solution is highly unlikely. India must clearly understand that China is dragging its feet because it doesn't want a settlement just now. Moreover, the public positions of the two sides are so far apart that it would be difficult to arrive at a compromise that is acceptable to the public in both countries. While the absurdity of China's claims on Arunachal Pradesh precludes any compromise solution, in the Ladakh sector the best hope—admittedly a long shot from today's perspective—is to convert the contested border regions into a frontier zone of cooperation, with transport and communication arteries running across the frontier for mutual benefit and interdependence.

Tibet as a Key Factor

Tibet is the key to understanding China's policy towards India in general and the India-China boundary question in particular. For too long India has viewed China as an East Asian country—an understandable perception, since China's heartland lies in East Asia and its strategic importance for the rest of the world is as an East Asian power. But from India's perspective, China's importance lies primarily in its Eurasian character. It is in Central Asia, specifically Tibet and East Turkestan, that the political borders of contemporary India and China meet. It is China's control of Tibet (and East Turkestan) that poses security threats to India. From China's security perspective, if Tibet were not a part of China, it would inevitably drift closer to India because of its geographical proximity as well as religious and cultural affinity to India. Unlike Tibet's relationship with China, there is no history of hostility or war between Tibet and India. Aware that in the past Tibet held sway over parts of China, China is wary of any foreign presence and influence in Tibet, as Britain had established in the nineteenth century to protect its Indian empire. Given Tibet's geography, any foreign influence there can only be Indian. When the Dalai Lama fled Tibet for India in 1959, China was uncertain about India's attitude and feared that India could become a platform from which attacks on Tibet could be launched. The content and the timing of Chinese prime minister Zhou Lai's reported package-deal offer to Prime Minister Nehru in April 1960 to let China keep Aksai Chin in return for recognition of the McMahon Line is significant: the strategic Aksai Chin area would not be given up, but China was willing to recognize the McMahon Line in order to get some breathing space to consolidate its hold over Tibet.

From a ground-level perspective, Tibet is crucial because it is the geographical link between India and China. Unless there is all-round agreement that Tibet is a part of China, there is only an India-Tibet boundary, not an India-China boundary. Even the 1914 Shimla Agreement that delineated the McMahon Line was signed between India and Tibet; the Chinese representative only initialled the agreement, which China later denounced. China rightly believes that a settlement of the India-China border has implications for the status of Tibet. From a political perspective, China would like to have Tibet recognized as an inalienable part of China, not only now but historically too; otherwise the Chinese takeover of Tibet will lack legitimacy and will always be considered an imperial conquest. As such, China is not likely to settle the boundary question with India, unless it has definitively resolved the question of Tibet on its terms and Tibet is firmly under its control. Whether and when this may happen remains to be seen. Arunachal Pradesh matters to China because the Chinese leadership has projected it as 'Southern Tibet', and therefore, China's inability to bring Arunachal Pradesh into China could be seen as weakening China's claim on Tibet itself. The specific claim to Tawang on the specious ground that this was the birthplace of the sixth Dalai Lama is not because the Chinese have any respect for this institution (quite the contrary) but because they see it as legitimizing their control over the institution of the Dalai Lama, and thereby, Tibetan Buddhism, which is seen by China as a threat to its rule over Tibet and a challenge to its goal of colonizing it. This line of thinking appears to have been reinforced as a result of the widespread disturbances and violence in Tibet and elsewhere over the last decade and a half.

India cannot, under any circumstances, accept such flawed Chinese reasoning for its claim on Arunachal Pradesh. Essentially,

China is adopting dilatory tactics in its boundary negotiations with India. There are no great issues of principle involved in the Chinese approach. It is illogical that China should not accept the McMahon Line as the boundary with India when it has done so with Myanmar in January 1960 and had made a similar offer to India in April 1960. In any case, by withdrawing to the McMahon Line after crossing it in 1962, China implicitly accepted its validity. Nor does China's argument that the 1914 Shimla Agreement be considered invalid carry any substance. After all, China scrupulously observed the ninety-nine-year lease on Hong Kong that the British imposed on a weak China in 1898 and patiently waited till 1997 to peacefully resume sovereignty over Hong Kong after holding lengthy and detailed negotiations with the British government.

China has already extracted significant concessions from India on Tibet through India's acceptance that China is a legitimate negotiating partner to settle the India-Tibet boundary, and that Tibet is a part of China. But China remains uncertain and somewhat anxious about India's Tibet policy and is highly suspicious of India's motives in providing refuge to tens of thousands of Tibetan refugees and a base for the Dalai Lama's activities. The Dalai Lama's periodic statements that India's policy on Tibet is over-cautious only reinforce China's suspicions and fears. It would seem that the Chinese leaders have made up their minds that a satisfactory solution to Tibet, from China's point of view, is unlikely while the Dalai Lama is still alive and that China's interests are better served by waiting till the Dalai Lama has passed away. The Chinese mistrust and suspicion of the Dalai Lama has only intensified since the March 2008 troubles in Tibet and other parts of China where there is a concentration of Tibetans. Besides, the harsh and vituperative language used by the Chinese leaders and official media to denounce the Dalai Lama, which is reminiscent of the days of the Cultural Revolution, makes it that much more difficult for the Chinese government to even have talks with the Dalai Lama, much less for such talks to be successful. In any case, the various rounds of talks that the Chinese government has had with the representatives of the Dalai Lama have not brought the two sides any closer. The talks have remained suspended for many years now.

Contrary to what the Chinese government may be thinking, the situation may deteriorate and go out of control after the present Dalai Lama is no more. When the troubles erupted in Tibet, in other parts of China and elsewhere in the world in March 2008, the Dalai Lama did not appear to be in control of the movement. Although he remains by far the most respected personality for the Tibetans, the younger generation of Tibetans who were born and have grown up outside Tibet has increasingly begun to question the efficacy of his middle path of seeking only genuine autonomy for Tibet as part of the People's Republic of China and keeping the resistance non-violent. They have been inspired by the new nations that have come up in Central Asia and Europe. Tibetans wonder why Hong Kong and Macao can have their autonomy but not the Tibetans, despite the fact that they have a much more distinct personality and enjoyed quasi-independence in the first half of the twentieth century. As he gets on in years, the Dalai Lama appears to have become conscious of the limits of his power and influence, which probably led him to play the card of threatening to resign if the violence should escalate. With this move, he may have temporarily restored the unity of the movement. But graver dangers lie ahead.

After the passing of the Dalai Lama, the Tibetan movement is likely to get splintered but also become far more radicalized, unpredictable and violent, as the Dalai Lama himself has conceded. The trigger for trouble would be the issue of selection of the next Dalai Lama. The Dalai Lama has explained that the very purpose of reincarnation is to carry forward the unfinished work started in the previous life, and if the he were to die while still a refugee, then logically his reincarnation should be born outside Tibet so that the next Dalai Lama can carry on the unfinished work from his previous incarnation. It is possible, as he has indicated recently, that the present Dalai Lama goes ahead with a referendum among the Tibetans in the Himalayan range, including China, Nepal and India, as well as Mongolia (although Tibetans living in China are unlikely to be allowed to participate) to decide whether he should himself select his successor from among the Tibetan diaspora. If this proposal does not find favour, there would be no future Dalai Lama! As opposed to this, the Chinese government, in a bizarre move, has arrogated to itself the absurd right to approve all reincarnations of Tibetan lamas! This will undoubtedly create a tricky situation for India, since the Dalai Lama lives in India and there is a high probability that his successor will be reincarnated in India, perhaps in Dharamsala or even Tawang. China could well demand that India hand over the new Dalai Lama to China, where he will no doubt disappear under mysterious circumstances. Even if it is not in India that the next Dalai Lama is reincarnated, it remains the main base of active followers who constitute his main body of support.

India has taken some welcome steps to review its Tibet policy. The first move was made in January 2008, when the statement issued at the end of Prime Minister Manmohan Singh's visit to China did not carry any reference to Tibet. It is now clear that this was a deliberate policy move, not a one-off measure, as this remains India's approach in subsequent India-China documents. The widespread disturbances in Tibet in March 2008 provided a welcome opportunity for India to continue with its subtle policy shift. India's official statement on 15 March 2008 was a step in the right direction. Clearly refuting official Chinese propaganda, it stated that innocent people had died in Lhasa. By expressing its hope that all those involved will work to improve the situation and remove the causes of such trouble in Tibet through dialogue and non-violent means, New Delhi conveyed its message to Beijing that there is merit in the demands of the Tibetans, that the onus is on Beijing to find a solution, and that such a solution requires dialogue, not use of force. In describing the Dalai Lama as a man of non-violence, Prime Minister Manmohan Singh signalled that India does not endorse the harsh and vituperative official Chinese denunciations of the Dalai Lama. Prime Minister Modi has gone further. He invited the *Sikyong*, leader of the Tibetan government-in-exile in India, to his swearing-in ceremony in May 2014. A few years later he met the Dalai Lama, news about which was leaked, and has been exchanging greetings with the Dalai Lama on their respective birthdays, much to China's chagrin and annoyance.

While formulating its policy on Tibet, India has to keep in mind that as it is uniquely placed vis-à-vis Tibet, it must have a unique policy that conforms to its national interests, irrespective of what the rest of the world says or does. No other country has comparable stakes in Tibet's peace and stability. A Tibet in ferment makes India's Himalayan frontiers unstable and insecure. As a democratic country hosting such a large number of Tibetans, India has a legitimate interest in what happens in Tibet. Tibet cannot be just an internal matter of China because it has direct consequences for India. India has to bear the burden of hosting nearly 1,20,000 Tibetan refugees because of China's repressive policies in Tibet. If there is a severe crackdown in Tibet, it will inevitably trigger a fresh influx of Tibetan refugees into India, whom it would be difficult to turn away on practical and humanitarian grounds. An increased Chinese military presence in Tibet has implications for India's security.

What could be the elements of India's Tibet policy? At a general level, in official statements and/or through authoritative but deniable unofficial channels, India could emphasize that while it firmly upholds the principles of supporting the territorial integrity of duly constituted states and non-interference in other states' internal affairs, its own experience shows that the peace and stability of multi-racial, multi-religious and multicultural societies require dialogue and accommodation within a democratic framework. Ethnic and separatist problems require political solutions that give every citizen the confidence that they are an equal stakeholder in the state. India expects that China will put in place policies that will stabilize Tibet and give the Tibetan diaspora in India the confidence that they can return to their homeland.

India also needs to take full advantage of an important nuance, perhaps unintended, in India's acceptance of Tibet as a part of China: India has merely conceded, during Prime Minister Vajpayee's visit, that the territory of the Tibetan Autonomous Region is a part of the People's Republic of China; it has not accepted that Tibet (whose borders historically and in the minds of the Tibetans extend beyond the Tibetan Autonomous Region) was always a part of China. In the past, it has signalled that Tibet is separate from China. Thus, despite Chinese protests, India invited Tibet as a separate delegation to the Asian Relations Conference convened in New Delhi in March 1947.

Traditionally, thousands of Indians have made pilgrimages to Mount Kailash and Mansarovar lakes in Tibet without needing any permission from the Chinese authorities in Beijing. Secondly, if at any time in the future the People's Republic of China were to give way to another entity, India could well argue that it is not obliged to recognize Tibet as part of any new political entity that may replace it. Of course, this is a hypothetical and somewhat unlikely scenario, but the Chinese, who are given to catching nuances and subtleties, would not miss this point.

India's new Tibet policy should also take into account China's routine and brazen violation of its solemn bilateral commitments. Contrary to the agreements reached during Prime Minister Vajpayee's visit to China in 2003 and in contravention of the Guiding Principles and Political Parameters for Settling the Boundary Question signed during Prime Minister Wen Jiabao's visit to India in 2005, China has reopened very aggressively its claim to Arunachal Pradesh, violated the 1993 and 1996 border agreements with India, not fully accepted Sikkim as a part of India, and does not want an early settlement of the boundary question. In launching a border war in 1962, China has also not followed in letter and spirit the 1954 Panchsheel Agreement. India needs to take a leaf out of China's book in this regard. India should also subtly reopen the whole question of the legitimacy of China's claim to Tibet, which is the basic foundation for any territorial claim to be made by China on Arunachal Pradesh. Technically, the 1954 Trade Agreement expired after eight years, since it was not renewed. In light of recent developments in Tibet, there could be other ways of signalling that India is introducing some nuances in its traditional policy. For example, India could state that it considers the territory of Tibet *as an autonomous region*, a part of the People's Republic of China—the implication being that it is only if Tibet is a truly autonomous region that India will recognize it as a part of China. India's understanding of Tibet's true autonomy should mirror the Dalai Lama's position on this question.

China's offensive and patronizing tone about India's stand on Tibet requires an appropriate riposte. It is evident that, notwithstanding India's reaffirmations that the Tibetans in India are not allowed to indulge in political activities on Indian soil, India remains the base from which they are conducting a political campaign against Chinese rule in Tibet. The Chinese have to understand that such practical deviations from India's stated policy will continue. India should be in no hurry to remove the ambiguities in its Tibet policy unless conditions are created in Tibet for the Tibetan refugees to go back in safety and dignity. Moreover, since China has shown no understanding of India's position on Kashmir, there is no reason for India to give China satisfaction on Tibet. As former minister of external affairs, Sushma Swaraj, put it pithily, if China wants India to follow a 'One China' policy, it should follow a 'One India' policy! If China has its core issues on which it will not compromise, so does India.

Chinese Perceptions of India

Traditionally, China has never looked at India as an equal but merely as an upstart wannabe. India's place, in Chinese eyes, is in South Asia only; it should not aspire to be an influential Asian, much less a global, player. While the May 1998 Pokharan-II nuclear weapons tests did make China sit up and take notice, it was not something over which the Chinese lost too much sleep. During US President Clinton's visit to China a month later, China got implicit US endorsement of its position as Asia's leading power, with a role to play in South Asia. However, what appears to be bothering China is India's impressive and consistent economic performance over the last decade. India has become an attractive economic partner for a large number of countries, which are beginning to look at India as a serious alternative to China. The rest of the world no longer regards China as the only game in town. Admittedly, the size of India's economy is much smaller than China's, but if India keeps growing steadily and China's economy falters (as it appears to be), the gap between India and China will narrow. India is the only other Asian country with the size, resources, demographic profile and all-round capabilities to pose a credible challenge to China's dominance over Asia in the long term. It has some definite advantages over China, such as its democratic structure, its legal system, its developed services sector, its sophisticated world-class finance and banking systems and, of course, its prowess in information technology and the English language. India has also made progress in some high-technology sectors, including space and biotechnology. Its defence modernization programme has made China sit up and take notice. India threatens to become a competitor to China for attracting investments, for access to energy sources and as a market for goods. There appears to be a return to the paradigm of the 1950s involving competition between India and China over which model of development is more successful. The ardour with which India is pursuing a strategic engagement with the United States has also unsettled China. India's diplomatic activism all over the world, most recently its successful hosting of the G-20 summit in September 2023 and its growing attractiveness as a partner for a growing number of countries signal that much of the world, and India itself, does not want India to remain in the South Asia box.

From China's point of view, therefore, it makes sense to keep India unsure about its intentions, as that will make it difficult for India to free up resources from defence for developmental activity. War is not necessary if psychological pressure and controlled border aggression serve the purpose. Steady economic integration of Tibet and Nepal into China's fold is also expected to strengthen China's bargaining position. In this way, China probably hopes that over time the military and economic gap between India and China may increase and that it may be able to drive a better bargain with India on the boundary question later rather than sooner.

Future Trajectory of Relations

Apart from the serious differences over Tibet and the boundary question between India and China, China's activities in India's neighbourhood give Delhi India cause for considerable concern. For more than four and a half decades, China has used its 'all-weather' relationship with Pakistan very effectively to keep India in check. It is attempting to do the same with India's other immediate neighbours. The Indian security establishment is concerned about many aspects of China's activities in South Asia—its railway network that has reached Kashgar and Lhasa and its proposed further extension to Xigatse near the Indian border as well as into Nepal; its rapid development of infrastructure in Tibet; its activism in Myanmar; its entrenched position in Pakistan, including the development of Gwadar Port as a Chinese base and the China-Pakistan Economic Corridor (CPEC) project; its success in developing considerable influence in Bangladesh, Nepal, Sri Lanka and the Maldives; and its base in Djibouti. Uncertainties in the India-China relationship reassure India's insecure neighbours that they have an alternative source of support against India. China's growing economic weight makes it an attractive partner for India's neighbours seeking to reduce their economic dependence on India. It suits China if India remains bogged down in relationships of suspicion and mistrust with its South Asian neighbours, as that would impede India's economic growth and limit its global influence.

The growing strategic and security cooperation in bilateral and trilateral frameworks, and now in a quadrilateral one too (the 'Quad') that has developed in recent years between India and the US, as well as between India and US allies like Japan and Australia, has stoked Chinese fears about India's strategic direction. China appears to have concluded that India has joined the US camp. It may be reviving Chinese memories of the Indo-US collaboration of the 1950s pressuring China over Tibet and stoking China's apprehension of a similar joint approach targeting not just Tibet but East Turkestan too. Unfortunately, China sees its relationship with India only through the prism of its rivalry with the United States. It mistakenly ignores India's deep concerns about many bilateral issues with China, which bear no relation to the state of India's relations with the United States. India has made it clear that it will not be a pawn in the strategic plans of the US, which can change rapidly. After all, there are too many linkages between the United States and China that the United States will be loath to disrupt for the sake of India. Realpolitik dictates that India should continue to develop closer relationships with China's neighbours like Japan, South Korea, the Philippines and Vietnam, including in the defence field. India also needs to beef up its presence and activity in the Indian Ocean and make increasingly frequent forays into the west Pacific Ocean too. Such measures will help India exert counter-psychological pressure on China.

Taiwan Issue

In accordance with India's 'One China' policy, India does not recognize Taiwan. It has no diplomatic relations with Taiwan, and it was not until 1995 that it even established unofficial relations. Today, India has established an office of the India-Taipei Association to handle its interests in Taiwan, while Taiwan does the same through a Taiwan Economic and Cultural Centre in New Delhi. Taiwan has since emerged as an important economic partner of India's in East Asia. As Taiwan has many technologies of interest to India, especially semiconductors, and significant investible resources, trade and investment is at a healthy level, though still below potential. Initially, India was very discreet about its contacts with Taiwan, which were mostly at the non-official and middle-level official levels. It is only since 2006, presumably as a signal of its displeasure with China on account of various political and military provocations by the latter, that India has been bold enough to have exchanges with Taiwan's political leaders, including on the occasion of Prime Minister Modi's election victory in June 2024. India is now actively courting investments by Taiwanese companies in India. Another significant development was the recent visit to Taiwan by retired chiefs of the Indian armed forces. This is welcome activism in India's Taiwan policy.

As Chinese and US rhetoric over Taiwan has built up in recent years, and there is increasing speculation about whether China will use force to invade Taiwan and what the US reaction to any such move will be, India has to have its ears on the ground to understand the Taiwan situation better. China's aggressive postures and actions towards its neighbours have now become routine. Many observers are speculating that in order to bolster his nationalist credentials, and as a diversionary tactic from the mounting economic and political troubles at home, Xi Jinping may try a risky gambit overseas. Taiwan and India are two target countries. The fear is that if China concludes that any invasion of Taiwan would be too risky, it may choose India as a target. On the other hand, any normalization of Taiwan-China relations would enable China to shift many of its missiles and other military equipment currently targeted at Taiwan to areas like Tibet and East Turkestan, where they would change the military balance and create security headaches for India. Thus, India will also have to keep a close eye on the state of Taiwan-China relations. Taiwan is also a useful perch for China-watching. While it is desirable for India to develop relations with Taiwan in diverse spheres, there is little to be gained from an open disavowal of India's 'One China' policy since Taiwan's position on India's border with Tibet is the same as that of the People's Republic of China.

Future Prospects

China will remain among India's most pressing, difficult and complex foreign policy challenges. India will have to deal with China at many levels. In the first place, China is a neighbour with exaggerated and preposterous territorial claims on India. It is suspicious of India harbouring the Dalai Lama and a large population of Tibetan refugees, since it is their presence in India that has principally kept alive the Tibetan issue, which is at the heart of India's festering border dispute with China. Besides, recent developments portend no early end to the mutual mistrust and suspicion between India and China. China could have been a possible partner for India in a cooperative endeavour to build a multi-polar world, but the prospects of this have receded as China has made it clear that it aspires to be a global leader with only the United States as a peer. As a strategic rival to India claiming leadership in Asia, China has made it clear that it will continue to create difficulties for India through Pakistan and India's other neighbours, as well as through its activities in the Indian Ocean. Strategically, China wants to keep India bottled up in South Asia and not have it rise as a major Asian and global power. India has managed to thwart such Chinese designs and is now recognized as a credible Asian power and global player. On the military side, India has built up its missile capabilities to bring China's major population centres within reach, as well as enhanced its naval strength to enable it, together with its strategic partners, to disrupt China's energy and trade flows in a crisis.

Despite tensions in bilateral relations, the two countries are together at many regional forums that provide them the opportunity to engage with each other constructively. These include the Shanghai Cooperation Organisation, BRICS, the East Asia Summit (EAS) and the trilateral Russia-India-China framework. Till the relationship started souring over the last decade or so, India took the line that there is enough space in Asia for both China and India. It is now abundantly clear that China, riding on the back of its economic strength and technological achievements, does not feel the same way. While some degree of mutual wariness and competition for economic and strategic space is inevitable, it is only if both countries are confident that the other is not engaged in a zero-sum game that there can be peace and stability in Asia.

On global issues, there is not much common ground between India and China. Allied as it is with Pakistan, China does not share India's perspective on countering terrorism. China is firmly opposed to India's bid to become a permanent member of the UN Security Council, nor was it openly in favour of modifying the Nuclear Suppliers' Group guidelines to accommodate India. The interests of India and China also diverge on other crucial issues. On climate change, China is a major polluter compared with India, and therefore, it is not in India's interest to be clubbed with China. In the WTO, India's interests also somewhat diverge from China's since India's economy relies more on services and China's on manufacturing.

While India must never let its guard down, prudence and common sense dictate that it is not in India's interest to have a relationship of perennial tension and antagonism with a large and powerful neighbour like China. It is not clear if China has a similar long-term perspective. As there is much to be gained from a peaceful cooperative relationship with China, India must keep the door open for a modus vivendi with

China, on the basis of equality and dignity, without any illusions that there can be any return to the so-called fraternal relationship of the 1950s. Of course, post-Galwan this has become more difficult and can be envisaged only if there is a radical change in the thinking of China's leaders. As of today, the outlook for a cooperative India-China relationship is bleak.

Chapter 8

'Act East' Policy and the Indo-Pacific

Historical Roots

It is generally thought that India started focusing on its eastern neighbours only about three decades ago when then Prime Minister Narasimha Rao proclaimed India's 'Look East' policy. However, that is not quite true. For centuries, India has had strong trading, cultural and people-to-people links with its eastern neighbours. There was a strong logic to this interaction. The lands to the east of India were fertile, prosperous, and sustained large populations. Monsoon winds facilitated the movement of ships and boats between the Indian subcontinent and South-east Asia. In this way, there evolved a vibrant Bay of Bengal community. Across this stretch of water, people moved back and forth easily. One of the important features of this interaction was that it was largely peaceful. Apart from some forays by the Cholas into South-east Asia in the eleventh century, there was no attempt at empire building, no history of war or conflict, only tales of extensive interaction through the flow of trade, movement of people and the intermingling of cultures and ideas. There were large and prosperous Hindu and Buddhist kingdoms in South-east Asia, such as those of Srivijaya, Majapahit, Java and Bali (Indonesia), Ayutthaya (Thailand), Bagan (Myanmar), Kedah (Malaysia), Angkor (Cambodia) and Champa (Vietnam). It is noteworthy that all of them were well-established, large, confident kingdoms with local roots, not colonies of India.

Despite this deep historical connection, South Asia and East Asia developed independently during the colonial period because India's traditional pattern of interaction with South-east Asia changed. The colonial powers broke the intra-Asian trading and people-to-people links; now the links were stronger between the colonies and the European colonizers. At the same time, the colonizers took Indians as agricultural labourers and plantation workers to South-east Asia, as a result of which a large Indian-origin population mushroomed in countries like Malaya and Burma. During the period of colonial rule, memories of shared commonalities of history and culture weakened. Nevertheless, South-east Asia played an important role in India's freedom movement, particularly as far as Netaji Subhash Chandra Bose's Indian National Army was concerned.

India's Post-Independence Perspective

When India became independent, its leaders fully understood the importance of South-east Asia for the country. In a note on India's foreign policy recorded on 12 September 1948, Nehru said:

> We are most intimately concerned with South East Asia and we should therefore develop these contacts as much as possible. This means that we should particularly help in every way in the freedom of the countries of South East Asia and their closer cooperation with India in political and economic matters, and ultimately in defence. South East Asia would include Australia and New Zealand . . . India is the natural leader of South East Asia if not of some other parts of Asia also.[1]

The importance of the Asian dimension of independent India's foreign policy was presaged in the Asian Relations Conference convened in New Delhi in March–April 1947, a few months before India became independent. South-east Asia and East Asia continued to occupy a prominent role in India's foreign policy over the next decade or so. India's independence gave a fillip to the anti-colonial movements across South-east Asia. India took a keen interest in the independence struggles of Indonesia (a conference was convened in Delhi in early 1949) and Burma, played a prominent role in trying to resolve the Korean conflict and was chairman of the International Control Commission in Indo-China. It was an active participant in the Bandung Afro-Asian Conference in 1955.

However, as the Cold War developed and military blocs like SEATO were set up, India and the South-east Asian countries found themselves on opposite sides of the Cold War divide. Other factors too contributed to India and South-east Asia drifting apart. The Indo-China states were engulfed in war and conflict, while Myanmar and Indonesia drifted away from India following military coups in 1962 and 1965 respectively. Overland linkages with South-east Asia, never easy because of the difficult terrain and poor communications, withered away as East Pakistan/Bangladesh blocked transit after the 1965 India-Pakistan war. India too was more focused on the greater opportunities in the West compared with opportunities the relatively less developed eastern neighbours could offer at the time. While this historical legacy has ensured that there is no baggage to act as a drag on India-East Asia relations in the twenty-first century, it has also led to a situation where neither region impinged very much on the other's consciousness and foreign policy priorities throughout the second half of the twentieth century.

'Look East' Policy

The imperatives for a change in India's perspective of South-east Asia that led to Prime Minister P.V. Narasimha Rao's Look East policy in the early 1990s were compelling and simultaneous: the collapse of the Soviet Union, which was India's valued economic partner; the financial and economic crisis faced by India that led to a change in India's inward-looking economic policy orientation; and the dramatic transformation in the global strategic environment following the end of the Cold War and the consequent absurdity of regarding South Asia and South-east Asia as separate strategic and economic regions with marginal interaction. As peace returned to Indo-China, new transport and other economic arteries started coming up in South-east Asia, which was being systematically hardwired with China and inexorably sucked into China's economic whirlpool. India was concerned that it was not a part of these mushrooming linkages that were creating new long-term political and economic interdependencies. There was the danger that India could remain strategically and economically boxed up in the South Asian region, mired in dealings with a fractious neighbourhood that offered limited opportunities for its growth. In order to fulfil its aspirations of playing a greater regional and global role, India needed an extended political and economic strategic space beyond South Asia. The East, with its dynamic economies, was the only direction in India's strategic neighbourhood where opportunity beckoned.

ASEAN was the focus of India's Look East policy in the 1990s. Progress in developing ties was halting and slow. India initiated a Sectoral Dialogue with ASEAN in 1992, and became a full Dialogue Partner and a member of the ASEAN Regional Forum (ARF) in 1996. But ASEAN did not yet regard India as a serious and credible partner. ASEAN's interest in India was limited, and India was kept out of organizations like the Asia-Europe Meeting (ASEM) and Asia Pacific Economic Cooperation (APEC), which were set up in the 1990s. (India joined ASEM in 2008, but is still not a member of APEC.) The year 1998 was a turning point. All countries, including the ASEAN nations, Japan, Korea, Australia and New Zealand, put relations with India on hold following Pokharan-II. For the next couple of years or so, India's diplomatic energies were directed at handling the fallout of this development and the Kargil war with Pakistan. Meanwhile, the faltering of the Doha Round of global trade negotiations and the proliferation of regional trading arrangements in Asia added urgency to India's quest to engage with ASEAN. Fortunately, perceptions within ASEAN about India had changed during this period. There was the reality of India as a nuclear weapons power. India had also weathered the Asian financial crisis quite well. Unsurprisingly, once the dust had settled down, ASEAN began to view India as a major Asian power with the economic and military potential to be a partner in trying to balance China, whose economic dominance was beginning to worry many Asian countries. Singapore's then prime minister, Goh Chok

Tong likened ASEAN to an airplane that could remain airborne and stable only if its two wings, China and India, were balanced.

By the turn of the century, the composition and orientation of ASEAN also significantly changed. Four new members were taken in between 1995 and 1999—Vietnam in 1995, Laos and Myanmar in 1997 and Cambodia in 1999, referred to as the CLMV countries. Now, for the first time, India had a land border with ASEAN. India was also seen as a country with skills and assets that could help in the development of the CLMV countries with which it had close cultural, religious and historical ties. Similarly, there was political change in India too. After the rickety coalition governments of the mid-1990s, India got a stable government led by Prime Minister Atal Bihari Vajpayee. With the setting up of a Department for the Development of the North-east Region in 2001, the Vajpayee government signalled its intention to give greater attention to this region of India. Geography dictated that development of the North-east region could be facilitated by the region's interaction with the CLMV countries and Thailand.

Evolution of the 'Look East' Policy

While India's Look East policy covered relations with all its eastern neighbours, including ASEAN and its ten member states (Brunei, Cambodia, Indonesia, Laos, Malaysia, Myanmar, Philippines, Singapore, Thailand, Vietnam), as well as Japan, South Korea, Australia and New Zealand, it is India's engagement with ASEAN that was central to its Look East policy in the early years. Nuances also developed in India's Look East policy. It became two-pronged. The first prong reached out to the original, wealthier ASEAN countries (Thailand, Malaysia, Brunei, Singapore, Indonesia, the Philippines) with whom connectivity was by sea and the focus on trade and economic cooperation. The second prong was directed at the CLMV countries. Here, the focus was on developing land connectivity and reviving cultural and people-to-people contacts.

The year 2002 was a landmark in India-ASEAN relations. ASEAN invited the Indian prime minister for a summit meeting with its leaders.

It was at this meeting that India offered to conclude a Free Trade Agreement with ASEAN, which gave credibility to India's Look East policy and ensured that ASEAN-India summit meetings became a regular feature. The next five years or so saw intensive India-ASEAN engagement, both with the group as a whole as well as with individual ASEAN members. In 2005, India became a founder member of the East Asia Summit (EAS). This was an important development, since India was recognized as an East Asian power that had a legitimate role in community building and security in the region. In a psychological, political and strategic sense, India's membership of the EAS bridged the gap between India and East Asia. One could say that this was the genesis of the concept of the Indo-Pacific.

Two developments during this period are noteworthy. First, while ASEAN remained at the heart of India's Look East policy, the geographical scope of India's Look East policy widened to include other countries in East Asia and the Pacific, like Japan, South Korea, Australia and New Zealand. Relations with them rapidly expanded. Particularly noteworthy was the swift upturn in relations with Japan. Second, while economic cooperation remained a core area of cooperation—and free trade/comprehensive economic cooperation or partnership agreements were concluded or initiated with ASEAN and BIMSTEC as well as with individual countries like Singapore, Japan, South Korea and Thailand—there was the beginning of cooperation in the security field, initially to counter terrorist threats, but later increasingly to counter Chinese threats.

India continued to attach high priority to developing ties with the ASEAN countries. In 2012, India became a Strategic Partner of ASEAN. In a small but important gesture, Prime Minister Modi converted the Look East policy to the 'Act East' policy. Signalling ASEAN's importance in its foreign policy, India invited all the ASEAN leaders as chief guests for its Republic Day function in 2018 to celebrate twenty-five years of India-ASEAN relations. The gesture was notable, but more significant was the decision of all the ASEAN leaders to accept the invitation and be present on the occasion. Clearly, China and its policies were bothering them, and their collective presence in

New Delhi showed that they were looking to India to provide leadership in countering China.

India has consistently reiterated that ASEAN is the central pillar of India's Act East Policy, that India fully supports ASEAN centrality and ASEAN's collective outlook on the Indo-Pacific, and that ASEAN holds a prominent place in India's Indo-Pacific initiative. This is not just symbolism. ASEAN acts as a buffer between the great powers of the region such as China, Japan, the United States and India. The ASEAN region is also the geographical link between the Indian and the Pacific Oceans, as well as between South Asia, East Asia and the Pacific Island nations, and between the individual members of the Quad. Thus, it is evident that there can be no meaningful Indian strategy for the Indo-Pacific region that does not take ASEAN into account. Currently, all regional economic and security cooperation structure have ASEAN at the core. From this perspective, an independent and united ASEAN is imperative to ensure that there's a stable regional architecture rather than one dominated by China.

Bilateral Relationships

India's Look East policy has not only strengthened its relationship with ASEAN as a whole but has also provided a complementary institutional framework and a catalyst for India's bilateral ties with individual ASEAN countries. Singapore was the principal shepherd for India in ASEAN and played a critical role in bringing about the India-ASEAN engagement at the summit level as well as India's membership of the EAS. In keeping with its policy of staying ahead of the curve, it took a strategic view of India in the early 1990s, at a time when not many countries were looking at India seriously. Singapore realized that with the rise of Shanghai as China's own financial centre and the transfer of Hong Kong back to China in 1997, it would be disadvantaged in doing business with China. It accordingly decided that it could play a catalytic role in India's economic transformation, similar to the role Hong Kong has traditionally played for China. It felt that if India and Singapore developed greater long-term mutual stakes in the form of investments, and exchange of knowledge workers, tourists and students, this would bring greater vitality to Singapore's economy and enhance its security. The result of Singapore's efforts, reciprocated by India, is the India-Singapore Comprehensive Economic Cooperation Agreement, the first of its kind for India, which has been operative since 2005. Over the last few years there has been a noticeable spurt in India-Singapore trade and economic relations. Singapore is India's largest trading partner in ASEAN and accounts for 95 per cent of India's inward and outward foreign direct investments with ASEAN. India also has an extensive defence cooperation programme with Singapore that is unmatched in the rest of ASEAN. Overall, between India and Singapore, there is considerable mutual trust and confidence, extensive people-to-people ties and frequent exchange of high-level official visits.

Apart from Myanmar (which as an immediate neighbour is a special case), Indonesia, Malaysia and Thailand are the three other ASEAN countries with which India has the greatest interaction. As by far the largest country in the region, Indonesia gives weight, credibility and stability to ASEAN. Given its strategic location linking the Pacific and Indian Oceans, and its sprawling size, extending from the borders of India to those of Australia, Indonesia is vital for regional stability. Indonesia is also the world's largest Muslim country, and whether it remains democratic, tolerant and secular or succumbs to incipient fundamentalist tendencies matters hugely to the rest of the world, including India. India had an indifferent relationship with Indonesia during the more than three decades of Suharto's rule, but since his overthrow in 1998 the tempo of relations has rapidly picked up under his successors. A lot of the old warmth that characterized India's relations with Indonesia in the 1950s, when India and Indonesia were leaders of the Non-Aligned Movement (NAM), has come back. In 2005, the two countries agreed to develop a 'New Strategic Partnership'. Since both India and Indonesia are large developing countries, Indonesia has been keen to learn from India's experience of managing a pluralistic democratic society. Trade and economic cooperation, including investments, are growing between the two, and Indonesia is India's second largest trading partner in ASEAN. India is keen to tap Indonesia's rich resources like gas, coal and timber. Defence and counter-terrorism are growing areas of cooperation. Indonesia and India are maritime neighbours who undertake regular joint patrolling. Indonesia has become a valuable friend of India in ASEAN, the more so as Indonesia is trying to regain its traditional leadership role in ASEAN and is a member of the G-20 grouping.

Malaysia is an important, complex and difficult country in ASEAN. It matters to India because of its economic dynamism (it is India's third largest trading partner in ASEAN), its Islamic orientation (it has a generally pro-Pakistan and pro-OIC view on many matters), its sympathetic orientation towards China because of the control of its economy by businessmen of Chinese origin, and its considerable weight in ASEAN. Malaysia has more than 2 million citizens of Indian origin, mostly descendants of the workers brought by colonial Britain from India to work on Malaysia's rubber, tin and palm oil plantations. The ruling ethnic Malay majority discriminates against this economically weak community at the lowest strata of Malaysia's society, which at times creates ripples among the public in India. The attitude of the ethnic Malays towards Malaysian citizens of Indian origin also, regrettably, seems to colour Malaysia's attitude towards India. Despite the high level of trade, growing defence cooperation and the extensive involvement of Malaysian companies in road-building, housing and other infrastructure projects in India, and of Indian companies in Malaysia's infrastructure and information technology sectors, for many years India's relations with Malaysia were marked by some tension and mistrust. This has begun to change after Anwar Ibrahim became the prime minister of Malaysia in 2022.

As maritime neighbours, and in view of the fact that many insurgent groups from the North-east region have been using Thailand as a base, Thailand and India understandably give each other special attention and cooperate closely on counter-terrorism and defence. Thailand remains an attractive tourist destination for Indians. Under Prime Minister Thaksin Shinawatra, Thailand was very aggressive in pursuing closer ties with India as part of its 'Look West' policy. In order to give a boost to the modest level of trade between them, India and Thailand signed a

Framework Agreement for Free Trade Agreement in goods in 2003, but both sides have gone slow in concluding negotiations. The operation of the Early Harvest Programme that has come into effect has created misgivings among some sections of Indian industry, which feel that import of some products from Thailand has put Indian manufacturers at a serious disadvantage. Thailand's geographical location gives it a natural advantage in facilitating India's engagement with the Indo-China countries. For a while, after the departure of Malaysia's long-standing prime minister Mahathir, Thailand tried to position itself as the natural leader of ASEAN and as India's principal interlocutor with the bloc. While that has not fructified because Thailand has been preoccupied with dealing with its domestic political situation, it does remain relevant for India's engagement with the CLMV countries and is the only developed member of ASEAN involved with India in sub-regional mechanisms like BIMSTEC and the MGC. On the whole, India's relations with Thailand are marked by warmth, cordiality and confidence.

Although the Philippines and Vietnam are the two largest ASEAN countries after Indonesia, the level of India's interaction with them was disappointingly low till not so long ago. Traditionally, India has not figured on the radar screen of the Philippines, which has generally been more focused on its relations with ASEAN members, other countries in East Asia and the United States. It is only as a result of India's summit-level dialogue with ASEAN, India's membership of the EAS and the exchange of Presidential visits in 2006–07, that there has been some movement in bilateral relations, including cooperation in the fields of defence and counter-terrorism.

Vietnam and India were close friends during the Cold War years, but the residual goodwill of that period has not translated into any concrete benefits for India as Vietnam has focused on rebuilding its economy and working out stable equations with its giant neighbour, China, and the United States. In many respects, India and Vietnam are competitors in the world market. Nevertheless, trade between the two has grown considerably, and Vietnam in India's fourth largest trading partner in ASEAN. There is growing defence cooperation between India and Vietnam. India is assisting Vietnam, both bilaterally and within the framework of ASEAN, in the areas of technical and scientific cooperation, in human resources development and in setting up projects funded by relatively cheap credit lines. India has also made profitable investments in Vietnam's hydrocarbons sector.

India's relations with the two smaller Indo-China countries of Cambodia and Laos are characterized by generous assistance on similar lines, as well as some defence cooperation. India's assistance to the CLMV countries is given both bilaterally as well as through ASEAN's Initiative for ASEAN Integration (IAI), which aims to bring the four new members of ASEAN to the same level of development as the original ASEAN members. Unfortunately, China's money power has enabled it to suck both countries into its sphere of influence.

Brunei, a small but extremely rich country that has extensive links with Malaysia, does not figure high on India's radar. Resident diplomatic missions were established only about three decades ago; trade is low and there is a small Indian community of a few thousand there. However, greater interaction within the ASEAN framework has helped push bilateral ties between the two nations.

Despite Japan being a country with which India has no direct conflict of interest, whether ideological, cultural or territorial, the two countries, strangely, remained distant from each other throughout the twentieth century. Jawaharlal Nehru made a gesture of friendship towards Japan in not signing the 1951 San Francisco Peace Treaty that Japan signed with forty-nine countries, as he felt it offended the dignity of Japan (India signed a separate Peace Treaty with Japan in 1952 in which all war claims against Japan were waived). The dissenting judgment of Justice Radha Binod Pal in the Tokyo War Crimes Tribunal holding Japan's wartime leaders not guilty generated goodwill for India in Japan. Unfortunately, neither of these gestures led to a meaningful all-round relationship commensurate with the fact that India was a large but developing Asian country and Japan the world's second largest economy. For many decades this relationship was relatively undeveloped in all respects, be it in trade, investments, tourism or just mutual awareness. The most substantial aspect of bilateral relations was the official development assistance (ODA) that Japan began to give India in 1958, perhaps in gratitude for India's support for it in international forums. India was the first country to get aid from Japan, and even today it remains the largest recipient of Japanese ODA. Japan was also very helpful at the time of India's financial crisis in 1991.

It was only with the visit of the Japanese prime minister Mori to India in 2000 that Japan began to look at India seriously. India's nuclear status, its growing economy and the fact that even the United States was beginning a serious engagement with India impelled Japan to take a second look at it. Since Japanese prime minister Koizumi's visit to India in April 2005, the relationship has begun to blossom and is steadily evolving into a 'special strategic and global partnership'. Former prime minister Shinzo Abe played an important role in taking the India-Japan relationship to new heights. The leaders of India and Japan hold regular summit meetings, at least once a year. Japanese business houses have begun to show interest in dealing with India. Japanese investors have been active in the Indian stock market. A Comprehensive Economic Partnership Agreement signed in 2011 is an important initiative with considerable long-term economic and strategic significance. India hopes to attract large-scale Japanese investments into India and access Japan's enormous strengths in cutting-edge technologies of the 'knowledge economy', while Japan wishes to gain access to India's large market and tap into its talent pool. India and Japan were together in the G-4 initiative to secure permanent membership of the UN Security Council. Japan was also extremely helpful in pushing India's case for membership of the East Asia Summit and shares India's vision of community-building in Asia. Defence and security cooperation has grown. For the last few years there have been regular meetings of the foreign and defence ministers ('2+2 Dialogue'), as well as annual meetings of the defence ministers and a Coast Guard dialogue. In 2020, the two countries signed an agreement on reciprocal provision of supplies and services between their armed forces (so-called Acquisition and Cross-Servicing Agreement, or ACSA). While, of late, there is a welcome official-level emphasis on developing more extensive cultural, academic and people-to-people ties between

India and Japan, at the popular level there is need to do more to convince the Japanese people about India's long-term value and reliability. At the end of the day, Japan's primary foreign policy focus remains China, and its attitude towards India is influenced to a great extent by the state of its relations with China.

There has been a similar rediscovery of India by the Republic of Korea, or South Korea, in recent years. Unlike in the case of Japan, it is South Korea's business and industrial sector that is driving the bilateral relationship. Leading South Korean companies have aggressively established themselves in Indian markets, in particular in the automobile, white goods and telecommunications sectors, and are actively pursuing possibilities in the steel and information technology sectors. Many of them have decided to use India as a global manufacturing hub that can cater to markets in Asia and elsewhere. Indian companies too are now buying into South Korean companies. Economic relations got a boost with the signing of a Comprehensive Economic Partnership Agreement in 2010. The two countries now have a 'special strategic partnership'. The interdependencies that are being forged today are likely to be long-term. Regular high-level political exchanges have consolidated economic relations. There is also a growing defence relationship with South Korea. With the coming into effect of South Korea's New Southern Policy, India-South Korea relations have received a boost. However, an important question that India will have to consider is whether any political contradictions are likely to develop in the light of China's importance for South Korea and India's frosty relations with China.

Relations with Australia, historically never very warm if not bordering on indifference, received a severe setback after India's nuclear tests of 1998. Over the last couple of decades there has been a dramatic shift in mutual perceptions, and relations are now cordial and close. Both sides signed a declaration of Strategic Partnership in 2009, which has been elevated to that of a Comprehensive Strategic Partnership in 2020. Today, there is a regular exchange of high-level visits and a wide array of agreements across diverse fields, including defence. As with the United States and Japan, India has a '2+2 Dialogue' with Australia too. Both countries are members of the Quad and the G-20, and have a mechanism of trilateral dialogues with France, Indonesia and Japan. India is interested in Australia's rich resources of oil, gas, coal, uranium and other minerals. Australia sees India as an attractive, growing market. There is a healthy level of trade amounting to over US$30 billion. In 2022, the two countries signed an Economic Cooperation and Trade Agreement (ECTA) and are negotiating a Comprehensive Economic Cooperation Agreement (CECA).

New Zealand, much smaller and more distant than Australia, was also neglected for many decades. After Indira Gandhi's 1968 visit, the only other prime ministerial visit from India to New Zealand was by Rajiv Gandhi in 1986. President Pranab Mukherjee, however, did visit New Zealand in 2016, and other high-level visits have been regularly exchanged over the last couple of decades. Needless to say, cricket also plays an important role in bringing India closer to Australia and New Zealand. As more students and tourists began to view Australia and New Zealand as attractive destinations and large numbers of Indians migrated to these two countries, relations have become much warmer. Even though the large and rapidly growing Indian diaspora (about 3 per cent of the population in both Australia and New Zealand) acts as a bridge, as in other English-speaking countries, to bring India closer to these two Pacific countries, their presence does create problems and tensions in bilateral relations from time to time. In 2009–10, there were widespread racially motivated attacks on Indian students in Australia. India is also concerned about the activities of Khalistani separatists operating in Australia.

Of late, India has been giving much greater attention to all the Pacific Island Countries—Cook Islands, Fiji, Kiribati, Marshall Islands, Micronesia, Niue, Nauru, Palau, Papua New Guinea, Samoa, Solomon Islands, Tonga, Tuvalu and Vanuatu. At present, India has resident missions only in Fiji and Papua New Guinea in this region. With Fiji, India has had a special relationship because of the large number (about one-third of the total population) of Indian-origin people settled there. They are the descendants of indentured workers taken to Fiji from India under British colonial rule. From time to time this has resulted in tensions in bilateral relations. Since 2014 there has been an institutional framework for cooperation with the Pacific Island countries—the Forum for India-Pacific Islands Cooperation (FIPIC)—and there have been more frequent bilateral visits.

Mekong-Ganga Cooperation

Two supplementary prongs of India's Look East policy are BIMSTEC (covered in Chapter 2) and the Mekong-Ganga Cooperation (MGC), an organization launched in 2000 that brings together India with Thailand and the CLMV countries of ASEAN. MGC is a sub-regional organization that aims to promote cooperation in ten identified areas: tourism, education, culture, public health and traditional medicine, agriculture and allied sectors, transport and communications, small and medium enterprises (MSMEs), water resources management, science and technology, and skill development and capacity building. The MGC is a valuable framework that India could use to come closer to the CLMV countries which are geographically and culturally close to India. One notable, successful project of the MGC has been the establishment in 2014 of a MGC Asian Traditional Textile Museum in Siem Reap. Unfortunately, in general the MGC has so far failed to live up to its promise. Meetings at the ministerial level have been sporadic. The MGC has been hobbled by problems like absence of clear timelines, uncertainty about sources of funding and inadequate implementation and review mechanisms. Keeping these constraints in mind, India launched in 2012 an India-MGC Quick Impact Scheme focused on projects of short gestation periods costing not more than US$ 50,000 each that can have a positive impact at the community level. So far, under this scheme, more than eighty projects worth over US$ 4 million have been successfully completed in Vietnam, Laos and Cambodia, and another twenty-odd projects are ongoing. Given their relatively larger weight in the grouping, India and Thailand have to be the main drivers and sources of funding for the MGC. However, Thailand became less enthusiastic about the MGC after it set up the Ayeyarwady-Chao Phraya-Mekong Economic Cooperation Strategy

(ACMECS), which brings together the same group of countries, minus India (which has joined ACMECS as a Development Partner in 2019), and Thailand's preoccupation with domestic politics after the departure of Prime Minister Thaksin Shinawatra in 2006. The military takeover in Myanmar in 2021 and the consequent ASEAN policy of ostracizing Myanmar have also reduced the relevance of the MGC.

Importance of the Indian Ocean

The Indian Ocean is vital to India's security and well-being, brought out dramatically by the fact that it was the route for India's colonization by the Europeans. In remarks that remain relevant even today, the well-known academic and diplomat, K.M. Panikkar, shrewdly observed many decades ago that for India the Indian Ocean is different from what it is for other powers. In his words:

> While to other countries, the Indian Ocean is only one of the important oceanic areas, to India it is a vital sea. Her lives are concentrated in this area; her freedom is dependent on this vast water surface. No industrial development, no stable political structure is possible for her unless the Indian Ocean is free and her shores fully protected. The Indian Ocean's strategic importance for India remains undiminished. It is worth emphasizing that it is called Indian because India dominates it. The Indian Ocean is like the Mediterranean Sea in that it is a large virtually enclosed space, with comparable choke points and civilizations flourishing around its rim. Over the centuries, India has been the most advanced civilization in the Indian Ocean area, exerting an influence on other regions on the periphery of the Indian Ocean like the Persian Gulf, the east coast of Africa and South-east Asia. It is central both to the potential threats it poses to India's security as well as the opportunities it offers for influence projection in various directions.[2]

After India became independent, the military and economic elements of India's maritime strategy were at a low level. There were no maritime threats; and India had neither the capability nor need for projection of military force. India had a relatively small share of the global trade and few offshore assets to protect. The navy was India's smallest military arm and the least visible component of its armed forces. Moreover, as its activities do not affect ordinary citizens' lives, its domestic constituency is limited. With their origins in Central Asia, having had to only deal with security threats from the land and ensconced in a capital far from the oceans and their continental empires, India's Muslim rulers did not appreciate the importance of the Indian Ocean for India's security and prosperity. For about a decade after India's independence its leaders continued with this mindset, since it was not till 1958 that an Indian was made the chief of naval staff!

The situation is different today. India has begun to give greater importance to maritime security. Speaking in Kolkata in June 2007, the then minister of external affairs Pranab Mukherjee said:

> For far too many centuries of our history has India either neglected or devoted insufficient attention to this relationship (between international relations and maritime affairs). Fortunately after nearly a millennia of inward and landward focus, we are once again turning our gaze outwards and seawards, which is the natural direction of view for a nation seeking to reestablish itself, not simply as a continental power, but even more so as a maritime power, and consequently as one that is of significance upon the global stage . . . it was only when the ruling Indian elites forgot the imperatives of maritime security that ancient and medieval India's dominance of world trade was lost. The realization that this gross neglect of maritime security eventually led to the colonisation of the sub-continent and the consequent loss of India's very independence for nearly three centuries should make a repetition of this strategic error utterly unaffordable. These harsh lessons of history are not lost on the modern, independent republic that is India.[3]

India has rightly drawn some lessons from the fact that its conquest by the West was from the sea. India today has to exercise control over at least its immediate maritime neighbourhood of the Arabian Sea, the Bay of Bengal and the north Indian Ocean. Of course, India's aspirations are much wider, ranging from the Persian Gulf in the north to Antarctica in the south, and from the Cape of Good Hope and the east coast of Africa in the west to the Straits of Malacca and the archipelagos of Malaysia and Indonesia in the east. The Indian navy's Maritime Security Strategy (2015) has identified the key choke points in the Indian Ocean as follows: the Ombai-Wetar Straits, Lombok Strait, Sunda Strait, the Malacca and Singapore Straits, the Strait of Hormuz, Bab-el-Mandeb, the Suez Canal, the Mozambique Channel and the Cape of Good Hope. The Indian navy and the Coast Guard have tasks to fulfil: working in the traditional defensive role of protecting India's coastline and territorial waters; conduct of military operations in India's neighbourhood whenever needed; keeping India's increasingly important trade and energy SLOCs secure; protecting the resources of India's large exclusive economic zone (EEZ) covering an existing area of more than 2 million square kilometres; ensuring the security of India's offshore assets, including oil and gas; safeguarding its deep-sea mining areas in the central Indian Ocean; and countering piracy and terrorism. There are legal obligations too, with the coming into force of the United Nations Convention on the Law of the Sea (UNCLOS) in November 1994, which sets out a legal international maritime regime.

Indo-Pacific Strategy

Under Prime Minister Modi, India has begun to give much more attention to maritime issues, including maritime security. In March 2015, in an address in Mauritius, Prime Minister Modi unveiled his vision of Security and Growth for All in the Region (SAGAR), envisaging the development of a climate of trust and transparency; respect for international maritime rules and norms by all countries; sensitivity to each other's interests; peaceful resolution of maritime issues; and increase in maritime cooperation. Prime Minister Modi developed this idea in an address at the Shangri-La Dialogue in Singapore in June 2018, when he said that India would promote a democratic and rules-based international order in which all nations, small and large, thrive as equal and sovereign. India would work with others to keep the seas, space and airways free and open, nations secure from terrorism, cyberspace free from disruption and conflict, an open economy, transparent engagement, and share its resources, markets and prosperity with its friends and partners. This, he said, translates in Hindi into sammaan (respect), samvaad (dialogue), sahayog (cooperation), shaanti (peace) and samridhdhi (prosperity). India would engage with the world peacefully, with respect, and through dialogue and absolute commitment to international law.

Among the various bodies that have been established to promote maritime cooperation in the Indian Ocean region, the oldest one, going back to 1997, is the Indian Ocean Rim Association (IORA). India was a prime mover in the setting-up of IORA. Today IORA brings together twenty-three Indian Ocean member-states (Australia, Bangladesh, Comoros, France, India, Indonesia, Iran, Kenya, Madagascar, Malaysia, the Maldives, Mauritius, Mozambique, Oman, Seychelles, Singapore, Somalia, South Africa, Tanzania, Thailand, the United Arab Emirates and Yemen) and eleven countries from outside the region as dialogue partners for promoting mutually beneficial regional cooperation through a consensus-based, evolutionary and non-intrusive approach. It has six priority areas—maritime safety and security; trade and investment facilitation; fisheries management; disaster risk management; tourism and cultural exchange; academic, scientific and technological cooperation; and two focus areas, viz., the blue economy and women's economic empowerment. The apex body is at the ministerial level. On the occasion of the twentieth anniversary of the founding of IORA, a summit level meeting was held in Jakarta in 2017.

In order to underline its seriousness in playing a more active role in matters related to the Indian Ocean, India took a welcome initiative to convene in February 2008 an Indian Ocean Naval Symposium (IONS) with the participation of the naval chiefs of about thirty littoral countries of the Indian Ocean region. IONS is a voluntary initiative intended to provide an open and inclusive consultative forum for flow of information and discussion of regionally relevant maritime issues between naval professionals. The objective of these confabulations is to arrive at a common understanding and possibly cooperative solutions to increase maritime co-operation and security among the navies of the littoral states of the Indian Ocean region. Its twenty-five-nation membership broadly overlaps with that of IORA, but excludes Comoros, Madagascar, Somalia and Yemen, and includes Myanmar, Pakistan, Qatar, Saudi Arabia, Timor-Leste and the United Kingdom. After languishing for a while, it has become more active from 2014 onwards, when Australia became the chair of the organization. Within India too, a lot more work remains to be done, both in terms of allocation of resources and in working out institutional mechanisms to better coordinate and integrate India's multifaceted maritime interests.

Speaking at the 14th East Asia Summit in Bangkok in November 2019, Prime Minister Modi took forward the concept of SAGAR and enunciated a new Indo-Pacific Oceans Initiative (IPOI), whose sweep ranges from the western coast of North America to the eastern shores of Africa. IPOI envisages seven dimensions of maritime cooperation and collaboration: maritime security; maritime ecology; maritime resources; capacity building and resource sharing; disaster risk reduction and management; science, technology and academic cooperation; and trade, connectivity and maritime transport. It does not envisage the setting up of a new institutional framework. Rather, it seeks to promote practical cooperation by drawing on the existing regional institutions like the EAS, IORA, BIMSTEC and the Pacific Islands Forum. India has taken the lead on two pillars—disaster risk management and maritime security. India has made it clear that it sees itself as a net security provider in the Indo-Pacific.

The Chinese Vector

In the early years of the twenty-first century, the Chinese vector was in harmony with the other elements of India's Look East policy since India-China relations were on an upward trajectory. Mid-2005 was the high point. Yet, notwithstanding statements about Asia having enough space for both China and India, the public rhetoric was at odds with the practical realities. The lingering mutual suspicions between the two countries found expression in the intensive diplomatic jockeying preceding the first East Asia Summit (EAS). China and some of its friends in ASEAN tried to prevent India from joining the EAS, but the other camp, where Japan and some ASEAN countries like Singapore played a leading role, managed to prevail over it in a touch-and-go affair. Henceforth, the China factor would be the dominant one in shaping India's Look East policy.

As India and the United States drew closer following the agreement on the India-US nuclear deal and Chinese self-confidence soared on the basis of its remarkable economic and military achievements, tensions began to rise in India-China relations. Other Asian countries too began to worry about the rise of China. Under President Obama, the United States too shook off its neglect of the region over the previous few years with its 'pivot to Asia' strategy, later termed as 'rebalancing'. India and Japan accelerated their strategic embrace from 2007 onwards. Bilateral military cooperation intensified. The Indo-US Malabar naval exercises became a trilateral Indo-US-Japan affair. In 2007, Australia and Singapore also joined them, raising concern in China about the emergence of a so-called 'Quad'. This idea was short-lived. New governments that came to power in Japan and Australia deemed it prudent not to challenge the Chinese so openly. Even India was cautious about the Quad initiative, which petered out. Moreover, given their huge economic stakes in China, none of the Quad countries wished to convey an impression of being part of an anti-China coalition. The incipient Chinese challenge to the established order in the Indo-Pacific region was not seen as serious enough—at least not yet. But the contours of a new geopolitical structure in Asia were visible.

The year 2008 marked a decisive turning point in China's attitude. On the one hand, the global financial crisis weakened the economic power and the moral authority of the West. On the other hand, China's successful holding of the Beijing Olympics had bolstered its self-confidence. It felt that its time had come to regain its perceived place in the sun, and it began to behave like a great power intent on having its way. Its attitude towards other countries was marked by hubris, arrogance, insensitivity and intimidation. The earlier slogans of 'peaceful rise' and 'harmonious development' gave way to 'China Dream', which threatened to become a nightmare for many countries! From 2009 onwards, tensions significantly rose between China and its East Asian neighbours, triggered primarily by China's aggressive moves to assert its territorial and maritime claims vis-à-vis a number of ASEAN countries in the South China Sea and vis-à-vis Japan over the Senkaku/Diaoyu islands. Unfazed, China continued its boorish and bullying behaviour. Although it had signed a Declaration on the Conduct of Parties in the South China Sea in 2002 with ASEAN, it has been dragging its feet on actually signing a Code of Conduct with ASEAN. At the ARF meeting in July 2010, then Chinese foreign minister Yang Jiechi arrogantly stated that China was a big country and the other countries small, and that was just a fact! The Philippines took its territorial dispute with China over claims to islands in the South China Sea to the International Arbitration Tribunal under UNCLOS, which ruled in favour of the Philippines in 2016. But China has simply ignored the ruling. The Philippines, disappointed at the US unwillingness to come to its aid despite its treaty alliance with it, thought it prudent to cut a deal with China. There was no unity within ASEAN on how to deal with China. As for Japan, China's muscular behaviour convinced newly elected nationalistic prime minister Shinzo Abe that Japan should accelerate the ongoing process of building up its military strength.

Unmindful of the mounting criticism against it, China relentlessly and swiftly continued to pursue its aggressive strategic moves, especially after Xi Jinping assumed power in 2012. In the South China Sea, China consolidated its hold on the various islands and rocks by undertaking extensive land reclamation work and rapidly set up extensive military facilities at various locations. The Chinese build-up in the South China Sea is worrying for India too, from a long-term perspective. If China controls the South China Sea, it can then move into the Indian Ocean with more confidence and thereby directly threaten India in its own backyard. There is also the danger that by controlling the South China Sea, China could create a counter-choke point for the energy and trade

SLOCs of its adversaries. A new challenge that has emerged is the revival of the idea of a canal across the Kra peninsula in Thailand, which would provide a shorter link between the Indian and the Pacific Oceans and also avoid the Malacca Straits. There is a distinct possibility that China may invest in such a project as part of its overall plan to have easier access to the Indian Ocean and thereby overcome the perceived vulnerability of its ships having to navigate through the narrow Straits of Malacca (China's so-called 'Malacca Dilemma'). India will have to be watchful and should closely consult with Thailand as well as Singapore, Malaysia and Indonesia, the countries that would be adversely affected were such a project to fructify.

'Act East' Policy and the Quad

After Prime Minister Modi came to power, India accelerated its defence and security cooperation with the ASEAN and other East Asian countries through a reinvigorated Look East policy, now called the 'Act East' policy. Recognizing that it could not meet the Chinese challenge on its own, India sought to develop a countervailing force by working closely with the United States and the countries of East and South-east Asia. India signalled its growing strategic convergence with the United States in 2015 by signing a Joint Strategic Vision for the Asia-Pacific and the Indian Ocean emphasizing the safeguarding of maritime security, ensuring freedom of navigation and over-flight, and settlement of territorial and maritime disputes peacefully in accordance with international law, including UNCLOS.

Japan, Vietnam, Indonesia and Australia came in for special attention. With Japan, the relationship was upgraded to a Special Strategic and Global Partnership, and with Vietnam to a Comprehensive Strategic Partnership. The key elements of the Indo-US Joint Strategic Vision were reflected in these relationships too. Trilateral maritime security mechanisms were established with the United States and Japan, as well as with Japan and Australia. It is no coincidence that in six out of the eight years between 2010 and 2017, the leaders of South Korea, Indonesia, Thailand, Japan, the United States and all ten

ASEAN countries were invited as chief guests for India's Republic Day celebrations.

In 2017, India shifted to another gear in its Act East and Indo-Pacific policies. The first important development was revival of the 'Quad', with a meeting of senior officials of the four Quad countries (United States, Japan, India and Australia) organized on the margins of the East Asia Summit in Manila in November 2017, followed up by a meeting of the naval chiefs of the four countries at the Raisina Dialogue in New Delhi in January 2018. This quickly developed into an organization that now regularly meets at the political level. Since 2019, the Quad foreign ministers have been meeting regularly, at least once a year. The leaders held their first virtual meeting in 2021. Starting from their first in-person meeting in September 2021, the Quad leaders have held three annual meetings so far. Whereas some other members of the Quad wanted to give the organization a sharp military and security dimension, India has not been in favour of it. One reason could be that it does not want to burn all its bridges with China. Secondly, perhaps India does not want to upset ASEAN, which is uncomfortable with having to choose between China and the Quad, an organization which, unlike all the existing structures in the region, is not ASEAN-centric.

Realizing that it was not in their interest to antagonize ASEAN, the Quad members changed direction and now acknowledge and respect the centrality, agency and leadership of regional institutions, including ASEAN, the Pacific Islands Forum and the Indian Ocean Rim Association, and will work within and alongside them to complement their efforts and advance shared interests. The Quad has emerged as a platform that supports a free and open Indo-Pacific that is inclusive and resilient, where no country dominates and no country is dominated. Its vision is a region that is peaceful and prosperous, stable and secure, respectful of sovereignty, free from intimidation and coercion, and where disputes are settled in accordance with international law, ensuring peace, prosperity, stability and security in the Indo-Pacific region. It voices strong opposition to destabilizing or unilateral actions that seek to change the status quo by force or coercion. It emphasizes the importance of adhering to international law, maintenance of freedom of navigation and over-flight, and of addressing challenges to the maritime rules-based order, including those in the East and South China Seas. It has expressed serious concern at militarization of disputed geographical features, dangerous use of coastguard and maritime militia vessels, and efforts to disrupt other countries' offshore resource-exploitation activities. Thus, there is a thinly veiled, but not direct, criticism of China. It is not a military alliance but a group focused on working together on issues like development of alternative supply chains, vaccine partnerships and other health programmes, infrastructure development, undersea cable networks, digital connectivity, cyberspace security, cooperation in outer space, enhancement of maritime domain awareness, and advancement of the UN 2030 Agenda for Sustainable Development and its Sustainable Development Goals.

Seeing that the strategic horizons of many of the East Asian countries converge with those of India in the eastern Indian Ocean, and keeping in mind the sensitivities of the South-east Asian countries, India has undertaken many confidence-building and cooperative measures, such as the India-sponsored biennial MILAN exercises, since 1995. Initially, only Thailand, Malaysia, Singapore, Indonesia, Bangladesh and Sri Lanka participated, but over the years participation has been widened to include other ASEAN countries as well as the western Indian Ocean and Persian Gulf states like Oman, Seychelles, Mauritius, Kenya, Tanzania, the United Arab Emirates, Saudi Arabia, Iran, Iraq, Kuwait, Egypt and Israel, as well as outside powers like the United States, Russia, France, the UK, Japan and South Korea. India's growing bilateral military ties with the countries of the region have also served to create a higher level of mutual comfort between India and these countries. India holds regular naval, military and air exercises with Singapore and undertakes coordinated patrolling with Thailand and Indonesia along its settled international maritime boundary with these countries. All these are integral components of India's maritime policy to its east.

India has beefed up its maritime capabilities by expanding and upgrading its naval bases on its own territory, both on the mainland as well as in the Andaman and Nicobar and Lakshadweep islands. India has also been active in acquiring facilities and promoting security cooperation with countries across the western Indian Ocean such as Oman, Seychelles, Mauritius, Mozambique, Madagascar, South Africa, Kenya and Tanzania. In the eastern Indian Ocean, defence and security cooperation is an important element in India's relationships with all ASEAN countries. For example, the Philippines is the first country in the region that has bought Brahmos missiles from India; India has got access to Changi Port in Singapore; it has set up satellite tracking and telemetry stations in Vietnam and Indonesia. India also has extensive maritime security cooperation with the United States, Japan and Australia, its partners in the Quad. As a result of agreements signed with the United States and France, India can make use of US facilities in Diego Garcia and French facilities in Reunion. Truly, India's security is now intimately tied up with developments in the Indian Ocean and the western Pacific regions. The Indo-Pacific strategic concept has become a reality.

Chapter 9

Persian Gulf and West Asia

Historical and Emotional Bonds

The Persian Gulf region is indeed very special for India. The Arabian Sea has linked rather than divided the Arab world and India. As a neighbouring region with very close people-to-people ties with India, it has historically always figured very high in India's external ties. Trade, culture, religion and language have bound the people of India and the Arab world over many centuries. No wars have been fought between Arabs and Indians. No bilateral disputes have marred the relationship. Arab traders have been visiting India since at least the eighth century. Kerala's Moplah community emerged from intermarriage between Arab traders who had settled down in India and the local women. There was movement of both traders and pilgrims in the other direction too, and many Arabs have Indian ancestry. To this day, there is a large community of Indians in Yemen and of Yemenis in Hyderabad. This peaceful interaction with the Arab world, which resulted in the confluence of ideas, of art, literature and much else, has left an indelible imprint on India's history, culture and civilization. Under British rule, the Arab Gulf states were further integrated with India as they were administered from India, and the Indian rupee was the currency in circulation locally in the Gulf. For the Arabs, India (particularly Mumbai) was their preferred destination for medical treatment and recreation, and many Arabs bought prime property in Mumbai pre-1947. Yet, for all the common factors that dictate a close relationship between this region and India, for many years post-Independence, India had only a modest presence and little influence or even interest in the Persian Gulf region. After Britain withdrew from the region in the early 1970s, its role was taken over by the United States, which maintained a formidable military presence to ensure the security of this rich oil-producing region.

People-to-People and Economic Ties

Oman, geographically the closest country in the Persian Gulf region, has historically had close and cordial connections with India. As early as in March 1953, India signed with the Sultan of Muscat and Oman (the earlier name of Oman) a Treaty of Friendship, Commerce and Navigation. Meaningful people-to-people and trade relations with the other sheikhdoms in the Persian Gulf began only after the oil boom of the early 1970s, which brought unprecedented prosperity to the region. Indians flocked to the region as new job opportunities opened up there. Today, there are around 9 million Indians working and living in the Persian Gulf states, of which approximately two-thirds live in the United Arab Emirates and Saudi Arabia.[1] Indians constitute the largest expatriate community in all the Persian Gulf states. They are among the favoured foreign workers because they are relatively more disciplined, do not get involved in local politics and create little trouble. If their numbers have not further increased, it is only because the host countries, for internal reasons, have imposed informal limits on the number of workers that can come from any one country. Indian workers, both blue and white collar, have played a tremendous role in ensuring the sustained growth and prosperity of the Persian Gulf countries. Behind the glitter of Dubai is the sweat and toil of foreign workers, including Indians. Indians have traditionally flocked to the Persian Gulf because of the comparatively better employment opportunities and higher wages available there. Earlier, it was mostly blue-collar workers who went to work in the region, but now the share of white-collar workers and professionals has increased.

Looking after the welfare of these Indians is a high priority for all Indian diplomatic and consular establishments in the region. This includes, in the first place, taking steps to ensure that unscrupulous local employers do not exploit Indian workers, working out suitable arrangements with the local authorities for setting up Indian schools, and a whole range of consular issues. The welfare of Indians working in the region is a politically sensitive issue for both the Central government and many state governments that send a large number of migrant workers. The remittances of workers constitute a sizeable proportion of India's foreign exchange earnings in the services sector. It is these workers' frequent travel to and from India that makes the India-Persian Gulf region the most profitable sector for airlines plying these routes. In the future, as their own populations grow, these countries will have to provide jobs for locals in the first instance. It is possible that the demand for labour from India may go down or that the skills required may change. India has to anticipate the possible trends and work out ways to handle a changed situation. Otherwise, the closing of an important traditional employment avenue could create social and political unrest in the affected regions of India.

India's trade with the Persian Gulf countries is also very significant. Most important is the oil trade, with this region supplying about half of India's oil imports. Non-oil trade too is rapidly growing, even though much of it is third-country trade routed via ports like Dubai. India and the Gulf Cooperation Council countries (Saudi Arabia, Kuwait, Qatar, Bahrain, United Arab Emirates, Oman) are also negotiating a Free Trade Agreement. This region is an important destination for setting up projects and for export of consultancy services and information technology. Education, healthcare and tourism are other promising areas of cooperation. There is a long-term congruence of the interests of India and the Persian Gulf countries, which realize that India offers a large and attractive workforce that brings them much needed workforce and skills. The oil-rich among them, especially Saudi Arabia and the United Arab Emirates, are now looking to diversify their investments away from the West and towards countries that offer economically attractive investment schemes and projects. This matches India's priorities. India is keen to attract the burgeoning Arab petrodollars for investments in infrastructure projects particularly in the oil, gas and petrochemicals sectors. Apart from the economic and financial benefits that such investments bring to both sides, they serve a larger strategic purpose. Through its large semi-permanent work force in the Persian Gulf region, India has acquired long-term stakes in the stability and prosperity of the region. If the Arabs were to invest their wealth in India, they too would develop stakes in India's continued economic growth. Such mutually profitable linkages will create long-term stability, development and prosperity for all sides.

Opening with Saudi Arabia

Saudi Arabia matters hugely to India. There is, firstly, Saudi Arabia's intrinsic importance—as a major player in a complex and fast-changing regional and global scenario, as the largest economy in the region, as a major global oil producer and exporter, as the world's largest holder of investible petrodollars, as a large global employer of Indians, and as an influential leader of the Islamic world (particularly after the decline of Egypt). Then there is the religious connection. Saudi Arabia, home to Islam's holiest shrines in Mecca and Medina, has understandably always had a special pull for Muslims, including those living in India. About 1,75,000 Indian Muslim pilgrims visit Saudi Arabia every year for Haj, and more than ten times that number for Umrah.[2] Undoubtedly, their interests and needs constitute an exceedingly important political parameter for any Indian government. That is why all Indian ambassadors to Saudi Arabia and Indian consuls general in Jeddah have been Muslim to enable them to travel to the holy cities and look after the interests of the Indian pilgrims. Unfortunately, for decades, just this concern rather than Saudi Arabia's geostrategic importance remained India's principal focus. It was not simply a matter of India's neglect and misplaced priorities. Pakistan's machinations too played an important role in feeding Saudi hesitation, ensuring that India's relations with Saudi Arabia remained strained for many decades. Pakistan has historically enjoyed considerable influence in Saudi Arabia for three principal reasons—its successful exploitation of the politics of Islam to prejudice the Arab countries against India; its assiduous and systematic cultivation of the Saudi royal family members; and its close cooperation in the security field with Saudi Arabia. Another factor that played a role in the coolness that crept into India's relations with the Arab states of the Persian Gulf was India's stand on Saddam Hussein's invasion of Kuwait in 1990.

After an exchange of visits by the King of Saudi Arabia and the Prime Minister of India in the mid-1950s, there was no high-level visit from India till 1982, when Prime Minister Indira Gandhi visited the country. Things went quiet after that for nearly two decades afterwards, till the visit of Jaswant Singh to Saudi Arabia in 2001, the first ever by an Indian foreign minister. As a result of this visit, Saudi Arabia signalled that it valued its ties with India on their own merits and did not view them through a Pakistani prism. The real breakthrough in bilateral relations came with the visit of the King of Saudi Arabia to India as the chief guest for India's Republic Day celebrations in January 2006, more than half a century after the last visit by a Saudi King to India. Recognizing the strategic significance of the visit, the Indian government extended special protocol honours to the Saudi King. In the Delhi Declaration which, unprecedentedly for the Saudi side, was signed by King Abdullah himself and Prime Minister Manmohan Singh, both sides recognized the visit as a historic one that heralded a new era in bilateral relations. It was for the first time in more than a quarter of a century that India was gaining direct access to the Saudi leadership, which till then had been hesitant to treat India in anything but the most routine way, notwithstanding the considerable commercial interests of Saudi Arabia in selling oil to India and of India in getting jobs for its workers in Saudi Arabia. As a result of the visit, new horizons opened up in energy sector cooperation. India acknowledged Saudi Arabia as a trusted and reliable source of oil supplies. There was agreement on developing a 'strategic energy partnership' based on complementarities and interdependence involving reliable, stable and increased volumes of crude oil supplies to India through 'evergreen' contracts, upstream and downstream investments in the oil sector in Saudi Arabia, India and third countries, and joint ventures for gas-based fertilizer plants in Saudi Arabia. Counter-terrorism, information technology, agriculture, biotechnology, educational and cultural exchanges were other areas identified for cooperation.

Important as the agreements on energy and other areas were, the principal significance of the Saudi King's visit was political. India's decision to honour the Saudi King by inviting him as the chief guest for India's Republic Day celebrations was imaginative and astute. His acceptance of the invitation and the conscious inclusion of India in his first trip outside the region, particularly his participation as chief guest at India's Republic Day celebrations, sent a very public message to the people of India and to the world that Saudi Arabia regarded its relationship with India as important. The important signal picked up by the rulers and the people of the Arab world was that India is a friend with whom more intensive and extensive contacts should be established. In this way, India managed to make a significant breakthrough in changing perceptions about it in the region. This landmark visit opened a new chapter not only in India-Saudi relations but also between India and the Persian Gulf states as a whole. A number of other Arab leaders visited India in the ensuing months and years to build closer ties. Against the background of the hitherto desultory India-Saudi Arabia relations, it was nothing short of revolutionary that the two countries should have agreed to develop a broad strategic vision and to recognize that the stability and security of the Gulf region and the Indian subcontinent are closely interlinked. However, the Saudi side had not yet given up its obsession with trying to play some kind of a role in resolving India-Pakistan differences over Kashmir. It was only after the terror attacks in Mumbai in November 2008 that the Saudi perspective on Pakistan and Kashmir changed.

Four years passed before Prime Minister Manmohan Singh paid a return visit to Saudi Arabia in 2010. The visit took forward, somewhat belatedly, the relationship, which was now elevated to that of a 'strategic partnership'. Both countries stepped up their cooperation on counter-terrorism. Since then, high-level visits have been regularly exchanged between India and Saudi Arabia: Crown Prince (now King)

Salman visited India in 2014, and during Prime Minister Modi's visit to Saudi Arabia in 2016, King Salman conferred Saudi Arabia's highest civilian honour on him as a signal of the importance Saudi Arabia attaches to relations with India. On becoming the Crown Prince of Saudi Arabia in 2017, Mohammed bin Salman (MBS), the de facto ruler of Saudi Arabia, imparted a new dynamism to India-Saudi relations. India acquired a prominent place in his long-term vision of Saudi Arabia's future. In the last four years, he has visited India twice (in 2019 and 2023), while Prime Minister Modi visited Saudi Arabia again, in 2019. The India-Saudi Strategic Partnership Council established in 2019 to steer the relationship held its first Leaders' Summit meeting in 2023. Among other things, Saudi Arabia has targeted investments in India amounting to up to US$ 100 billion, half of which is for a refinery project on India's west coast. This is a sharp jump from the current (2024) Saudi investments of about US$ 3 billion in India. Indian companies have invested US$ 2 billion in companies in Saudi Arabia. With a bilateral trade turnover of around US$ 43 billion, India is Saudi Arabia's second largest trading partner, while Saudi Arabia is India's fourth largest trading partner and third largest source of oil imports.[3] Both sides agreed to diversify the status of their hydrocarbons relationship into a 'comprehensive energy partnership' that would encompass the downstream sector, renewable energy, energy efficiency, hydrogen, electricity, strategic petroleum reserves and circular carbon economy. There is also some defence cooperation involving joint naval exercises, training and high-level visits, and the two sides are considering possibilities of joint development and production of defence equipment. Both are members of G-20, and their cooperation can be expected to grow, now that Saudi Arabia is also a member of BRICS.

United Arab Emirates a Key Partner

The United Arab Emirates (UAE) is today perhaps India's most important partner in the Persian Gulf region because it has the deepest and most extensive linkages with India, whether it is people-to-people, economic, defence and security or connectivity. The 3.5 million or so

Indians living in the UAE today constitute about 30 per cent of the country's total population and play a key role in its functioning.[4] Large numbers of Indians also visit the UAE for tourism and business. This has made the India-UAE air corridors among the busiest in the world. Given this staggering demographic, which inevitably entails deep mutual interest and high stakes in the continued stability, growth and prosperity of both countries, it is surprising that till Prime Minister Modi's visit in 2015, no Indian prime minister had visited the UAE for thirty-four years! This neglect has been more than made up by Prime Minister Modi who has visited the UAE six times (in 2015, 2018, 2019, 2022, 2023 and 2024). As a signal of the importance that the UAE attaches to relations with India, it has honoured Prime Minister Modi with the Order of Zayed, its highest civilian award. Contrary to its traditional policy, it has also allowed the construction of a grand Hindu temple in Abu Dhabi, which is seen as a symbol of interfaith and cultural harmony. During this period the UAE Crown Prince (now King) has visited India twice, in 2016 and 2017. On the second occasion he was the chief guest at India's Republic Day celebrations.

Trade and economic ties have also sharply increased over the last couple of decades. The UAE is India's third largest trade partner with a trade turnover of over US$ 85 billion, its second largest export destination and the fourth largest investor in India.[5] As a result of the signing of a bilateral Comprehensive Economic Partnership Agreement in 2022 with the UAE, India has obtained preferential market access there on over 97 per cent of its tariff lines, which account for 99 per cent of its exports to the UAE in value terms, particularly from labour-intensive sectors.[6] This agreement, and a subsequent decision in 2023 to promote trade and other cross-border transactions in the local currencies—that is, rupees and dirhams—are expected to give a boost to bilateral trade, which is expected to reach the level of US$ 100 billion over the next few years.[7] In order to benefit the citizens and residents of the two countries, there are plans to integrate the two countries' payment and messaging systems such as Unified Payments Interface (UPI), and acceptance of domestic credit and debit cards like Rupay. India is keen to attract more investments from the Abu Dhabi Investment Authority (ADIA), one of the world's largest sovereign funds, in diverse fields. ADIA has already committed to invest US$ 75 billion into India and has plans to set up a presence in Gujarat International Finance Tec-City (GIFT City), a financial free zone in Gujarat.[8] One of the priority areas for UAE investors is the food sector, where the proposed investments are in developing an India-UAE food corridor, cold storage, warehousing and food processing facilities, and fisheries and poultries, with the objective of tripling the value of UAE food imports from India in five years. From the Indian side, many Indian companies have set up manufacturing units for cement, building materials, textiles, engineering products, consumer electronics, etc., in the UAE. There are also significant Indian investments in the area of services, covering the tourism, hospitality, catering, health, retail and education sectors. India and the UAE have also moved away from purely buyer-seller relations in hydrocarbons to a broader energy partnership. In a breakthrough, an Indian consortium led by ONGC has been given a 10 per cent stake by the UAE in the rich Lower Zakum basin oilfield, and India is to get 2 million tons of crude from the field for a period of forty years.[9]

India and the UAE also engage with each other in various non-bilateral forums. Following the 2020 so-called Abraham Accords that normalized relations between Israel and the UAE, a new grouping of India, the United States, Israel and the UAE ('I2U2') came into being in 2021, to develop collaborative economic projects. At their first virtual summit in July 2022, the leaders of these four countries agreed on two major projects. One relates to food security, whereby the UAE, with supplemental funding by the private sector in Israel and the United States, would invest US$ 2 billion to develop a series of integrated food parks in India. Another envisages a hybrid renewable energy project in Gujarat that could provide a model with the potential to make India a global hub for alternative supply chains in the renewable energy sector.[10] In 2023, the four countries agreed to establish a new joint space venture that would leverage the space-based data and capabilities of the four countries to tackle environmental and climate change challenges.[11]

The most ambitious project, announced on the margins of the G-20 summit in New Delhi in September 2023, is the India-Middle East Economic Corridor (IMEC) project for infrastructure development and strengthening of connectivity, in its various dimensions, between India, the Middle East and Europe. An MOU to this effect was signed by India, the US, Saudi Arabia, the UAE, the European Union, Italy, France and Germany. The IMEC comprises an eastern corridor connecting India to the Persian Gulf region and a northern corridor from there to Europe. It will include a railway and ship-rail transit network and road transportation routes supplementing existing maritime and road transport routes. Along the railway route, the project envisages rail, digital, electricity and hydrogen corridors. The details of the project are being worked out. However, essentially this project will involve shipping links from India's west coast to the UAE (which already exist), a rail link from the UAE across Saudi Arabia to Jordan and Israel, and another shipping link from Israel to Europe. Israel is not specifically mentioned in the MOU, but there is the hope that if Saudi-Israel relations normalize, this project could become a reality. It is anticipated that financing will come from the UAE and Saudi sovereign wealth funds, US private equity and Indian private-sector infrastructure companies. Each country provides the investments required in its own sovereign territory and can levy a transportation or transit fee for use of its corridors.

India and Iraq

Iraq is the most important of the other Persian Gulf states. Even though India established diplomatic relations with Iraq in 1947 and signed a Treaty of Friendship with it in 1952, India was not happy with Iraq's participation in the West-sponsored Baghdad Pact (1955), a military alliance that brought together Iran, Iraq, Pakistan, Turkey and the United Kingdom. However, there was substantial Indian involvement in Iraq's development. Large numbers of Indians lived and worked in Iraq in the educational, industrial and financial sectors. Iraq's new military leaders noted India's recognition of the new government in Iraq following the 1958 coup in the country. Iraq's withdrawal from the Baghdad Pact in 1959 was a matter of satisfaction for India. During the 1960s, India-Iraq relations steadily improved. Indian companies got many large development projects in Iraq. There were also military ties between the two countries. Iraq remained neutral in the 1965 India-Pakistan war. Relations between India and Iraq improved dramatically in the mid-1970s as a result of a personal decision to this effect by President Saddam Hussein. Iraq supported India on vital issues like Kashmir. India, for its part, trained a large number of Iraqi defence personnel. Many Indian experts and professionals got work in Iraq. Indian companies too were very active and executed several construction projects in Iraq. India also developed an affinity towards Iraq as the only secular Arab country. Both collaborated within the framework of the Non-Aligned Movement. With India and Iraq both having close ties to the Soviet Union, India greatly benefited from a three-way swap deal whereby Iraq paid off its debts to the Soviet Union by supplying large quantities of oil to India, which was paid for by India through export of goods to the Soviet Union against rupees. Good relations were established between the ruling parties in both countries, a legacy that led to the eruption of a scandal in 2005 that kickbacks had been paid to India's Congress party and politicians under the UN-sponsored Oil-for-Food programme that permitted Iraq to export its oil in the world market for food and medicines. This legacy of mutual goodwill has not been lost.

Foreign Minister I.K. Gujral's public embrace of Saddam Hussein when he visited Iraq during the first Gulf crisis in 1990 may have been indiscreet, but it was nevertheless a spontaneous and heartfelt gesture that conveyed the warm feelings that India had for Saddam Hussein, who was regarded as a friend of India. It is noteworthy that the decision of the government of Prime Minister Chandrashekhar during the 1991 Gulf War to provide refuelling facilities to US military aircraft drew such a sharp protest in India that the government had to suspend the facility. India opposed sanctions against Iraq and supplied food and medicines to it. India, which was then a member of the UN Security Council, abstained on Resolution 686 that outlined the requirements for Iraq to comply with the ceasefire. In 1998, when India conducted its nuclear weapons tests, Iraq supported India.

If the First Gulf War of 1991 crippled Iraq, the US invasion of Iraq in 2003 shattered the country. By this time India was seriously trying to improve relations with the United States, which no doubt influenced its decision not to formally oppose the war against Iraq. India came under tremendous pressure from the United States to send troops to Iraq in 2003, and it was only the shrewdness and political sagacity of Prime Minister Vajpayee that prevented this from happening. It is also likely that India's traditional friendship with Iraq influenced its decision. At any rate, the goodwill for India among the people of Iraq was definitely an important factor that enabled India to secure the release of four kidnapped Indian truck drivers in Iraq in 2004. It also seems to have influenced India's decision to allocate a relatively generous $20 million in bilateral assistance for Iraq's reconstruction, and another $10 million to the International Reconstruction Fund Facility for Iraq launched in 2004 by the UN and the World Bank.[12] As the violence in Iraq escalated, and in order not to provoke the Iraqi groups fighting the military forces of the United States and its coalition partners, India thought it prudent not to replace its ambassador who came away when his term expired in 2005. But it kept open a small diplomatic mission in Baghdad.

Relations between India and Iraq are now steady. From 2006 onwards, India has resumed its purchase of oil from Iraq, which is today among the top three suppliers of oil to India. The ban on movement of Indian labour to Iraq imposed in 2004 was lifted in 2010. An Indian ambassador has been back in Baghdad since 2011. In 2013, there were several exchanges of high-level visits, including one by the Iraqi prime minister to India, a visit by the India foreign minister to Iraq and a meeting of the Joint Commission. The emergence of the Islamic State or Da'esh in 2014 did complicate bilateral relations as thousands of Indians in Iraq got stranded there. The Da'esh also took some Indian nurses and construction workers captive. While India managed to evacuate the nurses back to the country, it emerged many years later that the construction workers had been killed. Many Indian companies have resumed their business activities in Iraq and have got contracts for building power projects, hotels, sewage systems, etc. These enhanced exchanges led India to open a consulate in Erbil in the relatively peaceful Kurdistan region of Iraq, where many Indians are living and working. The foreign minister of Iraq visited India in 2017. There have been many visits exchanged at the minister-of-state level, and some Parliamentary exchanges too. Now that Iraq is more peaceful, India has been trying, with some success, to pick up the pieces of its relationship with that nation. After a gap of ten years, a meeting of the India-Iraq Joint Commission was held in India in 2023.

The Iran Conundrum

Although a dominant power in the Persian Gulf, Iran itself is primarily a land power. India's contacts with Iran have been traditionally over land, not across the Arabian Sea. With the formation of Pakistan in 1947, India and Iran (or Persia, as it was known till 1935) lost the geographical contiguity they had enjoyed for centuries. As a result, Indian policymakers to some extent failed to appreciate that from a strategic perspective India has to deal with Iran as a neighbouring country. The rhetoric frequently used about the historical ties between Iran and India has substance, certainly insofar as it concerns north India, whose history, culture and language have been shaped to a considerable degree by Persian influence. Nor should India and the world forget that despite its strategic location, Iran is one of the few major countries in Asia that managed to maintain its independence and was never colonized. It is also the only country in the Persian Gulf region that takes care of its own security. In the West's demonizing of Iran after the 1979 Revolution, some inconvenient realities are ignored. One is that the Revolution itself was a reaction to the CIA-sponsored coup that overthrew the Iranian prime minister, Mossadegh, in 1953 and the subsequent savagely autocratic rule of the Shah of Iran, who became the darling of both the West and Israel. A second is that the

West, by eliminating Saddam Hussein and weakening Iraq, enhanced Iran's power in the region. Besides, Iran is not a country that can be casually dismissed or ignored. As a sophisticated people with a strong sense of national pride and self-confidence, drawing inspiration and strength from their rich and deep-rooted heritage of civilization and culture, Iranians expect their country to be treated with respect and want it to be recognized as a genuine regional power. It is logical that Iran seeks to follow an independent foreign policy.

The development of India's relations with Iran has been uneven. Iran was one of the first countries with which India signed a Friendship Treaty (March 1950) after Independence. The early promise of friendship could weather neither the politics of the Cold War nor India-Pakistan animosity and conflicts. After the overthrow of Mossadegh, Iran under the Shah got enmeshed in the strategic plans of the West and became a member of various Western-sponsored regional military alliances—like the Baghdad Pact which later transformed into the Central Treaty Organization (CENTO)—while India's orientation was more towards the Soviet Union and the Non-Aligned Movement. Nor did Nehru's friendship with fellow-NAM founder and socialist President Nasser of Egypt go down well with a conservative monarchy like the Iranian Shah's. Iran's role in supporting Pakistani machinations to prevent India from attending the 1969 Organization of Islamic Conference (OIC) Summit at Rabat added to the strains in India-Iran relations. It was only after Pakistan's defeat in the 1971 war, which changed the balance of power in South Asia decisively in India's favour, and the passing away of Nasser that both sides took steps to improve relations. Prime Minister Indira Gandhi and the Shah of Iran exchanged visits in 1974. However, India's own turbulent domestic politics of the second half of the 1970s, followed by the Iranian Revolution of 1979 and the almost decade-long war that Iran fought with Iraq (then a close friend of India's) in the 1980s once again derailed this relationship, even though there is great mutual interest and benefit in closer India-Iran ties. For India, relations with Iran also have a domestic political dimension. As the largest Shia country and home to some of the holiest shrines of the Shia community, Iran remains influential among India's large Shia population.

From the early 1990s, starting with Prime Minister Narasimha Rao's visit to Iran in 1993, relations steadily improved. Iran and India closely cooperated in supporting the Northern Alliance in Afghanistan against the Taliban in the 1990s. There was a regular exchange of high-level visits, including the highly symbolic visit of President Khatami to India as the chief guest for India's Republic Day celebrations in 2003. Unfortunately, relations took a sharp dip in 2005 following India's position in the International Atomic Energy Agency (IAEA) in September 2005 and February 2006 on transfer of the dossier on Iran regarding its nuclear programme from the IAEA to the UN Security Council. The decision generated resentment and mistrust of India in Iran, jeopardized the future of the already-concluded liquified natural gas (LNG) contracts between India and Iran, and probably led Iran to conclude that India was not a serious or reliable strategic partner. It also polarized political and public opinion in India. The handling of its relations with Iran has become an important benchmark to assess India's willingness and ability to follow an independent foreign policy. The cloud in bilateral relations lifted only as a result of Iranian President Ahmedinejad's brief stopover in New Delhi in April 2008, when the Indian side went out of the way to reassure him that it would follow an independent policy towards Iran and not succumb to US pressure.

As Pakistan's neighbour and a very influential actor in the Persian Gulf, Iran matters greatly to India from a strategic perspective. It is a key country for India's access to Afghanistan and Central Asia, for which India has built a road from Zaranj on the Iran-Afghanistan border to Delaram on Afghanistan's girdle road which skirts Afghanistan. India also agreed to develop Iran's Chabahar port and connect it by rail with Iran's existing railway network, but both the scope and progress of the project have been constrained by US sanctions on Iran and India's unwillingness to finance the construction of the railway line from Chabahar to Zahidan. Moreover, with the return of the Taliban to power in Afghanistan in 2021, India's ties with Afghanistan languished and the value of the Iran route to Afghanistan was regarded as not relevant for the immediate future. It is only in May 2024 that Iran and India signed a ten-year contract for India to develop and manage

Chabahar port. India, Iran and Turkmenistan have an arrangement to facilitate transit of Indian goods via Iran to Turkmenistan, while India, Iran, Russia and some Central Asian states have taken steps to develop an International North-South Transport Corridor (INSTC), which is intended to provide faster and cheaper connectivity between India and Russia via Iran and the Caspian Sea.

Possessing enormous reserves of both oil and gas, Iran was traditionally one of India's major sources of oil, but US sanctions on Iran have made it difficult for India to maintain its economic links with that nation. Iran's nuclear programme and the animosity in US-Iran relations have cast a deep shadow on India-Iran relations since 2005. A couple of decades ago, India took the significant step of delinking the Iran-Pakistan-India (IPI) gas pipeline project from its overall relationship with Pakistan. With the deterioration of both India-Pakistan and US-Iran relations, and the constraints imposed by India's decision to give high priority to its relations with the United States, this project has died a natural death. It was hoped that US-Iran relations would get normalized and international sanctions on Iran lifted after the signing of the Joint Comprehensive Plan of Action in 2015 and its endorsement by the UN Security Council. Prime Minister Modi and Iranian President Rouhani exchanged visits in 2016 and 2018, respectively. There was now an air of optimism in India-Iran relations, though India was cautious in responding to Iran's keenness to develop defence cooperation, as this was likely to complicate India's valuable defence and intelligence cooperation with Israel. Unfortunately, US President Donald Trump's decision in 2018 to withdraw from the deal had a negative fallout on India-Iran relations. In 2019, after the United States stopped giving waivers to India from the sanctions regime it had imposed on Iran, bilateral India-Iran relations began to languish and India completely stopped its oil purchases from Iran, the main pillar of their bilateral relations. Even though the United States had indicated that the Chabahar project would be exempt from Iran-related US secondary sanctions, India slowed progress on the Chabahar project; did not take up Iran's offer to participate in the Farzad-B offshore gas field project, and put on hold plans to set up railway, steel, aluminium, petrochemical and fertilizer projects in Iran.

The Palestine Question

India's policy towards Israel has been intimately linked to its support for the Palestinian cause and the impact India-Israel relations have on India-Arab relations. India's position on the Palestine question has its roots in India's freedom movement. As a party that was opposed to the partitioning of India on religious grounds, the Congress could hardly be expected to endorse the goals of the Zionist movement that eventually led to the creation of Israel. Mahatma Gandhi expounded India's perspective clearly and in detail in an editorial in the *Harijan* of 11 November 1938, a major policy statement that continues to guide India's policy on Palestine to this day. Despite his sympathy for the Jews who had been subjected to discrimination and persecution for centuries, Mahatma Gandhi was clear about the rights of the Palestinians:

> My sympathy does not blind me to the requirements of justice. The cry for the national home for the Jews does not make much appeal to me . . . Why should they not, like other peoples of the earth, make that country their home where they are born and where they earn their livelihood? Palestine belongs to the Arabs in the same sense that England belongs to the English or France to the French. It is wrong and inhuman to impose the Jews on the Arabs . . . Surely it would be a crime against humanity to reduce the proud Arabs so that Palestine can be restored to the Jews partly or wholly as their national home.[13]

The Palestinian problem, which has defied solution for seven and a half decades, has become more intractable than ever. More than anything else, it centres on the fact that Palestinians, who had been living in Palestine for centuries, have been evicted from their land, becoming refugees in other countries or living as virtual prisoners in the West Bank and Gaza or as second-class citizens in Israel. It is ironical that Israel, which is fanatical about the right of Jews anywhere in the world to migrate to Israel, refuses to countenance that the Palestinians driven out of their homes too have a similar right to return to their traditional homes where they have lived for centuries. Frustration and hopelessness among the Palestinians has led to desperation, reflected in the suicide bombings and terrorist attacks and two uprisings, or intafadas (1987–93 and 2000–05), that have happened. As the latest fierce and unprecedented Hamas attack on Israel (October 2023) shows, Israel is not secure.

India joined the Arab countries in opposing the partition of Palestine. India was the first non-Arab country to recognize the Palestine Liberation Organization (PLO) as the sole legitimate representative of the Palestinian people, and later gave the PLO office in New Delhi full diplomatic recognition. Similarly, India was the first non-Arab country to recognize Yasser Arafat as the president of Palestine. India voted for Palestine to become a full member of UNESCO and co-sponsored and voted in favour of the 2012 UN General Assembly resolution that enabled Palestine to become a 'non-member observer state' at the UN without voting rights. Arafat had a special rapport with India's leaders, especially Prime Minister Indira Gandhi. Of late, as India has become more open about its relations with Israel, there has been a change in India's voting pattern in the United Nations on issues related to Palestine. In contrast to the activist role that India had traditionally played in drafting and steering resolutions on this subject at NAM, India is now more neutral and less critical of Israel. Thus, in 2022, India abstained from voting on a UNGA resolution that was critical of Israel. At the same time India has become more open about high-level Indian visits to Palestine (former President Pranab Mukherjee visited Palestine in 2015 and Prime Minister Modi in 2018), which have been delinked from visits to Israel.

India does continue to endorse the Palestinian right to self-determination and supports the Palestinian people in their pursuit of economic and social development with dignity and self-reliance. India's traditional position for many decades has been to advocate a two-state solution. It seemed that there had been a change in nuance in India's stand on Palestine when Prime Minister Modi, in a message on the occasion of the International Day of Solidarity with Palestine in November 2022, said that India was hopeful that direct talks between the Palestinian and Israeli sides will resume to find a comprehensive and negotiated solution. Moreover, in his reaction to the October 2023 war in Gaza, initiated by Hamas and responded to with unprecedented ferocity by Israel, Prime Minister Modi expressed his 'solidarity with Israel at this difficult hour' while adding that India strongly and unequivocally condemned terrorism in all its forms and manifestations. In response to widespread criticism that there was no mention of India's support to the Palestinian cause, the argument given out informally was that this was a statement focused on the unacceptability of terror, an issue on which India, given its own experience, has to be forthright and unambiguous. However, India has not agreed to Israel's request to declare Hamas as a terrorist organization. India's official spokespersons have subsequently clarified that there is no change in its long-standing and consistent policy that favours resumption of direct negotiations between Palestine and Israel towards establishing a sovereign, independent and viable state of Palestine, living within secure and recognized borders, side by side in peace with Israel.[14] India has now reverted to its traditional position that the only way forward for enduring peace is a two-state solution, where the Palestinian people are able to live freely in an independent country within secure borders, with due regard to the security needs of Israel. In what is seen as a veiled criticism of the unprecedented ferocity with which Israel has attacked and besieged Gaza, the spokesman added that there is a universal obligation to observe international humanitarian law. While acknowledging that the large-scale civilian casualties and overall humanitarian situation continue to be cause for extreme concern, and calling for safe and timely delivery of humanitarian aid and assistance, India has not endorsed calls for a ceasefire in Gaza. This is probably out of deference to the stand on this matter taken by its close partners, the United States and Israel.

Strategic Relations with Israel

It was only in 1950, two years after the State of Israel came into existence, that India granted it de jure recognition. However, India did not establish full diplomatic relations with Israel. Initially, Israel was permitted to have only an immigration office in Mumbai, subsequently upgraded to a trade office and then a consulate, not the exchange of embassies with India it so dearly wanted. This situation lasted for many decades, and Israel used its resident embassy in Nepal, opened in 1961, as a useful window to India. Israel's collaboration in the attack on Egypt during the 1956 Suez crisis hardened India's stand towards it. However, Jawaharlal Nehru himself candidly and publicly acknowledged in 1958 that recognition of Israel was not a matter of high principle, and this attitude was adopted after a careful consideration of a balance of factors. In the late 1970s, under Prime Minister Morarji Desai's Janata government, India began to deviate from its policy, presumably as part of Desai's own pro-West orientation and his desire that India should follow a policy of genuine non-alignment. Israel's foreign minister, Moshe Dayan was invited to India in 1977 on a secret visit. India's interests were primarily to explore the possibilities of cooperation with Israel in intelligence sharing on terrorist and separatist organizations and in getting defence supplies. The visit did not lead to any substantive outcome as word of it leaked out to the Indian media and this, predictably, sparked off a political controversy about India's support to the Palestinian cause and India-Arab relations. It was not till 1992, after the Middle East Peace Process at Madrid in 1991 between Israel and the Arab states had begun and the break-up of the Soviet Union had changed the geopolitical balance decisively in favour of the United States, that India felt emboldened to exchange diplomatic missions with Israel.

Since then, relations have rapidly grown in all fields, especially in defence and security, which is underplayed by India and overplayed by Israel. Israel has emerged as a significant and reliable source of military equipment and many advanced sensitive defence technologies that are unavailable to India from elsewhere. India particularly appreciated Israel's willingness to supply military equipment and ammunition during conflict situations such as the Kargil operations in 1999 and Operation Parakram in 2002. There is also useful, mutually beneficial cooperation in the intelligence domain, as well as a vibrant relationship in non-military sectors, including agriculture and science and technology. Two-way trade (excluding defence) exceeds US$ 10 billion, a large proportion of which is accounted for by the trade in diamonds.[15] There are also growing investments by the two in each other's countries, the most promising being the investment by an Indian company in the acquisition of Haifa Port.

The valuable political support that the Jewish lobby provides in the United States makes Israel a desirable partner for India. An understanding and supportive US attitude has facilitated the transfer to India of many technologies and equipment produced by Israel over which the United States has a veto. As India and the United States have come closer over the last few years, there have been some tentative moves to forge a trilateral strategic relationship between the three countries. Speaking to the American Jewish Committee in May 2003, India's former national security adviser Brajesh Mishra seemed to hint at a trilateral grouping of—or at least close cooperation among—India, Israel and the United States based on the complementarities and common interests that bring India closer to both. In practice, the Jewish lobby in the United States was used to garner support in the US Congress for the Indo-US nuclear deal. The formation of the I2U2 grouping of India, Israel, United States and United Arab Emirates, and the proposal for an India-Middle East Economic Corridor show how India, Israel the United States and the larger and most influential Persian Gulf states are working together.

Whatever other benefits that an overtly close relationship with Israel may have for India, for a long time it was politically difficult and risky for any Indian government to ignore negative public perceptions within India, especially among Muslims, about Israel's harsh and unjust treatment of the Palestinians. This was a particular dilemma for the UPA government, which depended on the outside support of the left parties, who had been regularly calling for ending India's defence and security cooperation with Israel. Although nothing in India's relations with Israel changed in practice, an impression gained ground that there was a certain cooling in India's relations with Israel under the UPA government. There were relatively few high-profile political-level exchanges between India and Israel during UPA rule. From the Israeli side, there was a visit by Israeli President Weizman in 1996, and another by Israeli prime minister Sharon in 2003, but these were not reciprocated by any visit from India to Israel at the level of head of state/government, though Indian ministers (except the defence minister) and chief ministers of states visited Israel regularly.

India's approach changed when Narendra Modi became the prime minister in 2014. His government has dehyphenated India's relations with Israel from the Palestine issue, and there is no longer any shyness about India's engagement with Israel. Over the next few years, high-level visits were exchanged, first at the Presidential level. These laid the ground for Prime Minister Modi's visit to Israel in 2017 and a return visit by Israeli prime minister Netanyahu in 2018. Relations were upgraded to a strategic partnership. Given that a growing number of Arab countries themselves are normalizing relations with Israel, they do not object to India developing its relations with Israel. It does appear that there is some change in the attitude of the Arab states as a fallout of the latest Israel-Hamas conflict that erupted in October 2023. This very serious development calls into question the viability of the so-called Abraham Accords, and has become a roadblock in the incipient efforts by the United States to bring about a Saudi-Israeli rapprochement. It is also likely to put strains on the I2U2 grouping and will, at the very least, delay the plans for an India-Middle-East-Europe Economic Corridor (IMEC). Nor can one rule out the Israel-Hamas war broadening into a wider regional conflict that would have a global impact.

Organisation of Islamic Cooperation (OIC) Politics

The role of the OIC has become a minor irritant in India's relations with the Arab world. The OIC was set up in 1969 to promote solidarity among the Islamic countries following the arson attack on the al-Aqsa mosque in Jerusalem. India was invited to its first conference in Rabat in 1969, and the Indian Ambassador did participate and make a speech. However, when a high-level Indian delegation arrived in Rabat, it was not allowed to participate because of Pakistan's objections. Over the last four decades, the OIC has become a sprawling organization of fifty-seven members and is more in the nature of a club that is useful for networking and conducting business on the sidelines than for any intrinsic worth it may have. The OIC does, however, regularly adopt resolutions on Kashmir reflecting the Pakistani position. These are routinely adopted without any discussion. India has wisely not allowed the OIC issue to cloud its real interests with its member countries. In a strange twist of irony, former Indian minister of external affairs, Sushma Swaraj, was invited to speak at the OIC foreign minister-level meeting in Abu Dhabi in 2019 as a guest of honour, much to the annoyance and dismay of Pakistan, which boycotted her address!

From time to time, suggestions have been made that India should seek to become an observer or even a member in the OIC. This is neither a viable nor desirable option, because as an observer, India would have to tacitly accept OIC resolutions in whose formulation it plays no role. It also does not become India, with the second largest Muslim population in the world, to be a mere observer in an organization that claims to represent the interests of Muslims. Moreover, India would have to battle Pakistan to get itself associated with the OIC, which is not worth India's while since there are no great Indian interests at stake in the organization. Perhaps the most compelling reason for India to stay away is a domestic, political one. It would be politically risky for India to formally associate itself with an avowedly religious international organization as that could create a political and communal backlash within India.

Future Prospects

India's policy towards the Persian Gulf region is based on the fundamental assumption that the destinies of India and the Persian Gulf are intertwined as this region is very much part of India's extended and strategic neighbourhood. What happens here directly affects India's vital interests. India would like this region to remain peaceful and stable. Any widespread disorder here would affect India's energy security and, more importantly, displace millions of Indians living and working here, creating enormous social and economic disruption, with unpleasant political consequences within India. India had a taste of this when thousands of Indians fled Kuwait in the aftermath of the 1990–91 Gulf War. Since then, the number of Indians working in this region has increased manifold. There is simply no way that India can evacuate its people from the Gulf in a hurry, whether by ship or by air.

The Persian Gulf region is also of global strategic importance. Earlier, Britain deemed it essential to have control over this region in order to secure the sea route from Britain to India. When the United States took over the role of primary security provider in the Persian Gulf, the local sheikhdoms and monarchies entered into military alliances or arrangements with the US, which, in turn, acted as a guarantor securing these regimes from any possible popular upheavals. An important aspect of the deal was that oil would be priced in US dollars. Unfortunately, this created only superficial stability in the Persian Gulf, as it did not take into account the long-term problem of rapid population growth, which has created a large demographic bulge of young people whose economic expectations and political aspirations may be difficult to fulfil. The local rulers are no longer as confident of US commitment to their security as before and are keen to diversify their options. China and India are today major players with huge stakes in the region.

Many complex, messy and contradictory relationships compound the potential instability of this region. The most long-standing and intractable of these is a psychologically embattled, small but militarily dominant Israel versus a large and belligerent Iran and its regional proxies, like the Hezbollah in Lebanon, the Hamas in Gaza and the Houthis in Yemen. Shia-dominated, militarily superior and revolutionary Iran poses a serious challenge to the hitherto unquestioned leadership of the Islamic world by a rich Sunni Saudi monarchy, even though both countries restored diplomatic relations in 2023 after a seven-year rupture and agreed to normalize relations. There is the deep but unspoken fear of the large, perceived predatory states of the Persian Gulf like the United Arab Emirates and Saudi

Arabia among the oil-and-gas-rich minnow states like Qatar and Kuwait. Syria and Lebanon remain divided and unstable, with the Hezbollah always looking for opportunities to create trouble for Israel. One should not forget rich and strategically located Iraq, perhaps supine today but which can decisively swing the regional balance of power, and a resurgent Turkey flexing its muscles and engaged in fishing in the troubled waters of the region. As the only large power located in the geographical proximity of the Persian Gulf, with more than 9 million of its citizens living there and huge economic stakes, India has necessarily to be more involved in ensuring the region's prosperity, stability and security. However, it has to tread cautiously.

Chapter 10

Russia and Eurasia

The Soviet Legacy

With the focus of Indian public attention on the foreign policy front in recent years having been on India's relations with the United States, it is easy to miss the value of India's traditionally close and friendly ties with Russia, the successor state to the former Soviet Union. The deep roots of this relationship go back to the early twentieth century, when India was under British rule and the Tsars ruled Russia. The Russian Revolution of 1905 inspired Indian freedom fighters. Mahatma Gandhi, then in South Africa, was struck by the similarity in the prevailing conditions in Russia and India. He developed a close bond with Leo Tolstoy and carried on a lengthy correspondence with him. Lenin followed with interest and sympathy the nascent Indian freedom struggle. Following the 1917 Bolshevik Revolution, the Soviet leaders understood that their revolution stood a better chance of success if India too were to be free and independent. Even though many Indian freedom fighters, greatly inspired by the Bolshevik Revolution, established personal contacts with the Soviet leaders, it was Jawaharlal Nehru's thinking, more than anything else, which laid the foundation of the policy of the Indian National Congress towards the Soviet Union. After visiting the Soviet Union in 1927, on the occasion of the tenth anniversary of the Bolshevik Revolution, Nehru came back deeply impressed with the Soviet experiment. Convinced that poor, developing countries like India needed to follow not the capitalist path but a development model that emphasized social justice, equality and human dignity, Nehru was emphatic that India must develop close and friendly relations with the Soviet Union. It is noteworthy that even before India's Independence, an official announcement was made on 13 April 1947 on the establishment of diplomatic relations between India and the Soviet Union. However, during the Stalin era, there was considerable mutual suspicion and mistrust between the two countries. Stalin thought that India was ruled by a bourgeoisie that was too much under British influence. Nehru was upset with Soviet political interference in India through the Indian communist parties. It was only in the mid-1950s when Khrushchev came to power and together with the Soviet prime minister Bulganin made a landmark visit to India in 1955 that the air was cleared and relations took off.

Over the next few decades, the Soviet Union gave India valuable political, diplomatic and strategic support, bilaterally as well as at international forums, on Kashmir and other vital issues affecting India's national interests. There were some blips in the second half of the 1960s when the Soviet Union mediated the Tashkent Conference after the 1965 Indo-Pakistan war and considered selling arms to Pakistan. Fortunately, these dark clouds did not last long. It was Soviet diplomatic backing and material support, and the confidence provided by the 1971 Indo-Soviet Treaty of Peace, Friendship and Cooperation, which enabled India to successfully undertake the operations that led to the creation of Bangladesh. This political understanding was underpinned by a strong economic and strategic relationship. Beginning in the 1950s, India received from the Soviet Union generous assistance for its industrialization as well as in the sensitive areas of defence, space and atomic energy. Short of capital, foreign exchange and technology, India appreciated that it received from the Soviet Union cheap economic credits repayable in rupees for setting up infrastructure projects in India; reliable, affordable and good-quality military supplies, also on credit; and large-scale supplies of crucial items like oil and oil products (mostly via a swap deal with Iraq), fertilizers, metals, etc. Some of today's globally competitive Indian public-sector companies like Bharat Heavy Electricals Ltd, Oil and Natural Gas Corporation, as well as pioneering steel behemoths like the Bhilai and Bokaro plants, were set up with Soviet cooperation. The Soviet Union assisted in setting up the Indian Institute of Technology in Bombay, the first to be established with foreign collaboration. In Soviet times it was a truly strategic, if somewhat unequal, partnership, which helped India become more self-reliant. For all these reasons, the Soviet Union enjoyed a favourable public image among ordinary Indians and across the Indian political spectrum, even though the Soviet Union was most comfortable with the Nehru-Gandhi family in power in India.

New Priorities in the Post-Soviet Era

With the breakup of the Soviet Union, the whole edifice of India's relations with it, built up over decades, came crashing down. Both sides scrambled to adjust to the new realities. India and Russia drifted apart in the 1990s as each had different priorities. While Russia struggled to cope with the wrenching shift from a state-controlled economy to a free-market economy and from a centralized, authoritarian regime to a multi-party democracy, India too embarked on a process of economic reforms. The business communities in both Russia and India focused their energies and attention on the West, which was seen as the source of technology, capital and management. Oil deliveries from Russia to India stopped. Military supplies to India were badly disrupted as many defence establishments in the integrated Soviet military-industrial conglomerate shut down, jacked up prices unrealistically, or were simply unable to coordinate supplies with other defence manufacturing units sprawled all over the post-Soviet space. Neither Russia nor India could devote much time to learning how to deal with the other in the vastly changed circumstances. Political relations too reached a nadir during the Yeltsin era because the Russian leadership was too obsessed with the West and did not consider relations with India a sufficiently important foreign policy priority. Overturning its traditional policy, Russia supported the Pakistani proposal for a nuclear-weapons free zone in South Asia. Under US pressure, Russia reneged on its deal to supply cryogenic engines to India. A decade or so was lost in this period of transition and readjustment. In retrospect, perhaps this was unavoidable.

Following the breakup of the Soviet Union, Russia's main foreign policy concerns were its immediate neighbourhood, the United States, Europe and China, regions from where the main threats to Russia's security emanate. Russia was keen to regain political and economic primacy in its 'near abroad' and was concerned about the threat of Islamic fundamentalism and incipient instability in some of the newly independent states of Central Asia and the Caucasus. This task became more difficult because of the efforts of the United States to permanently weaken Russia by expanding NATO to Russia's western periphery, actively instigating Ukraine, Georgia and Azerbaijan against Russia and locating missile defences in Poland and the Czech Republic.

Outside its immediate neighbourhood, Russia had the West as the reference point for its foreign policy, both because of security considerations and also because Russians have traditionally regarded the West as the 'civilized world' and want to be accepted as 'Europeans'. Integration with Europe has been an enduring Russian theme and aspiration since the time of Peter the Great. Gorbachev had spoken of a common European home. Europe has been also the principal enemy and threat to Russia in the centuries after the Mongol invasion of Russia. Post-Soviet Russia sought access to Europe's lucrative markets and advanced technology in many spheres. Russia also tried to keep Europe dependent on Russian oil and gas and to prevent the consolidation of a common United States-Europe approach towards Russia. At the same time, as a country with a vast Eurasian expanse, Russia had to look towards Asia where most of its natural riches are located. This meant having to resolve its border disputes with China and establish a stable, mutually profitable economic relationship with it. The two countries' interests also converged in the matter of curbing the presence and influence of the United States in Central Asia, even though Russia fears that China's economic pull and demographic expansionism in Siberia, the Far East region of Russia and Central Asia pose a threat to Russia's traditional political influence and economic dominance in this region. Given these more urgent preoccupations, Russia had little time for India.

India-Russia Relations in the Twenty-First Century

At a time when India-Russia relations were at an important crossroads, the replacement of Yeltsin by Putin in 2000 brought to the helm in Russia a new leader who appreciated the strategic importance of Russia's relationship with India and took note of the fact that, unlike the West, India had not tried to humiliate Russia when it was weak. Putin put in place policies that helped to revive the staggering relationship and steer it in the right direction in the new millennium. Even though the days of cheap credits were over, oil flows had stopped, and rupee trade was sputtering to an end, Russia and India once again began to regard each other as relevant to their respective national priorities. The relationship evolved into a more equal one, since Russia was no longer a superpower and India a mere developing country. Both India and Russia acquired a new self-confidence arising out of their rapid economic growth, their large foreign exchange reserves, their respective strengths and their sense of destiny. In 2010, the two countries elevated their relationship to a 'Special and Privileged Strategic Partnership'. For two decades, until the Covid-19 pandemic and the war in Ukraine disrupted this rhythm, India and Russia had annual summit meetings.

Now that India is a global player with a large and fast-growing economy, Russia would like to keep India as a friendly, independent-minded power. The vital interests of the two countries do not clash. Rather, there is reciprocal support for and understanding of each other's priorities and policies in their respective strategic neighbourhoods—South Asia in the case of India and countries of the former Soviet Union in the case of Russia. Russia has given India valuable political, diplomatic and strategic support at critical times—on Kashmir in the UN, during the 1971 Bangladesh Liberation War, at the time of the merger of Goa and Sikkim with India, and when Article 370 was revoked. Now that India's relations with the West have improved, Russian support to India on political issues is perhaps less critical. But times could change. In deference to India's sensitivities and concerns, Russia has not given any advanced defence equipment to Pakistan that would upset the military balance in South Asia. Russia has also given India unique access to advanced technologies in many sectors.

India, for its part, did not criticize Russia's crackdowns in Chechnya (1994–96 and 1999–2000), its military operations in Georgia that led to the secession of Abkhazia and South Ossetia (2008) or its takeover of Crimea (2014). While it has been unhappy over Russia's invasion of Ukraine in 2022, India has abstained on UN resolutions condemning Russia, resisted the West's pressure not to trade with Russia, and managed to work out a formulation on Ukraine at the 2023 G-20 summit that satisfied all sides.

As rising powers likely to play an increasingly larger role on the world stage in the coming decades, Russia and India share the goal of creating a multipolar world. India is happy that Russia has recovered economically and militarily, and is reasserting itself on the international arena. Russia pushed for India's membership of the Shanghai Cooperation Organization. Both countries are members of BRICS. However, as India and the United States have drawn closer, Russia and India seem to have drifted apart somewhat. Russia is unhappy with the concept of the Indo-Pacific espoused by India and the United States and with India's membership of the Quad. For India, Russia getting too close to China is a matter of some concern, though it is highly unlikely that in its dealings with China Russia will sacrifice its interests with India or become too dependent on China. The approach of both countries is pragmatic, dictated by national interests rather than ideology or sentimentalism. In today's complicated and fast-changing geo-political situation, both countries have wisely diversified their foreign policy options, yet have been careful not to jettison a mutually beneficial partnership of trust built up over decades, even though the inescapable reality is that today for both Russia and India, the other country figures only in the second rung of foreign policy priorities.

The defence relationship with Russia is vital for India, which is heavily dependent on Russian equipment and spares, especially for the navy and the air force. Although India has diversified its defence purchases, Russia still remains India's most important foreign supplier of military equipment. There are many problems in this area, some of them very difficult ones. Price negotiations are tough and the era of friendship prices is over. Product support and supply of spares and maintenance for several important acquisitions by India are still inadequate. There are delays and price escalation. The problem has been aggravated after Russia launched its 'special military operations' in Ukraine. Yet, it is neither easy nor desirable for India to put at risk a defence relationship of long standing. Russian military equipment remains competitive, sturdy and reliable. India also appreciates Russia's willingness to sell state-of-the-art equipment to it, such as the S-400 missile defence system, nuclear-powered submarines and an aircraft carrier, the latter two being items that no other country is willing to give India. Russia and India are also engaged in joint research and development of new products like the Brahmos cruise missile. India's legitimate worry is that without a substantial defence relationship, the whole edifice of India-Russia relations would be greatly weakened. For Russia too, considering the large volume of business with India and its record of timely payments and scrupulously settled Soviet-era debts, India is a large and valuable customer for defence equipment. At a time when Russia's economic situation was fragile, defence sales helped to keep Russia's own defence industry afloat. Concerned that India has diversified its defence purchases, Russia understandably does not want to lose the lucrative Indian market to fast-rising and tough competition from Israel, France and the United States, whose powerful arms lobbies have scored notable success with the Indian defence services in demonstrating the attractiveness of their products and services. Hence, Russia is now more receptive to establishing joint ventures in India for producing military equipment and spares.

With synergies arising out of India's energy deficiency and Russia's energy surplus resulting from the country having lost its most lucrative energy market in Europe because of the Ukraine conflict, energy is an important area of future cooperation. Following up on the success of its investment in the Sakhalin-I project in 2001, India is seeking more investment opportunities in Russia's upstream oil and gas sector, including in the Arctic region. India's growing strategic relationship with the United States may complicate efforts to expand India-Russia energy ties. From a commercial perspective, Russia's oil companies want a share in India's petrochemicals sector. As a result of Western sanctions on Russia arising out of the war in Ukraine, Russia has suddenly emerged as the largest supplier of oil to India because of the lower price of its oil. This situation may not be a long-term trend since the attractiveness of Russian oil depends on Russia continuing to offer competitive prices. Besides, Western sanctions have made it very difficult for India to pay for Russian oil. Rupee payment is not very attractive to Russia, which is finding it difficult to use its rupee holdings. In order to resolve this problem, India has permitted Russia to invest its rupee holdings in Indian government securities, treasury bills, corporate bonds and infrastructure schemes. In the nuclear energy sector, following the revision of the Nuclear Suppliers Group guidelines to accommodate India, Russia has contracted to build six units of the Kudankulam nuclear power plant, two of which are already operational.

The big problem in India–Russia relations is the relatively low volume of trade. Two-way trade, excluding oil, is at a worryingly low level of only about US$ 10 billion.[1] Both sides recognize the desirability of increasing and diversifying bilateral trade, as that would lay a sound foundation and give long-term stability to bilateral relations. Even the modest trade target of US$ 30 billion for 2025 is not easily attainable. In both countries, business is now mostly in the hands of a largely West-oriented private sector, which governments can try to nudge and persuade but not compel or push in a particular direction. This Western orientation is partly the result of a historical legacy. Mainstream Indian traders and industrialists were never involved in trade and economic relations with the Soviet Union. Indo-Soviet trade was conducted on the basis of annual trade plans, heavily influenced by political considerations and drawn up by the Central authorities. A whole generation of businessmen, industrialists and trade officials—a rather specialized group—learnt how to work this system and made enormous profits. It was an esoteric activity requiring special expertise and contacts, not the normal skills required to do business along market principles. After the Soviet Union broke up, the more reputable Indian industrial and business houses somehow never ventured seriously into the Russian market. A few brave souls who tested the waters in the early years after the breakup of the Soviet Union were badly scalded and beat a hasty retreat. Bureaucratic complexities and rigidities on both sides present additional hurdles. Indian businessmen have poor awareness of the opaque and frequently changing tax, customs and other rules and regulations in Russia. The difficulties faced by Indian businessmen in getting visas for Russia have been persistent. Recently, as a fallout of the imposition of Western sanctions on Russia because of the Ukraine war and the severe disruption in Russia-West business and people-to-people contacts, Russia has taken steps to make it easier for Indians to visit and do business with it. The fundamental problem is that other than raw materials, there is little that Russia can competitively export to India, and Indian manufactured products are not attractive to Russia. Besides, the already weak banking links between the two countries have been seriously disrupted by Western sanctions.

India continues to regard Russia as a reliable friend and strategic partner. Over the years, successive Indian leaders have taken special care to nurture this relationship, which has survived political vicissitudes, neglect and drift during the Yeltsin era, pressures and attempts by outside powers to create rifts, and occasional misunderstandings over Pakistan. At the official level, both countries are making efforts to restore vigour and dynamism in the relationship, but neither Russia nor India has a wide domestic constituency driving the relationship. This is a fundamental weakness in the bilateral relationship. Perceptions on both sides tend to be shaped by Western prejudices and do not conform to contemporary realities. The new generation of Russia's ruling elite views India quite differently and, understandably, does not have any nostalgia for the Soviet times. It has tended to look essentially to the West for business linkages, in part because the West has traditionally been the benchmark for most Russians of what constitutes a 'civilized' society, and also because a lot of the windfall profits made in the privatization scams of the 1990s have been invested in Western banks, stocks and properties. Russian perceptions of India are outdated and stuck in the time warp of mid-twentieth-century India, and there is little understanding of the much richer, more self-confident and savvier India of the twenty-first century. The situation may change as

Western sanctions on Russia have cut it off from the West and it is now looking afresh at seriously exploring possibilities with partners elsewhere, including India.

The Indian elite's thinking and lifestyle too remains West-oriented. Culture, language and a democratic polity bring India and the West together. India's links with the West have been strengthened in many other ways—through the rich, well-educated and substantial Indian diaspora settled in Western countries; the rapidly growing linkages of Indian business and industry with their Western counterparts; and the large-scale movement of visitors and students between India and the West. Similar people-to-people linkages do not exist between Russia and India. The image that most Indians have of Russia is outdated. Russia is no longer the crushed, dispirited nation of the immediate post-Soviet period, but most Indians have yet to register Russia as a strong, modern and stable country, much less show understanding of its problems. India is also ignorant of, and lacks confidence in, Russian technological capabilities, since Russia is weak in transferring them on a cost-effective basis to the civilian sector. India's elite has fallen under the spell of new suitors who appear more attractive than a known and trusted old partner. Another factor is that Russia does not affect the lives of most ordinary Indians as does, say, the United States or the Persian Gulf region. Of course, these perceptions could change over time.

Despite the many difficulties, irritants and limitations in the relationship, India should not lose sight of Russia's many positive elements. Its relationship with Russia remains very important. If the strategic relationship is to move forward meaningfully, both India and Russia will have to make conscious efforts to understand the other's priorities and become more relevant to each other. The coming into power of a new generation of leaders in both countries adds to the uncertainties in India-Russia relations. There is need to create wider public interest in and understanding of the relationship, particularly among the younger generation. Without such public support, it will be difficult to keep this long-standing, mutually beneficial strategic partnership on a sound and stable foundation. India is rightly building direct contacts with the entire spectrum of stakeholders and interest groups in the political, economic, military and other spheres not only in metropolises like Moscow and St Petersburg but across Russia, including Siberia and the Far East region. Similarly, Russia will have to learn how to deal with the new centres of power and influence in India.

Imperatives in Eurasia

Eurasia is the swathe of land extending from the Mongolian grasslands, Siberian forests, Arctic tundra and Kazakh steppes to the Urals, the Persian Gulf and the Arabian Sea. It includes the Central Asian Republics (CARs) of the former Soviet Union ('Central Asia'), Afghanistan, northern Iran, Caucasia, Tibet, East Turkestan, Mongolia, as well as Ladakh and Pakistan-occupied Kashmir. From a historical, cultural and geopolitical perspective, Eurasia needs to be viewed as a vital strategic, rather than a mere geographical, region.

Throughout India's history, India's principal land connection to the outside world has been via Central Asia, earlier known as Turkestan and East Turkestan. Of all of India's neighbouring regions, whether across land or maritime frontiers, it is with Central Asia that India has had the longest association. The resultant intermingling of cultures and peoples has imbued north India with many elements of Central Asian culture. Historically, Kashmir has had equally intensive trading and cultural contacts with Central Asia and the plains to the south. Ladakh has more in common with the culture and lifestyle of the neighbouring regions of East Turkestan, like Khotan and Kashgar, than with South Asian regions. Central Asia has not just deeply influenced north India's history, culture and polity; till the European colonial powers came to India via the sea route, the traditional threats to India's security too emanated from Central Asia.

In dealing with the CARs, India has many advantages. Unfortunately, links with East Turkestan have weakened considerably since that region is now occupied by China. Unlike their view of China and Russia, the CARs' view of India is that of a benign power that does not pose any direct contemporary threat, whether ideological, demographic or territorial. In fact, India has always held a tremendous cultural attraction, a certain romance and mystique, for the people of this region. India's soft power, which has captivated Central Asia in the past, has the potential to be a powerful tool of India's diplomacy in this region. In an overall perspective, however, India's interests in Central Asia are fundamentally strategic. India wants that Central Asia should be stable and secular, since weak, unstable states with centrifugal tendencies could become a haven for terrorists, separatists and fundamentalists who could link up with similar elements in Afghanistan and Pakistan. Moreover, instability and chaos in Central Asia carry the danger of having a domino effect across the entire region. Among other things, India must track any military presence in the region that could potentially be a threat to it. India does not want this strategically located region to become an area dominated by China or other forces that are inimical or hostile to India. On the economic side, while the Central Asian market is relatively small, India would very much like to gain access to the rich natural resources of the region such as oil and gas, uranium, rare earths and minerals, copper, gold and diamonds; and to acquire, if possible, some specialized defence technologies and defence production facilities available in the CARs. While there have been many proposals for energy corridors from Central Asia to India, these have not taken off because of perceived security risks to the transit routes passing through unstable countries like Afghanistan and Pakistan, or geopolitically problematic countries like China and Iran.

From the perspective of the CARs, India is not regarded as a country that has been able to show that it is relevant, much less make a significant contribution, to their immediate priorities, such as their search for national identity, security and, more recently, regime survival. Nor have they received any large-scale assistance from India for their economic development. Even though India occupies a somewhat low priority among them, the CARs would like India to have a bigger presence in Central Asia, as they consider India, albeit somewhat vaguely, a potential balancing factor to other major players who carry considerable baggage. Foremost is Russia, a country they can neither ignore nor do without. Russia's takeover of Crimea and the war in

Ukraine have deepened their misgivings about Russia, whose influence they are seeking to reduce. Even though they have strong economic ties with China, especially with neighbouring East Turkestan, they view China as an expansionist and domineering power. The United States is welcomed insofar as it keeps the influence of both Russia and China in check, but the US propensity to work for regime change whenever it suits it is worrisome.

Evolution of Bilateral Relations

When the CARs attained independence, they looked forward to India playing a prominent role as a major partner in all spheres of activity. Former President Nazarbaev of Kazakhstan, for example, made it a point to visit India immediately after Kazakhstan's independence. Unfortunately, in the early years following the independence of the CARs, India was unable to optimally convert the traditional goodwill into contemporary influence. Relatively few people in India had any serious knowledge about or interest in Central Asia. Although this is changing of late, even today very little news about Central Asia is to be found in the Indian media, and Indian presence and visibility in this part of the world remain quite poor. At the governmental level, Central Asia was not a region that was given high priority. While resident embassies were opened in all the CARs, high-level visits were infrequent, conveying the impression to these countries that India was not looking at this region as seriously as other major global powers were. On the non-governmental side, India's businessmen, industrialists and bankers evinced only mild interest in Central Asia for the first couple of decades after the CARs became independent. There were objective reasons for this. The emergence of the CARs as independent countries coincided with India's own economic liberalization, when the focus of attention of Indian business and industry was understandably on the developed countries from where India hoped to get investments and technology. It's not that Indian companies did not try to do business in Central Asia, but they became cautious after many Indian companies burnt their fingers in the region during the chaotic years following the breakup of the Soviet Union. Poor air connectivity in the first couple of decades, after the CARs became independent countries, contributed to reinforcing the mutual ignorance among India and the CARs.

Today, India is somewhat more engaged with Central Asia. India sent a good signal about its seriousness in engaging the CARs through its invitation to former Kazakh President Nazarbaev to India as the chief guest on India's Republic Day in 2009. Similarly, Prime Minister Modi's five-nation trip to Central Asia in 2015 was a welcome initiative. In recent years, there have also been some visits at the level of President and Vice President to the CARs. But it has not been possible to sustain the momentum. Visits at the highest levels have tapered off in both directions; high-level ministers and officials meet only at forums like the Shanghai Cooperation Organization (SCO) or the Conference on Interaction and Confidence-Building in Asia (CICA).

India's trade with the CARs remains negligible. The largest partners are Kazakhstan and Uzbekistan, from whom India has been buying uranium of late. As a sparsely populated large geographical area, Central Asia does not figure in the global strategy of most major Indian companies. India's economic ties with the CARs have lagged, principally because India is not economically rich enough, nor its business, industrial and financial community sufficiently motivated or aggressive to be able to overcome India's geographical and other handicaps in dealing with Central Asia. India has to focus on areas other than traditional trade in order to pursue its interests in Central Asia. India's technical-economic assistance programmes like ITEC, particularly in areas like information technology, are seen as very relevant and useful by the CARs. Some of the other ongoing areas of cooperation are: investments in the oil and gas sector; small-scale projects; culture and education; training and capacity building; science and technology; defence and security; and parliamentary, media and academic exchanges. But India's engagement in these areas is not sufficiently deep. Tourism is a promising area of cooperation with considerable potential. Of late, air connectivity with the region has vastly improved, and the rich cultural heritage and natural beauty of Central Asia and Caucasia are attracting an increasing number of tourists from India.

The most important reason for India's limited presence and influence in the CARs is the lack of easy overland access. This severely constrains India's options, particularly in promoting trade. Traditionally, India's contacts with Central Asia have been mainly via Afghanistan, which provides the easiest land route to the region. But given the situation in Afghanistan, and the necessity of having to cross Pakistan to reach Central Asia, India cannot realistically hope to have overland access to Central Asia by this route in the foreseeable future. Pakistan's attitude does not hold out any hope that it would be willing to cooperate with India on Central Asia, since this negates its traditional objective of checking India at every opportunity and of seeking 'strategic depth' against India. India has also been trying to access the CARs via Iran. However, Iran does not provide a reliable or economically efficient access route. Transit to Central Asia via Iran involves cumbersome multi-modal transport, first by road or rail to a port in India, then by ship to an Iranian port, then again by road and/or rail to Central Asia. All connectivity projects via Iran—whether it is the International North-South Transport Corridor leading to Caucasia, the Caspian Sea and Russia, the trilateral India-Iran-Turkmenistan agreement, or the Iran-Afghanistan route—have so far turned out to be sub-optimal. Poor infrastructure, multiple trans-shipments involving different modes of transport, and inefficiency and corruption are the ills that plague all legs of the transport corridors in this region. International sanctions and pressures on Iran impose additional limitations on use of the Iran transit route. The recent sharp deterioration in India-China relations rules out any revival of the traditional trade routes to Central Asia via Leh and Kashgar in the foreseeable future.

More attention and resources need to be devoted to Central Asia in the government, media and academia. India also needs to change its image among the CARs, whose people, particularly the older generation, are attracted by India's history and culture. That is a good starting point and a positive factor; but it also reinforces old stereotypes about India. Today, India needs to project the image of a modern, industrial, scientifically and technologically advanced country that can serve not merely as a role model for these countries (just as India did for many Asian and African countries in the immediate aftermath of their independence from colonial rule) but also greatly help them in their integration with the contemporary world. India's task is much easier today because its image has indeed changed in the West—only the CARs have little direct experience of this, except in the information technology sector. India has to attract the younger generation in particular, target them to visit, study and do business in India, and create economic and people-to-people linkages between India and Central Asia.

A New 'Great Game'?

For many centuries, till the opening of the sea route from Europe to India in the late fifteenth century, Eurasia dominated global geopolitics. The reason was simple. It was a huge territory—the largest, most populous and richest of all possible land combinations. It was in the middle of the Eurasian continent, wedged in by maritime powers in the Atlantic, Indian and Pacific Oceans. Whenever strong leaders managed to unite the Eurasian tribes and people, they acquired an extensive territorial base. Equipped with the most formidable military technology of the time, namely horses, they successfully conquered territories across Eurasia, China, Russia, central Europe, Persia and India. The most successful and famed conquerors were the Mongols. On the other hand, when Central Asia was relatively weak, surrounding powers like Persia and India competed for influence in the region, as the Safavids and Mughals did in the sixteenth century.

As a geographical area into which the back doors, so to speak, of major Asian powers open, Central Asia has always attracted, and will continue to attract, the presence of outside powers. Central Asia is a 'negative security space'—in other words, an area where the major powers cannot afford to let competing major powers or forces exercise a dominating influence because that would pose a threat to their own security. The British, when they ruled India, understood well the strategic importance of the trans-Himalayan territories of Tibet, Afghanistan, Turkestan and East Turkestan. They made forays into Afghanistan and established a presence in Tibet and East Turkestan—all to protect the Indian heartland against the expanding empire of Tsarist Russia, which had taken over Turkestan and clashed with Manchu China, resulting in what the Chinese call the 'unequal treaties' of the mid-nineteenth century. These were the principal elements of the 'Great Game' in the second half of the nineteenth and early twentieth centuries.

The ever-present threat emanating from Central Asia has been fundamental to shaping the history and psyche of both the Russians and the Chinese. Lacking any natural frontiers to its east, Russia, in its search of security from marauding Turks and Mongols, expanded its frontiers to Central Asia, Siberia and the Pacific coast. Of course, Russia had imperialist designs too. China too has traditionally been concerned about threats emanating from the west and north, though it felt somewhat less insecure than Russia since it had the protection of the cold deserts and the Tibetan plateau. Generations of Chinese emperors periodically sought to control East Turkestan, Turkestan and Tibet, but met with only partial and fitful success; at other times they simply hunkered down behind the defensive fortification of the 'Great Wall' stretching thousands of miles. Unlike China and Russia, India was fortunate to have the Tibetan plateau, the Pamirs, the Karakoram and the Himalayan ranges as formidable natural barriers to its north. It did not need to expand its territory to ensure its security, but it had to deal with frequent invasions by tribes of Turks, Mongols and Afghans from this region through the narrow north-west opening of the Khyber Pass.

The impermeable borders of Central Asia during the Cold War era temporarily dulled strategic perceptions about this region. In view of Soviet-Chinese rivalry during this period, there was no danger of a single entity emerging as the dominant power in the Eurasian strategic space. That period was an aberration. Today the Central Asian Republics are once again at the centre of global geopolitics. In the words of Zbigniew Brzezinski, the well-known former US national security adviser and political thinker, this region has become

'The Grand Chessboard'.[2] As frozen borders have thawed after the end of the Cold War and the Soviet Union has disintegrated, connectivity has dramatically improved across the region. Roads, railway lines, oil and gas pipelines and power transmission lines are rapidly crisscrossing the region. Of course, good connectivity has also made movement easier for drug smugglers, terrorists and fundamentalists. China has benefited hugely from the breakup of the Soviet Union and the loosened grip of Russia over Central Asia. It has swiftly and systematically spread its tentacles into Central Asia, economically integrated the CARs with itself, and has built extensive transport and communications links with this region. From Central Asia, China has extended its reach to Iran and Afghanistan. One would have thought that it would be in the interest of the United States to follow a policy to ensure that the two Eurasian powers, Russia and China, don't get together and dominate the Eurasian continent. By provoking the Russians into a war in Ukraine and imposing sanctions on Russia, the United States has only pushed Russia and China into a tighter geopolitical embrace, which is in the interest of neither the United States nor India.

Nevertheless, it is far from smooth sailing for both Russia and China. Having lost its buffer zone of Central Asia, Russia once again feels vulnerable on its southern frontier. For China, East Turkestan could turn out to be its Achilles' heel. Among all the people of Turkic origin in Central Asia, the Uighurs are intellectually the most sophisticated, culturally the richest, and politically have the most developed sense of national identity. It does rankle that they don't have autonomy, much less independence, when much smaller Turkic tribal groups with a poorer sense of identity, like the Turkmen and the Kyrgyz, have managed to get their own independent states. Compared with the Tibetan diaspora, the Uighur diaspora is larger and more influential. Moreover, unlike Tibet, which has limited people-to-people contact with its neighbours India and Nepal, East Turkestan has more economic, social and other ties with its immediate neighbours. Any instability in Central Asia could affect East Turkestan's security since the traditional homelands of the ethnic Uighurs, Kazakhs and Kyrgyz straddle the present-day political boundaries of East Turkestan with Kazakhstan and Kyrgyzstan. Tajikistan's rugged border regions with China are poorly policed. Historically, all these areas had been one region. The old Sino-Soviet border in Central Asia, now the border between China and the Central Asian states, is unnatural since it runs along a rough north-south axis while the rivers flow from east to west. A more natural division of the combined region of Turkestan and East Turkestan would be between the north and the south. The northern regions of East Turkestan and adjoining north Kazakhstan are basically steppe lands inhabited by nomadic tribes, while the oasis settlements in the southern regions of East Turkestan around the Tarim Basin, such as Khotan and Kashgar, have much closer cultural and economic links with Ferghana Valley and the oasis towns of Samarqand, Bukhara and Merv than with northern East Turkestan.

More than three decades after they became independent, the CARs are inherently fragile states. Their nationhood is weak, and their nation building incomplete. Nor is there an accepted mechanism for periodic peaceful transfer of political power. Political institutions and traditions in all these countries are grossly underdeveloped. For most of the 1990s, Tajikistan was in a state of civil war, and it continues to face serious internal security challenges. Kyrgyzstan has had multiple coups, and Kazakhstan faced a coup attempt in 2022. Once again, the Central Asian states face a threat from the Taliban in Afghanistan. Their internal differences and rivalries are mostly unresolved. Uzbekistan, Kyrgyzstan and Tajikistan are the most vulnerable, because they share the strategically important, economically rich and politically volatile Ferghana Valley, which holds the key to stability in Central Asia. Nor is there long-term stability in East Turkestan, currently occupied by China. Were Beijing's control over Tibet and East Turkestan to weaken, this would have direct and far-reaching implications for India's security since these regions are geographically contiguous to India. A China that is more preoccupied with keeping Tibet and East Turkestan under its control would relieve some pressure on India. Hence, India must carefully monitor the situation in Central Asia.

In formulating its broad strategy for Central Asia, India, given its current handicaps, would be unrealistic to think that it can achieve its objectives by acting on its own. In order to protect and preserve its interests in the region, it may be wise for India to consult and cooperate with Russia. There are many reasons for this. In view of the support that Russia gives India in South Asia, India cannot be seen as pursuing policies in Central Asia that Russia considers inimical to its interests there. Russia's actions in recent years, such as its takeover of Crimea, its involvement in the ongoing war in Ukraine, and its role in swiftly suppressing the attempted putsch in Kazakhstan in 2022, have made the CARs fearful of it. Even though Russia's influence in the region has diminished, it remains hugely influential. It cannot be pushed out of Central Asia as it still retains many advantages and leverages with respect to this region. In many countries, especially Kazakhstan, there is a significant and influential ethnic Russian population. Russia is extremely well networked in the region and hosts many political dissidents from these countries who could be used to create difficulties for their local ruling elites. The economies of smaller and poorer countries like Tajikistan and Kyrgyzstan are significantly dependent on the remittances of migrant workers in Russia. All the CARs are landlocked countries whose access to the outside world still greatly depends on Russian transit facilities, including rail, road and energy pipelines constituting the old Soviet-era infrastructure. Russia also gives loans and grants to many CARs. Finally, a significant proportion of their trade is with Russia, which could economically squeeze them, if needed. Given the close India-Russia strategic partnership and the need to ensure that Russia doesn't come too much under China's influence, India should be mindful and supportive of Russian interests and sensitivities in Central Asia. The alternative scenario of the CARs becoming overly dependent on China is not at all in India's interest.

Chapter 11

United States and the West

Five Decades of Estrangement

Despite the Indian ruling elite's fascination with the United States and Jawaharlal Nehru's well known but little publicized attempts to get closer to the country in the 1950s, India's relations with the United States remained mostly frosty for the first fifty years after India's independence. At a time when India was deficient in food grains, the United States, through its PL-480 programme in the 1950s and 1960s, did help India overcome its food shortage by selling India its surplus agricultural produce against Indian rupees. However, at a strategic level the two countries were on different sides. India's policy of non-alignment irked the United States. Pakistan, on the other hand, was a US ally and got political and diplomatic support on the Kashmir issue, as well as generous military assistance. The United States also opposed the integration of Goa and Sikkim into India. In taking the positions it did on Kashmir, Goa and Sikkim, the United States undermined India's territorial integrity. Indo-US relations reached their nadir during the 1971 Bangladesh War, when the United States sent an aircraft carrier into the Bay of Bengal to intimidate India. One of the considerations behind the US move was the need to be seen as supportive of Pakistan, which had been a valuable conduit for the US opening to China. India's first nuclear test (Pokharan-I) in 1974 also greatly annoyed the United States and led, among other things, to its imposing a technology denial regime on India. During the 1980s and 1990s, the United States ignored Pakistan's terrorist activities against India and turned a blind eye to Pakistan's nuclear weapons programme. On the other hand, it actively encouraged Kashmiri separatism, questioned the validity of the accession of Jammu and Kashmir to India, tried to coerce India into signing the Nuclear Non-Proliferation Treaty and tried to scuttle India's space programme. There was also widespread suspicion in India that the United States was actively interfering in India's domestic politics.

Pokharan-II a Turning Point

It was only after India became a nuclear weapons power in 1998 that the nature of India's relationship with the United States qualitatively changed. This event, together with Pakistan too becoming a declared nuclear weapons power, gave an unexpected and unpleasant jolt to the United States. Unlike the situation a few years earlier, when the United States got wind of India's plans to conduct a nuclear test and forced India into abandoning them, this time the United States was completely blindsided. Furious, it imposed sanctions on India. But this also forced the United States, for the first time, into taking India—and indeed the whole of South Asia—seriously from a security and geopolitical perspective. Two other factors that added to India's importance in US eyes were India's economic reforms and its consequent growing economic weight, and the increasingly influential role of the Indian American community in the United States. South Asia was no longer a geopolitical backwater that could do without high-level US attention. India and the United States began their unprecedented serious and intensive high-level interaction with a series of meetings in different parts of the world between the designated representatives of the two countries namely, Jaswant Singh and Strobe Talbott from 1998 to 2000. President Clinton's visit to India in March 2000, the first by a US President to India after more than two decades, signalled the decidedly higher priority being given by the United States to India. If there were any doubts that South Asia had emerged prominently on the US foreign policy radar screen, these were removed after 9/11 and the ensuing US war on terror in Afghanistan that necessitated getting Pakistan's cooperation without alienating India.

From the US side, the focus of its strategic dialogue with India was on preventing India from enhancing its nuclear weapons capabilities. The Clinton administration's mantra was to 'cap, rollback and eliminate' India's nuclear weapons programme. The Bush administration in its first term tried to achieve the same objective, though not so aggressively. Essentially, the US objective was to put pressure on India to sign the Comprehensive Test Ban Treaty (CTBT), join the negotiations on the Fissile Material Cutoff Treaty (FMCT), strengthen controls over export of sensitive technologies and equipment in line with the guidelines of the Nuclear Suppliers Group (NSG) and the Missile Technology Control Regime (MTCR), and work to reduce tensions with a nuclear Pakistan since Kashmir was viewed as a 'nuclear flashpoint.' In return, the United States promised to lift its sanctions and give India access to high technology. The United States was also very keen on strengthening Indo-US defence ties, including through sale of military equipment. From the Indian side, the National Democratic Alliance (NDA) government in power from 1998 to 2004 was enthusiastic about forging a strategic partnership with the United States. As external affairs minister, Jaswant Singh tried hard, but in vain, to seal a strategic partnership with the United States by extending support to it on matters the latter considered to be of political and strategic importance. The Indo-US dialogue lost some momentum for a while as the US concentrated on the ongoing war in Afghanistan and India turned its attention to tackling the security threats from Pakistan following the attack on the Indian Parliament in December 2001. In November 2002, an Indo-US High Technology Cooperation Group was set up. India thought this might improve its access to items of both civilian and military application ('dual use technologies') from the United States. In 2003, President Bush pressed India to send troops to Iraq, but a canny and politically savvy prime minister Vajpayee saw the long-term dangers in this and adroitly managed to stave off the pressure. Although Vajpayee considered the United States a 'natural ally', he was understandably reluctant to agree to terms that would compromise India's strategic autonomy. The continuing search for a mutually acceptable basis for a strategic partnership found expression in the bilateral dialogue under the rubric of Next Steps in Strategic Partnership (NSSP) announced in January 2004, which was intended to increase cooperation in civilian nuclear activities, civilian space programmes and high-technology trade. Later, missile defence was added as a fourth component to the NSSP. It soon became clear that US laws and regulations would make it almost impossible for the NSSP to achieve its objectives, unless India could somehow be fitted into the non-proliferation regime.

On coming to power in 2004, the UPA Government, keen to leave its mark on foreign policy, grew impatient with the incremental progress being made under the NSSP. Prime Minister Manmohan Singh made nurturing of the relationship with the US his most important foreign policy priority. This coincided with the new strategic focus on India under the second Bush administration with Condoleezza Rice as Secretary of State. During her visit to India in March 2005, her offer to 'make India a great power' appealed to the vanity of Indian policymakers. President Bush and Prime Minister Manmohan Singh were determined to forge a new strategic relationship between India and the United States, unencumbered by the disappointments and suspicions of the past. In order to convince the United States of its bona fides, India pushed through comprehensive export control legislation in May 2005, agreed to a wide-ranging and far-reaching defence agreement (New Framework for the Indo-US Defence Relationship) with the United States in June 2005 and, at a critical moment, presumably not wishing to spoil the atmosphere on the eve of the prime minister's planned visit to the United States in mid-July, did not press for a vote in the UN General Assembly on a G-4 (India, Japan, Germany, Brazil) resolution seeking a reform of the UN Security Council.

Nuclear Deal

This set the stage for the Indo-US nuclear deal outlined in the 18 July 2005 joint statement issued during Prime Minister Manmohan Singh's visit to the United States. It was abruptly declared that the NSSP had been satisfactorily completed, without quite explaining how. The Indian side saw the nuclear deal as the centerpiece of a blossoming Indo-US strategic partnership. Conscious of the baggage of US dealings with India over half a century, Indian policymakers were astute enough to realize that it would not be politically easy to sell a strategic relationship with the United States, but simplistically concluded that public and political scepticism on this count could be overcome if the United States were to recognize India as a nuclear weapons power and lift the restrictions on technology transfer to India. Crafted in stealth and secrecy by a small cabal, the 18 July statement was thrust upon the Indian public and even the Indian nuclear establishment at the last minute, and perhaps without fully thinking through its consequences and implications. The statement stipulated that India would assume the same responsibilities and practices and acquire the same benefits and advantages as other leading countries with advanced nuclear technology, such as the United States. India agreed to separate its civilian and military nuclear facilities; voluntarily place its civilian nuclear facilities under IAEA safeguards; sign an Additional Protocol with respect to civilian nuclear facilities; continue its unilateral moratorium on nuclear testing; work with the United States for the conclusion of a Fissile Material Cutoff Treaty; and not transfer enrichment and reprocessing technologies to states that do not have them. Despite these severe restrictions on India's nuclear programme, the country at that time accepted the government's contention that the overall balance was favourable to India and that the agreement did not compromise India's national and strategic interests. Had the spirit of the 18 July statement been maintained in the negotiations, there would have been no problem.

Not unexpectedly, trouble started immediately thereafter as the United States successfully coerced India into toeing its line in September 2005, when the International Atomic Energy Agency (IAEA) adopted a resolution finding Iran non-compliant with its safeguards agreement with the IAEA and that this was a matter that fell under the purview of the UN Security Council. India followed the US line when the IAEA actually referred the matter to the UN Security

Council in February 2006. India's votes conveyed the impression that it was a soft state that could be arm-twisted even on matters concerning India's vital interests in its own neighbourhood. This reassured the US Administration and Congress that India would be a reliable long-term strategic partner willing to adjust its foreign policy to converge with the US global agenda.

India's foreign policy focus throughout 2006 was on relations with the United States in general and the Indo-US nuclear deal in particular. With External Affairs Minister Natwar Singh having become a victim of the Volcker Report on Iraq's oil-for-food controversy, Prime Minister Manmohan Singh did not appoint a new external affairs minister and personally guided the Indo-US relationship for nearly a year. During President Bush's visit to India in March 2006, a separation plan for India's civil and military nuclear facilities was finalized. Quietly, Indo-US defence relations were given a boost with the signing of the Framework Agreement on Maritime Security Cooperation. The two countries also agreed to conclude an agreement similar to the Acquisition and Cross-Servicing Agreements (ACSA) that the United States had concluded with its numerous allies. Presumably, in order to hide its true intent from the Indian public, this was labelled as a Logistics Support Agreement. But because of the opposition of the left parties, on whose support the UPA government was dependent, the Logistics Support Agreement could not be signed.

Political attention in the United States and India now turned to the US administration's efforts to get the US Congress to pass enabling legislation permitting the United States to engage in civilian nuclear cooperation with India. The debate within the US Congress seemed to confirm the fears of the sceptics in India that the United States would try to load unacceptable conditions on the US legislation. Sharp divisions within the Indian establishment and public on the nuclear deal engendered a heated and wide-ranging political and public debate in India. When the Hyde Act, as the enabling legislation came to be called, was passed by the US Congress in December 2006, it turned out to contain extraneous and prescriptive provisions that revealed wide gaps between Prime Minister Manmohan Singh's assurances to the nation and the Act. However, the US government disingenuously averred that the Hyde Act was an internal piece of legislation and that India would only be concerned with the bilateral Indo-US Agreement (the so-called 123 Agreement) that was under negotiation.

While the controversy continued to rage in India and the nuclear deal became a political football, the government engaged in protracted and difficult negotiations on the 123 Agreement. India's negotiators tried some semantic jugglery to bridge the seemingly irreconcilable gaps between the Hyde Act and Prime Minister Manmohan Singh's assurances to Parliament. Many senior Indian officials were resigned to the collapse of the deal because of the domestic political constraints. But both the Indian and US leaders gave a decisive political push, showing extraordinary keenness and doggedness to somehow reach an agreement. Why Prime Minister Manmohan Singh pursued the deal with such zeal is unclear. Perhaps there were considerations of prestige, ego and the 'legacy' he would leave behind. Thus, India went ahead and finalized the negotiations on a Safeguards Agreement with the IAEA Secretariat even without the approval of the UPA-Left committee that had been set up to examine this matter. As anticipated, the Left withdrew its support to the UPA government in July 2008, but the government nevertheless managed to survive thanks to support from the Samajwadi Party.

Indian official statements, including at the highest level, took the lofty line that this deal was all about civilian nuclear energy and would give India energy security; it was not about India's nuclear weapons programme. That is far from true. Getting US support for India's civilian nuclear energy programme was merely one element, and not the most important one, of this deal. In a candid observation during a private conversation with Indian interlocutors in September 2008, Bush admitted that the deal was not about selling reactors to India but about the larger significance of the US-India relationship. The unprecedented secrecy surrounding the negotiations for an ostensibly civil nuclear energy cooperation agreement only added to the misgivings. One secondary consideration for India to go in for the deal could have been that import of uranium for its civilian nuclear energy programme (now possible under the deal) would free up indigenous uranium for its nuclear weapons programme. It is true that the NSG waiver has paved the way for India to engage in nuclear trade. India has since signed civilian nuclear cooperation agreements with a number of countries for import of uranium. But because of the conditions imposed by the 2010 Nuclear Liability Law, US suppliers of nuclear plants have not yet come forward to set up nuclear plants in India.

The essence of the problem was that the United States and India had different objectives in signing the nuclear deal. From the US side, the first objective was to ensure that India's foreign policy was congruent with its own and to integrate India as a constructive actor and shareholder in a US-led international system. This ran counter to India's desire to see a multipolar world, with India itself as one of the poles. Another important area of difference was that whereas the United States' hope was to corral India into the non-proliferation framework in a way that would curb India's strategic capabilities, the Indian national consensus was for India to preserve its strategic autonomy and to continue to pursue its strategic nuclear weapons programme. India hoped the nuclear deal would at least open the doors to the privileges enjoyed by the nuclear weapons powers that are signatories to the NPT, even if it is not recognized as a nuclear weapons power under the NPT. This has not happened. India is still not a member of the NSG, and India has accepted implicit and irreversible curbs on its strategic weapons programme. There remain serious ambiguities on many technical points about the deal, such as India's practical ability to conduct nuclear tests should the situation so require; India's right to reprocess spent fuel; safeguards in perpetuity; guaranteed supplies of fuel; and the nature of corrective measures India can take if fuel supplies from abroad are disrupted.

Lessons for the Future

Even if the original objectives of the nuclear deal were not achieved, it did serve an important and useful purpose. Both sides drew valuable lessons from it to help guide Indo-US relations in the future. The first lesson was that there was a flawed assumption behind the deal—that the nuclear issue was the only major issue that had kept the US and India apart for so many decades, and that with the removal of this 'elephant in the room', relations would develop smoothly. This reasoning ignored the reality that the nuclear factor came into the Indo-US equation only after India's peaceful nuclear explosion of 1974 and that other fundamental factors had been at work in creating a divide between India and the United States for so many decades. From the very outset, the United States was unwilling to accept India's desire and right to pursue an independent foreign policy. There was constant pressure on India to align its foreign policy with that of the United States. The position that the United States had taken on Kashmir, Goa and Sikkim undermined India's territorial integrity. Its attitude towards India during the Bangladesh crisis was hostile. By assigning Pakistan a key role in its long-term strategic plans for the region and in seeking to ensure a military balance in South Asia, the United States had been working against India's security. In its Cold War rivalry with the Soviet Union, the United States was also wooing China, much to India's discomfort. Thus, it was evident that if India's national and foreign policy priorities and real interests in its immediate and wider strategic neighbourhood did not coincide with US policies, there could not be a sound basis for an Indo-US strategic relationship.

A second lesson was that in a vibrant democracy like India, a lasting strategic partnership with the United States could not be crafted by stealth and subterfuge. There must be trust, accompanied a wider public support base. This requires time and patience. There is little doubt that India's urban elites—the corporate sector, students, professionals, the urban middle class and the English-language media—have always favoured a closer strategic partnership with the United States. For them the United States remains the most attractive destination for education, work opportunities and migration. Then there is the Indian-American community, whose interests considerably overlap with those of India's urban elite. Their political activism on the nuclear deal probably arose from a combination of do-goodism, selfish political ambition and perhaps a subconscious wish to see the United States and India as allies so as to avoid having to make hard choices between India, their land of birth, and the United States, their adopted home. The support of Indian elites and the Indian-American community was not a strong-enough factor for the crafting of a strategic relationship.

A third lesson was that it was premature at that time for India to have a close military relationship with the United States centred on sales of military equipment and on developing 'interoperability' of the armed forces of the two countries. As a military relationship follows, not precedes, a convergence of strategic interests and objectives, this seemed to be a case of putting the cart before the horse. In any case, it was unrealistic for the United States to expect that India would jettison its hardwired decades-old defence ties with Russia.

A fourth lesson was that in order to craft a lasting strategic partnership, it would be essential to do so on more equal terms rather than with India positioned as a submissive junior partner. The terms of a dialogue, and the framework for a strategic engagement, could not be set by the United States, with India merely reacting to US proposals, unable or unwilling to put its own agenda on the table. The goal and interests of the two countries would have to converge, or at least be respected by the other side. India had to get over the assumption that the United States' overall global domination was destined to continue and therefore India had no option but to get closer to it. It became clear that India would have to situate the dialogue with the United States in the changing overall global scenario where US power has peaked and other countries, including India itself, are becoming more influential. It had to accurately gauge and leverage the compulsions of the United States to seek a better relationship with India. It would have to wait till the relative balance of power between the United States and India is less tilted in favour of the United States.

A fifth lesson was that it would require tremendous effort and compromise on both sides, and a steely determination at the highest level, to craft a truly strategic partnership. A fundamental problem—for any country—is that no strategic relationship with the United States can ever be one of equality. No ally or partner of the United

States has ever been treated as an equal by the latter. On issues where the United States feels strongly enough or exerts sufficient pressure, all are expected to fall in line, and they invariably do. On the other hand, India is firmly committed to pursuing an independent foreign policy. It would be necessary to find ways to reconcile these competing perspectives.

The final lesson was that, with all its weaknesses, the Indo-US nuclear deal did take forward Indo-US relations and brought out the high desirability for India to have a strong, stable and friendly relationship with the United States. India could not ignore the fact that the United States was the pre-eminent global power, a large investor in India, an important technology provider and India's largest market for goods and services. There were shared concerns about China, though it would have been unrealistic to expect the United States to sacrifice its relationship with China for the sake of India. Closer ties with the United States also opened the doors for India's engagement with many other countries that take their foreign policy cues from the United States. It gave India some leverage in dealing with other major global players.

The Obama Years

The Obama administration, which took office in January 2009, did not bode well for Indo-US relations. Unlike Bush, Obama was not personally invested in better Indo-US relations. In an article in *Foreign Affairs* in 2007, Obama opined that he would like to encourage dialogue between Pakistan and India to resolve their dispute over Kashmir, and that if Pakistan could look towards the east with greater confidence, it was less likely to believe that its interests could be best advanced through cooperation with the Taliban. This formulation hinted at a re-hyphenation of India and Pakistan and possible US diplomatic intervention on the Kashmir issue in order to get Pakistan's cooperation to fight the Taliban and al-Qaeda. Moreover, Obama as senator had pressed for stringent amendments to the Indo-US nuclear deal. India's apprehensions that Obama's priority in South Asia was to deal with

Afghanistan and Pakistan ('Af-Pak') seemed to be confirmed when, just a couple of days after his inauguration, Obama appointed Richard Holbrooke as special representative for Afghanistan and Pakistan. Although, because of vehement Indian opposition, Holbrooke's mandate did not include India, the direction of US policy was clear. India also noted that Secretary of State Hillary Clinton skipped India during her first visit to Asia and visited the country only in July 2009. Even worse, Obama, during his visit to China in November 2009 (the first time ever that a US president had visited China during his first year in office), agreed to a formulation for the United States and China to ready to strengthen communication, dialogue and communication on issues related to South Asia and work together to promote peace, stability and development in the region. This US-China joint approach on South Asia ('G-2') was a throwback to an earlier, similar attempt in 1998 after India's nuclear tests. Realizing its blunder, the United States tried to make up with India through the optics of upgrading a scheduled visit by Prime Minister Manmohan Singh to the United States later that month to a 'state visit', and the announcement of a new phase in the India-US global strategic partnership.

The next three or four years were comparatively better years in Indo-US relations. The big event during this period was President Obama's visit to India in November 2010, during which he pressed all the right buttons with praise for India's democracy and support for India's bid for a permanent seat in the UN Security Council and for India's membership of the multilateral export control regimes (the Nuclear Suppliers Group, the Missile Technology Control Regime, the Australia Group that controls chemical and biological weapons, and the Wassenaar Arrangement that controls dual-use technology). There was also some easing of controls on export of dual-use and high-end technologies from the US to India and removal of DRDO and ISRO (and the organizations under them) from the Entities List, a US government compilation of foreign individuals, companies and organizations deemed a national security concern, subjecting them to export restrictions and licensing requirements for certain technologies and goods. Obama flattered India by acknowledging that the US and India were equal partners and that India was a trusted and indispensable friend. The two countries also agreed to step up cooperation on counter-terrorism and initiated strategic consultations on all regional and global issues of mutual interest. India also increased its military exercises with the United States and its purchases of US military hardware. In 2012, the two sides launched a new initiative, the Defence Technology and Trade Initiative (DTTI), an ambitious new joint endeavour to facilitate bilateral defence trade and create opportunities for US-India co-production and co-development in various sectors, including aircraft carriers and jet engines. During Prime Minister Manmohan Singh's farewell visit to the United States in September 2013, the two sides signed a Joint Declaration on Principles of Defence Cooperation whereby, among other things, the United States agreed to treat India on par with its closest partners in terms of technology release. All these steps undoubtedly did create a better atmosphere in Indo-US relations and were incremental steps in taking the relationship forward.

Yet many differences, disagreements and disappointments remained on both sides. India remained unhappy with several aspects of US policy and attitude, such as its Af-Pak policy that ensured money and advanced weaponry for Pakistan and ignored India's interests in Afghanistan. Other issues that upset India were: US foot-dragging over bringing the perpetrators of the 26/11 Mumbai terror attacks to justice; US policy towards Myanmar and Bangladesh; US pressure on India to reduce oil imports from Iran; trade disputes that the United States took to the WTO; restrictions on H-1B visas for Indian professionals; and US unwillingness to conclude a 'Totalization Agreement' that would enable Indians who were unable to get immigration status to benefit from the social security contributions they had made while working in the United States. On the US side, the principal grouses were that the stringent conditionalities imposed by the Nuclear Liability Act passed by the Indian Parliament made US companies lose interest in setting up nuclear power plants in India; the elimination of US companies in trials for fighter aircraft purchases; India dragging its feet on signing the 'foundational agreements' that were intended to increase interoperability between the armed forces of the two countries and facilitate US sale of high-tech military equipment to India.

One factor that impacted the relationship was the absence of high-level oversight on both sides. The United States was preoccupied with crafting an exit strategy from Afghanistan, while in India, the Manmohan Singh government was increasingly enmeshed in domestic controversies that left no time or appetite for economic reforms in order to attract US investments. Relations reached a dangerous low in December 2013 when Devyani Khobragade, India's deputy consul general in New York, was arrested on charges of not paying her housekeeper minimum wages as per US law. In a predictable tit-for-tat response, India imposed restrictions on some dodgy privileges and practices of US diplomatic and consular establishments. This episode brought out the difficulties in crafting a closer Indo-US relationship. After a few tense months, and a realization on both sides that it would be foolish to derail a burgeoning relationship over this incident, creative and imaginative diplomacy found an honourable exit for both countries from this needless controversy. It served as a timely reminder to the US side that it could not deal with India going by its existing templates and would have to be mindful of Indian sensitivities.

Modi, A Game Changer

Given the earlier US hostility towards Narendra Modi, who was denied a US visa for a decade for his alleged complicity in the 2002 Gujarat riots, it was thought that there might be a cooling in the Indo-US relationship when Narendra Modi became prime minister. US and Indian officials and analysts were taken by surprise when, in fact, the opposite happened. Pragmatism and realism marked Modi's approach to the United States. Brushing aside possible misgivings over the US attitude towards him in the past, and wanting to move beyond the unfortunate Khobragade incident, he quickly reached out to the United States with dramatic overtures, including an early visit to that country in September 2014, less than four months after becoming prime minister. Obama, now under pressure because of low approval ratings and wishing to avoid any further deterioration in US relations with India, accepted Prime Minister Modi's bold invitation to him to be the chief guest at India's Republic Day celebrations in January 2015. He made a judgement call that the United States could do business with the Modi government, which it had been unable to with the Manmohan Singh government during the last few years. Moreover, it wouldn't have been lost on Obama that it might be politically useful to be friendly to Modi, who had demonstrated that he enjoyed considerable support among the affluent and increasingly influential Indian community in the United States.

Modi realized that India needed the United States by its side for two main reasons. One was to tackle the challenge of China. That was the logic behind the bold Joint Strategic Vision for the Asia-Pacific and the Indian Ocean Region announced during President Obama's visit, which enunciated the far-reaching proposition that a closer Indo-US partnership was indispensable for peace, prosperity and stability in the Asia-Pacific and Indian Ocean regions. It included a specific mention of 'ensuring freedom of navigation and overflight' in the South China Sea. The second was the need to have a friendly and cooperative United States—not just the administration, but also the Congress, corporate America, technology leaders and civil society, including the American Indian community—for India's economic rejuvenation, defence modernization and access to technology in order to realize its ambition to become a global power. During his visits to the United States, which became an annual feature, Prime Minister Modi reached out to all these stakeholders. The Indo-US Strategic Dialogue was upgraded to a Strategic and Commercial Dialogue involving the ministers of both external affairs and commerce. Even as the two sides tried to see how US companies could get over the obstacles the Nuclear Liability Law had created in making it not worthwhile for US companies to set up nuclear plants in India, nuclear issues were no longer the central element in the Indo-US relationship. The quest for a new Indo-US strategic partnership was now based on other considerations. As Modi put it, it was time that both countries overcame the 'hesitations of history', even though India's misgivings about US policy on Afghanistan and Pakistan, and US efforts to get closer to China, remained.

Over the next few years, defence and security cooperation was the main driver of the relationship. The 2005 Defence Agreement was extended by another ten years. A Defence Policy Group was set up headed by the defence ministers on either side. India stepped up its military exercises with the United States as well as its purchase of defence equipment from it. In 2016, the United States recognized India as a 'Major Defence Partner,' a new category of military relationship that was expected to facilitate defence trade and technology sharing with India to a level at par with that of US's closest allies and partners. Over the next four years, India also signed the three foundational agreements intended to facilitate military cooperation between the two countries—the Logistics Exchange Memorandum of Agreement (LEMOA) in 2016; the Communications Compatibility and Security Agreement (COMCASA) in 2018; and the Basic Exchange and Cooperation Agreement for Geospatial Intelligence (BECA) in 2020. The two countries began to work much more closely on other security issues like counter-terrorism and cybersecurity.

At the same time, India made it clear that it would not be arm-twisted by the United States on issues that mattered to India. One example was in the matter of the Trade Facilitation Agreement of the WTO, which India signed only after the United States agreed to a formulation that protects India's interests. India pushed back against US pressure on various issues such as intellectual property rights for US pharmaceutical giants, as well as on Iran, where India signed on to develop Chabahar port despite US murmurs of disapproval. India rejected motivated allegations of discrimination against and maltreatment of religious minorities in India and began greater scrutiny of the activities of prominent and influential American NGOs like the Ford Foundation and Greenpeace.

Dealing with Trump

The unexpected election of the unpredictable and mercurial Donald Trump as US President in 2020 threatened to undo all the hard work of the previous decade and a half that had gone into building a US-India strategic partnership. The traditional rules of functioning and reliance on credible interlocutors no longer applied to the US administration. Frequent changes of key personnel added to the confusion and uncertainty. Under these circumstances, India did well by not only managing to avoid a shipwreck in the relationship, but in also taking it forward in many respects. Prime Minister Modi's trip to the United States within months of Trump assuming office was intended to gauge the new administration's priorities and thinking, but it turned out to be quite productive. Shared concerns about China, which had triggered the Doklam standoff with India and was continuing its aggressive activities in the South China Sea, accelerated the coming together of the two countries. Much to China's annoyance, the United States started using the term 'Indo-Pacific' instead of 'Asia-Pacific', renamed its Pacific Command (PACOM) as INDO-PACOM and, like India, took a negative view of China's Belt and Road Initiative. The National Security Strategy released by the Trump administration in December 2017, while declaring China as a strategic competitor, welcomed the emergence of India as a leading global power and a stronger strategic and defence partner of the United States. There was also mention of the US giving priority to deepening its strategic partnership with India and supporting India's leadership role in Indian Ocean security and throughout the broader region. On Pakistan, President Trump began to take a hard line on aid to the country, though this position began to soften in the later years of his administration as it struggled to find an early exit from Afghanistan.

On some trade issues, however, Trump exerted considerable pressure on India. He withdrew the Generalized System of Preferences (GSP) concessions from India in 2019, imposed higher duties on steel and aluminium imports on national security grounds, and challenged India's export subsidies in the WTO. He also berated India for its high duties on medical equipment, dairy products, chicken legs and poultry, and for some reason, was obsessed with India's duties on Harley-Davidson motorcycles! In a bid to assuage US concerns, India started importing oil from the United States too and reduced its oil imports from Iran. Another potential, serious source of tension in bilateral relations was the passing of the Countering America's Adversaries through Sanctions Act (CAATSA), which was targeted at Russia but also mandated sanctions against countries that were buying Russian defence equipment. This had the potential to hurt India, which had struck a deal with Russia for buying its S-400 air defence system and some other military equipment. Fortunately, as a result of pressure from India, the law was amended to allow a waiver if the President were to certify that India was weaning itself away from Russian defence equipment, and so far, in practice, this has not been applied to India. In order to address US concerns and soften US opposition to India's substantial defence relationship with Russia, India increased its imports of defence equipment from the US, facilitated in part by the Trump administration's decision to give India Strategic Trade Authorization Tier 1 (STA-1)-facilitated export of some high-end technologies. It was during President Trump's tenure that many measures were taken to cement the bilateral strategic partnership. These included: India signing the second foundational defence agreement, COMCASA; Australia joining the Indo-US-Japan Malabar exercises; initial moves for revival of the Quad; and initiation of an Indo-US dialogue involving both the foreign and defence ministers ('2+2 Dialogue'), replacing the Strategic and Commercial Dialogue between the foreign and commerce ministers.

India quickly understood that as the traditional rules of diplomacy and channels of influencing decision-making did not apply to the Trump administration, it had to resort to unorthodox means to get through to President Trump. Appealing to his vanity and love of showmanship, Prime Minister Modi suggested that Trump might join him in a rally in Houston in November 2019 with an anticipated turnout of tens of thousands of Indian Americans. Trump accepted the offer, and was duly impressed with the show that had been put up. In a risky but politically crafty move, Modi flattered Trump by endorsing the latter's candidature in the forthcoming Presidential election of 2020. Trump also accepted Modi's invitation to visit India in February 2020, and was duly impressed by the huge rally organized in his honour at Ahmedabad. Obviously, the Democratic Party was upset, and some of their representatives in the Congress were openly and loudly critical of what they saw as official complicity in incidents of communal violence and alleged discrimination against minorities. India pushed back or ignored such criticism. It was focused on ensuring that the United States should remain supportive on issues that mattered to India, like the abolition of Article 370, and supply of real-time geospatial intelligence and equipment to it during the Galwan clashes with China in the summer of 2020. No doubt, both the Democrats and the Republicans had noted that India had signalled that it could, if it wanted, play a role in influencing political behaviour in the United States.

A Strategic Partnership?

There is now a consensus across the political spectrum, both in the United States and in India, that closer Indo-US relations serve the national interests of both countries. If, on the Indian side, Modi in 2014 had brushed aside earlier US antagonism towards him and actively sought better relations with it, on the US side the Democrats ignored the seeming endorsement of Trump by Modi and went on to consolidate the Indo-US relationship. The apogee was reached during Prime Minister Modi's state visit to the United States in June 2023, in the course of which he addressed for an unprecedented second time, and to all-round acclamation, a joint session of the US Congress. The key factors responsible for the turnaround in relations today are a much greater convergence of interests, growing mutual trust and a leader driven engagement that can cut through bureaucratic thickets.

Technology and defence are the two principal drivers of the relationship. India now considers the United States to be a reliable and very important defence partner. The driver for this is the initiative of Critical and Emerging Technologies (iCET) to elevate and expand strategic technology partnership and defence industrial cooperation between the governments, businesses and academic institutions of the two countries. On the defence side, a Roadmap for US-India Defence Industrial Cooperation has been signed, and a Defence Acceleration Ecosystem (INDUS-X) set up as a network of universities, startups, industry and think tanks to facilitate joint defence technology innovation for co-development and co-production of advanced defence technologies, including in the areas of space and artificial intelligence. There are agreements for transfer of technology for jet engines and sale of high-altitude drones from the US to India. Other areas identified for collaboration are artificial intelligence, quantum technologies, advanced wireless communications, high-performance computing technology, resilient semiconductor supply chains, space, development of STEM (science, technology, engineering and mathematics) talent, next-generation telecommunications, biotechnology, advanced materials and rare- earths processing technology. It remains to be seen how efficaciously these plans are implemented.

Keen to remove needless irritants in the relationship, the United States and India agreed to end the trade disputes that had been taken to the WTO. However, differences remain on other trade issues and on data localization. In order to facilitate growing people-to-people contacts, new consulates will be opened in Ahmedabad, Bengaluru and Seattle. On the war in Ukraine, the United States and India are clearly not on the same page. India successfully resisted US pressure to condemn Russia, and it is noteworthy that the United States did not let this adversely affect bilateral ties. India's response to gratuitous remarks by some on the US side, including former President Obama, about human rights and democracy, was firm and combative. It was ready for a two-way dialogue but would not accept any lecturing or finger wagging by the US side, whose own handling of such issues in its country left much to be desired. Similarly, India has strongly pushed back with a sharp and blunt response to unwarranted remarks by the US official spokesperson on India's Citizenship Amendment Act. Notwithstanding such irritants, the two sides are conscious of the need to not lose sight of the big picture.

Europe and the United Kingdom

Europe and the United Kingdom are important for India principally as valuable economic partners. India's need for capital, markets and technology necessitates closer ties with the affluent and developed West. There is also extensive people-to-people interaction, what with hundreds of thousands of Indian tourists, businessmen and students travelling to Europe. Although the share of Europe in India's external trade and economic contacts has gone down, in relative terms, over the last few years, Europe does remain an important market and source of technology for India. Since 2000, regular India-EU summits have been held, alternately in India and Europe, the last one being in 2021. While this does signal the mutual desire among the Europeans and Indians to engage with each other, the summits are rather ritualistic and often lightweight, depending on the composition of the EU 'Troika' (countries holding the present, immediate past and next Presidency of the EU).

For some years now, India and the European Union (which handles the EU's external economic relations) have been trying to conclude a Free Trade Agreement, but without much success so far. Wide differences remain on key issues. India is unwilling to give concessions on data, intellectual property and government procurement, and to evergreening of patents in the pharmaceutical sector. Starting from 2026, the European Union proposes to introduce a Carbon Border Adjustment Mechanism (CBAM) under which tariffs, estimated to be in the range of 20–35 per cent, can be imposed on imports of steel, aluminum, fertilizer, electricity, cement and hydrogen from countries using carbon-intensive methods of production.[1] The list could be expanded to cover other items too. Other unilateral protectionist measures that go against free trade and WTO rules, similarly lacking in clarity and leaving considerable scope for arbitrariness, are also on the anvil. These include deforestation-free product regulation, Foreign Subsidies Regulation (FSR), and the Supply Chain Due Diligence Act (SCDDA). India has warned the EU that this could trigger retaliatory measures by India, like imposition of a carbon tax on goods from countries that have high per-capita emissions. After Brexit, India has also been in talks with the United Kingdom for a free trade agreement, but significant differences remain to be bridged. However, India has taken the first step to concluding FTAs with Western countries by signing in March 2024 a Trade and Economic Partnership Agreement (TEPA) with the European Free Trade Association (EFTA) comprising Iceland, Liechtenstein, Norway and Switzerland. Any serious political interaction with Europe is done with individual European countries, among which the most important are the United Kingdom, France and Germany, all members of the G-7 and having some kind of a global footprint. India's presence at the G-7 summits, where it has been a regular invitee for the last two decades or so, provides further opportunities for interaction with the Europeans. India under Prime Minister Modi has engaged at the highest level with even the smaller European countries, many of which had been ignored by India for decades.

While giving primacy to economic factors in its dealings with Europe, India does not ignore some important political considerations. The United Kingdom and France are both permanent members of the UN Security Council and recognized nuclear weapon states, while Germany is a major economic power. All the European countries are members of the NSG, and most of them also members of the Missile Technology Control Regime (MTCR). As some of them, in particular the United Kingdom, have been hosting Indian extremist and secessionist groups and leaders, India has to engage with them in an effort to curb their activities. Thanks to their aid packages and otherwise large economic clout, European countries exercise considerable influence among India's neighbours, requiring India to be vigilant to ensure that the policies of these countries are not inimical to India's interests. Many European countries are preachy and intrusive about democracy and human rights, which they frequently use as pressure points or non-trade barriers against India. Some European countries, especially France, are also important suppliers of defence equipment and technologies to India.

On the whole, however, India does not give the Europeans undue political importance because the Europeans do not, individually or collectively, significantly affect India's core political and security interests. For the Europeans, a large portion of whose energies are spent in any case on intra-EU integration problems and more recently on the war in Ukraine, India has traditionally not figured prominently on their radar screens since it has neither been a major economic partner nor a permanent member of the UN Security Council with which they have to cut deals. Of late, things have started to change as India's economic growth has accelerated and Europe's concerns about its over-reliance on China have grown.

On paper, while India has developed strategic partnerships with the EU as well as with many individual European countries, it is only with France that India has had a genuine strategic partnership going back more than a quarter century. France had the most understanding attitude following India's nuclear tests in 1998, as a consequence of which, it became the first country with which India established a strategic partnership. France and India share a common belief in strategic autonomy and a multipolar world. There is coincidence of views and interest on an Indo-Pacific strategy, in which France has an active interest and role because of its islands and territories in the Indian Ocean. The two countries have a trilateral dialogue with Australia and the United Arab Emirates. As France has been more willing than other countries to transfer technology to India, it is hardly surprising that France won the contract in 2016 for supply of thirty-six Rafale fighter aircraft in flyaway condition. Defence cooperation with France is very robust and wide-ranging. Space is another growing area of cooperation. France and India have helped each other in launching each other's rockets and are working together on satellite programmes for scientific studies.

Chapter 12

Strategic, Military and Economic Constraints

Strategic Culture

The primary task of India's foreign policy is to ensure the country's security and territorial integrity, and a peaceful external environment for it. This means protecting the country's borders and establishing cordial relations with foreign countries. India's strategic culture has been shaped by its history, philosophy and traditions. Historically, India has never been an aggressive power, simply because it did not need to be. Blessed with abundant water, sunshine and fertile land, protected by the seas to the south, virtually impassable mountain ranges to the north, thick forests to the east and deserts to the west, India was a self-contained, self-satisfied and rich civilization that had no urge to conquer foreign lands since it had nothing to gain by making forays beyond its natural frontiers. The only threats and invasions it periodically faced were from marauding tribes and empires from the north-west—the Greeks, the Huns, the Persians, the Turks, the Afghans and the Mongols. India's deep hinterland served as an enormous cushion absorbing the impact of foreign invasions. Just as the raging fury of a rushing torrent cascading down a mountain gradually peters out in the plains and the sands, so too the energy of invaders streaming into India via the Khyber Pass got gradually and inexorably exhausted by the time they reached the lower reaches of the Gangetic plains in Bihar and Bengal. The Rajputs, Marathas and Sikhs fought them bravely in north-west and north India, but whenever they could not repel the attackers, India's rulers as well as ordinary people typically worked out prudent compromises. Many converted to Islam and became collaborators or beneficiaries of the ruling elite. Over time, the invaders, along with their retinue of administrators, traders, men of letters, artisans and others, were assimilated into India's fold and became stakeholders in a prosperous and pluralistic India. In large parts of the Indian subcontinent, rulers did not have to worry about crafting a strategy to tackle foreign threats that could potentially upset the everyday social and economic life of their people. This led to the development of a defensive mindset on national security issues.

In ancient times, India had a well-developed understanding of statecraft and diplomacy. In his classical treatise *Arthashastra*, Kautilya, also known as Chanakya, (375–283 BCE) listed six measures of foreign policy *(sadgunya)*: policy of peace *(samdhi)*; policy of hostility *(vigraha)*; policy of keeping quiet *(asana)*; marching on an expedition *(yana)*; seeking another's protection *(samsraya)*; and a dual policy of seeking peace with one and waging war against another *(dvaidhibhava)*. Alongside the six policies, four techniques *(chatur upayay)* have also been mentioned by Kautilya: a) *Sama*, or the use of friendliness, persuasion, polite argument or reason; b) *Dana*, or the resort to gifts, concessions or compromises; c) *Bheda*, or the fomenting of discord, dissension and divisions through use of propaganda and other means; d) *Danda*, or the use of force when all else fails.[1] These lessons of statecraft did serve India well. For more than a millennium India's was a sophisticated, well-run polity and society. However, centuries of peace and prosperity made Indians complacent, selfish and arrogant. India stagnated and ossified. That is why it could be so easily conquered by invaders, first by land and then by sea in the second millennium. The scale and brutality of the invasions of the Turks, Mongols and Afghans crushed the spirit and destroyed the self-confidence of Indians.

Then came the European colonists. Its historical experience left India unprepared for the vastly different kind of challenges that the European powers posed in the eighteenth century. For the first time the external challenge was different in vital respects from the earlier security threats faced by India. First, it came not from the land but from the sea, which was unprecedented in India's experience. India's maritime contacts with people across the seas, whether it was the area of modern-day Oman and the Persian Gulf, or Yemen and the Red Sea, or the coast of east Africa, or the territories and islands of South-east Asia, had been largely peaceful, with a focus on trade and culture. Second, the threat came not from the north-west but from the east, making eastern India a frontline region for the first time in its history. Unlike the people of north-west and north India, who had developed over time the instincts and the ability to tackle the frequent security challenges emanating from the Hindu Kush region, the response of the inhabitants of eastern India was conditioned by their considerably different historical experience and temperament. They misread the Europeans and underestimated them. Thus began the colonization of India.

India's strategy to shake off the yoke of colonial rule was largely shaped by Mahatma Gandhi's philosophy of non-violence, moral behaviour and satyagraha, which drew upon India's moral, ethical and philosophical traditions such as the Vedas, the Ramayana, the Mahabharata and the teachings of the Buddha. Gandhiji's own experiences in South Africa contributed to his understanding that India's freedom was linked to that of other Asian and African colonies. For decades, the widely accepted narrative of India's freedom movement was as a Gandhi-led peaceful and non-violent struggle. No doubt it was Gandhiji who made the freedom struggle a mass movement. At the same time, the reality, now increasingly recognized, is that revolutionaries like Bhagat Singh, Veer Savarkar, Sri Aurobindo and Subhas Chandra Bose, whose approach was militant, also made significant contributions to the success of the freedom movement. The setting up of Azad Hind Fauj (Indian National Army) and the naval mutiny of 1946 were important triggers that forced the British to hastily quit India.

Gandhiji influenced Jawaharlal Nehru's world view. The basic flaw in Nehru's strategic thinking was to regard India as merely the successor state to British India, not as a great civilizational state whose security and interests had historically extended far beyond its artificial post-Partition borders. Thus, he had a narrow and minimalist view of

India's security interests. Had he carefully analysed Britain's strategic perspective on ensuring the security of its Indian empire, he would have realized that India could not afford to vacate the trans-Himalayan strategic space that would inevitably be occupied by rival powers. He ignored Sardar Patel's advice on the long-term implications of the rise of communist China and its takeover of Tibet,[2] gave up India's possessions in East Turkestan and Tibet,[3] turned down suggestions by members of Parliament that India should lay claim to Kailash and Mansarovar (1962),[4] didn't seize the opportunity to take over Nepal when King Tribhuvan sought refuge in India (1950),[5] and turned a deaf ear to Khan Abdul Ghaffar Khan's pleas for the North-West Frontier Province (NWFP) to be part of a unified India (1947).[6] He also refused to consider the plea of the Khan of Kalat (now part of Baluchistan) for his kingdom to be recognized as an independent state (1948),[7] didn't take up Oman's offer of Gwadar Port (1958)[8] and dithered on taking over the French and Portuguese possessions in the subcontinent for more than a decade. On more than one occasion, Nehru was ready to agree to a partition of Jammu and Kashmir.

India's defensive and narrow mindset resulted in missed opportunities offered separately in the 1950s by the United States and the Soviet Union for India to become a permanent member of the UN Security Council. These have cost India dearly. Defence was neglected, resulting in India's inability to resist the Chinese invasion of Tibet in the 1950s, and later the Chinese aggression against India in 1962. The defining characteristics of India's foreign policy in the first few decades after Independence were non-alignment, anti-colonialism, anti-racialism, non-violence, disarmament and peacemaking. India indulged in moralistic posturing and had an air of self-importance and self-righteousness as it strutted on the world stage making lofty statements that did not match its real strength. Multilateral diplomacy acquired an aura beyond its real importance. Indian diplomats became greater experts in trying to work out compromise positions than in playing hardball to preserve and promote India's national interests. More attention was given to elegant formulations on paper than to the substantive outcome of negotiations.

This deeply ingrained attitude lingered on in the post-Nehru era too. The 1972 Shimla Agreement with a defeated Pakistan, and the puzzling willingness of various governments to conclude an agreement with Pakistan that would entail India withdrawing from the Siachen Glacier (located in Ladakh, which is a part of India) underscore this trend. Fortunately, some good strategic decisions were also taken, such as the takeover of Sikkim and the full integration of Arunachal Pradesh into India. These have served India well. While under Prime Minister Modi India's policies have become much more hard-headed, more clarity in strategic thinking is needed. For example, even after the revocation of Article 370, India's leaders and spokesmen continued to talk only about ensuring that Pakistan vacates the territory occupied by it in Kashmir. It was only in 2024 that the official spokesman reiterated India's rejection of China's illegal occupation of territory in Pakistan-occupied Kashmir (Shaksgam Valley) under the so-called China–Pakistan Boundary Agreement of 1963.

One can argue that the internationalist perspective in India's foreign policy did serve India's broader national interests. Would India have survived as a united, sovereign and independent state if it alone had been decolonized? Undoubtedly, the spread of the movement against colonialism and racism, leading to the emergence of large numbers of independent countries, buttressed India's own independence. The pride and self-respect that Gandhi engendered among the people of India gave India the moral courage to stand up and follow an independent foreign policy rather than submit to pressures to join one of the Cold War blocs. The conviction that an independent foreign policy is the right policy for India to follow is deep-rooted and widespread.

Ironically, it is India's experience under colonial rule that created the idea of India as a modern nation. Macaulay's educational reforms were intended to create an Indian elite who, cut off from the deep roots of their own rich heritage of culture and achievements, would become loyal subjects of the British empire. While Macaulay's strategy did succeed, an unintended outcome of educating Indians was the rise of Indian nationalism. The Indian elite educated in the Western mould drew inspiration from the great ideas of nationalism, communism and socialism that were sweeping across Europe in the second half of the nineteenth and first half of the twentieth century. Both Gandhi and Nehru were part of this elite. It is very likely that if the thinking represented by the revolutionaries mentioned above or even of the realists within the Congress like Sardar Patel could have influenced to a greater degree India's Gandhi-inspired and Nehru-directed foreign policy, it would have been imbued with a greater dose of realpolitik.

One of Nehru's enduring legacies is the personalized conduct of foreign policy. An obvious handicap was that no one among the political leaders or in the bureaucracy had experience in handling foreign affairs. Among the leaders, Nehru was the only one with an interest in and understanding of foreign affairs. His personal rapport with many of the world's leaders was undoubtedly genuine and sometimes effective, but he was so self-assured about his judgement on various issues that he was prone to summarily brush aside or ignore dissenting views by his officers on foreign policy issues. Indira Gandhi continued the personalized approach of her father and made the dubious contribution of undermining the weak foreign policy institutions she had inherited. It was during her time that the office of the prime minister became a source of enormous power. Personalized decision-making cost India dearly in the 1972 Shimla Agreement, where Indira Gandhi, relying on her personal instincts rather than professional advice, reached an unsatisfactory deal with Pakistani prime minister Zulfikar Ali Bhutto. Rajiv Gandhi too had an imperious style. In foreign affairs, he relied less on the established institutional structures and chain of command and more on trusted officials in his own office and in the wider bureaucracy. During his tenure, the prime minister's office became unprecedentedly powerful, with mid-level officials exercising power far exceeding their formal positions in the bureaucratic hierarchy. Sonia Gandhi, who effectively ran Manmohan Singh's UPA government, continued the Nehru-Gandhi legacy of personalized foreign policy formulation and execution. 'Loyalty' to the Nehru-Gandhi family was the watchword. An unelected National Advisory Council emerged as an alternative power centre, and no important decisions were taken by the government without her approval. The UPA government was also prone to cronyism. To this day, Indian leaders delude themselves that foreign policy successes, both real and imagined, are due only to the 'personal rapport' they enjoy with foreign leaders. Good personal relations do facilitate inter-state relations, but the ultimate driver is national interest. Like his predecessors, Prime Minister Modi too has put his definitive stamp on India's foreign policy and indubitably drives foreign policy decisions. But even though foreign policy has become much more focused and result-oriented, it still remains heavily reliant on inputs and advice from a handful of key individuals who enjoy the prime minister's trust and confidence.

In every country, the chief executive of the government, the prime minister in India's case, necessarily has to get intimately involved in foreign policy matters. As India's standing in the world has improved, so have the visibility and the international commitments of its prime minister. This makes the relationship between the prime minister and the minister of external affairs a delicate one, particularly if the external affairs minister is a political heavyweight. However, it is in the very nature of things that the prime minister, particularly one experienced and interested in foreign affairs, ultimately determines the extent of leeway and freedom of action given to the minister of external affairs. At the same time, no prime minister can ignore the voices of other important stakeholders. In practice, many foreign policy choices and outcomes are influenced by the predilections of state governments, particularly in respect of neighbouring foreign countries with which they share borders. As an example, it was only through the intercession of the then chief minister of West Bengal that India and Bangladesh could sign the treaty on sharing of the Ganges waters in 1996, and today it is the chief minister of that state who has successfully prevented the signing of an agreement with Bangladesh on the Teesta waters. For a long time, India's Sri Lanka policy was influenced by pressure from Tamil Nadu politicians on whose support the Central government was heavily dependent. India's attitude towards Myanmar is dictated in large part by considerations of the development and security of Mizoram, Manipur and Nagaland; Sikkim and Arunachal Pradesh have a huge stake in India's relations with China; India's policy towards Pakistan is influenced by what Jammu & Kashmir and Punjab think; Kerala keenly follows developments in the Persian Gulf region. In recognition of this reality, over the last few years the Ministry of External Affairs has opened offices in a number of state capitals and started outreach programmes there.

It has been rightly said that nations have no permanent friends or enemies, only permanent interests. Thus, India's relationships and priorities have changed over time. For example, during the Cold War, India's interests were best served through a close relationship with the Soviet Union, which gave India much-needed political and diplomatic support on key issues in the UN, as well as valuable economic and defence assistance. Today the relationship remains warm, though not as effusive as it used to be. By contrast, India's relations with the United States were quite strained throughout the twentieth century. Today, however, India and the United States have a much greater congruence of interests. Similarly, India-Japan relations, which were low-key and insubstantial for many decades, are now very vibrant and dynamic. On the other hand, the euphoria of the 1950s has given way to deep suspicion and mistrust in India-China relations. Similarly, the Commonwealth, NAM and the G-77 were important for India in the early decades after Independence but are largely irrelevant today, whereas the Persian Gulf region, the Indian Ocean rim, South-east and East Asia, which earlier occupied a relatively minor place in India's foreign policy, are now extremely high-priority regions.

Is foreign policy all about realpolitik, or do morality, truth and justice have contemporary relevance in a world that is seeing escalating levels of violence, oppression and inequality? The realist or pragmatic school of foreign policy scoffs at any suggestion that morality has a role in world affairs. It believes that power flows out of the barrel of a gun. It is true that power matters. Powerful nations get their way with impunity. Double standards are all too common in international relations. Nevertheless, morality cannot be wished away. It remains the core principle of all religions and continues to guide individual human behaviour. In politics and international affairs, it is a widely employed strategic psychological tool. Practitioners of realpolitik in all countries, including India, invariably rely on moral arguments—be it to persuade, convince or justify. The veneer of morality is what gives legitimacy to arbitrariness. At the same time, a moral approach can sometimes make a difference. Morality engenders boldness. Leadership implies not just economic and military strength but also ideas that inspire and motivate. Should India be a conscience-keeper of the world? Though there does remain a strong moral and idealistic strain in India's thinking, India's foreign policy is no longer hobbled by ideology or sentimentalism since India's rulers realize that their primary duty and responsibility is to protect India's national interests.

Military Power and Diplomacy

Military power is a sovereign state's principal instrument to protect and defend its national interests, especially to ensure its security vis-à-vis foreign powers. Unless a country has a credible military deterrent, of which a hostile country is aware, the latter could be tempted into launching an attack. Military power is also a critical, in some cases the most important, element of a state's offensive arsenal to influence the behaviour of other states and to promote its own interests on the international stage. It was the British navy's 'gunboat diplomacy' that successfully advanced Britain's national interests overseas and created the British empire. Today, it is the ability of the United States to project military power all over the globe, in the sea and in the air, which gives credibility to its claim to be a superpower with global interests that it can and will protect. Russia is taken seriously by the United States in its strategic calculus because of its military capabilities that have the potential to annihilate the United States. Military power is certainly an essential element of being a great power. For all their economic weight, Japan and Europe do not figure as prominently in the strategic calculations of other powers as they would have had they shown an ability and willingness to project military power. By contrast, China does have military and strategic clout.

Inescapable though military power may be for success on the world stage, it is an insufficient and imperfect instrument of state policy. It is only one of the determining factors in seeking favourable outcomes. In inter-state relations, politics drives decisions; war is merely an instrument of state policy, and usually the instrument of last resort. It has been said, with a degree of truth, that war is too serious a business to be left to the generals! Diplomacy, or the management of international relations by negotiation, is the preferred means of keeping relations between states smooth and friction-free. War breaks out when diplomacy fails or deterrence weakens. In any case, war cannot be waged indefinitely. War has to ultimately lead to a political settlement, which has to be negotiated diplomatically. Very often, during the course of a war, diplomatic negotiations are simultaneously under way, whether to settle the conflict or to weaken the enemy. Incidentally, the concept of diplomatic immunity evolved in the context of war. Warring sides looking for a peace settlement had to exchange emissaries, whose person and belongings had to be inviolate in order to enable them to carry confidential messages from one side to the other.

For military power to be effective and for diplomacy to be successful, there has to be synergy between these two instruments of state power. Exercise of military power has to be part of a larger military-diplomatic strategy. A couple of examples from India's recent experiences would illustrate this point. In 1971, it was diplomacy—through the instrument of the Indo-Soviet Treaty of August 1971—that created favourable political conditions for the successful Bangladesh operations of December 1971. Unfortunately, because of poor political judgement and negotiations, the diplomatic options that the military victory opened up could not be converted into a favourable peace settlement at Shimla in July 1972. In Sri Lanka, on the other hand, the Indian military establishment's overconfidence about its capabilities and the induction of the IPKF in 1987 in Sri Lanka turned out to be a political and diplomatic disaster.

Military thinking has also influenced diplomatic technique. For the school that thinks diplomacy is simply war by other means, the goal is a triumphant victory. In pursuit of this goal, the enemy is outflanked and weakened by attacks from behind the lines; wedges are drawn between the principal opponent and his allies; there is the resort to tactics like feint and surprise attack, sometimes even strategic retreat; and intimidation and propaganda are used to weaken the opponent's resolve and confuse him. On the other hand, another school of thought considers that fairness and honesty are more effective than deceit and trickery in achieving the desired results. The example of the Treaty of Versailles, which imposed a crushing peace on a defeated Germany after World War I, thereby sowing the seeds for German rearmament and World War II, is often cited as making the case for the second approach. Such thinking appears to have guided India when it gave generous terms to a defeated Pakistan at Shimla in 1972—without, however, achieving the desired results.

There is today a much better appreciation among India's political leaders and strategic community of how military power is an essential component of the overall strategy in advancing India's national interests and the need for self-reliance in this respect as far as possible. Other countries' perceptions about India's military capabilities too have changed. Pakistan no longer makes exaggerated claims about how each of its soldiers is equal to ten Indian soldiers. The Balakot strikes against Pakistan terrorist camps showed how India is now willing and able to take the war into enemy territory. China's hitherto contemptuous view of India's military capabilities changed somewhat after India became a declared nuclear weapons power. The losses China suffered during the 2020 Galwan clashes may also have given it a reality check about India's military preparedness and willingness to respond to its aggression. The United States started taking India seriously only after India became a nuclear weapons power. In inter-state relations, perceptions matter as much as reality. Invariably, states deal with one another with one eye on the military power of the other. Today, apart from nuclear weapons, the demonstration effect of India's missiles, its high-resolution satellites, its aircraft carriers, its submarine fleet, large numbers of combat aircraft and hundreds of thousands of well-trained and motivated men in uniform is clear for any adversary to see. The Indian armed forces' combat skills, both against foreign adversaries and in the conduct of counter-insurgency operations at home and their capabilities in areas like anti-piracy operations, high-altitude and jungle warfare, training, joint exercises, peacekeeping operations, airlift operations and disaster relief—all project India's military power, engender respect for it and thereby create more space for diplomacy.

Development of credible military capabilities requires both economic strength and a self-reliant defence industry. Currently, India's own resources are inadequate and have to be supplemented by foreign investments and technology. Excessive reliance on foreign countries for military equipment and supplies is India's big vulnerability. It makes India dependent on the goodwill of foreign countries, which could be a critical weakness in times of war. Admittedly, much work remains to be done in both areas and it will take time to build India's infrastructure, create indigenous defence capabilities and a healthier, better skilled work force. The encouraging aspect is that at least the process has started in earnest with the 'Make in India' programme and the call for 'Atmanirbharta' or self-reliance. The private sector is being increasingly involved in defence production. Implementation of stated policies is the key to success. One cannot underestimate the constraints on resources for defence and security, since the competing demands of development are enormous. In the early years after Independence, Nehru focused more on economic growth than defence. The result of this neglect was the humiliating outcome of the 1962 border war with China. The choices are difficult. In the traditional argument of guns versus butter, a judicious balance will have to be found, based on India's political-military objectives and threat perceptions. Much will depend on whether India is looking to expand its military footprint globally, or to keep its goals purely defensive.

Successful diplomacy involves using all aspects of national power, in particular military power, as instruments of diplomacy. Which elements of military power are more important depends on the circumstances. Nuclear weapons, missiles, satellites, drones and cyber capabilities have added new dimensions to warfare. Nowadays war is also a battle of narratives. India has to give greater attention to developing capabilities in these new areas of technology, as well as to special operations for ensuring its security. Newer technologies do reduce the salience of older technologies, but rarely do the latter become redundant. The ongoing war in Ukraine is a good case study, illustrating the continuing relevance and importance of traditional warfare involving artillery and infantry, self-reliance in weaponry, critical technologies and maintenance of weapons. India now also has a more focused plan for utilization of civilian infrastructure for defence (for example, the use of highways as airstrips). Given that the principal security threats to India so far have been at its land borders, it is understandable that in military matters India's overwhelming emphasis has been on its army and air force. Air power plays an important demonstrative role in psychologically intimidating the adversary, but it has its limits since only boots on the ground can capture and hold on to land. For extending influence abroad, a strong navy is critical, which is why of late the navy has begun to receive greater attention and resources in India.

Defence cooperation with foreign countries illustrates well the close inter-relationship between foreign and defence policy. Foreign defence cooperation is the most sensitive aspect of any bilateral relationship. By its very nature, it presupposes a certain level of trust, confidence and understanding between the cooperating partners, as well as a broad coincidence of strategic objectives. It therefore flows from and reflects a good political relationship, not the other way round. Defence cooperation—whether in training, buying or selling of defence equipment, conduct of joint exercises or joint operations—cannot, or at least should not, be independent of the overall thrust of a country's foreign policy. Thus, India has a long-standing and robust defence relationship with Russia, but not with Pakistan or China. In between these two ends of the spectrum there are many shades of grey. After decades of mutual suspicion and wariness, India and the United States are now engaged in a rapidly intensifying military relationship, underpinned by regular joint interaction between the foreign and defence ministers of the two countries ('2+2 Dialogue'). As a major buyer of defence equipment, India factors in political considerations, apart from pricing and other terms, in decisions on high-value defence purchases. India also seeks to effectively leverage its defence imports not only for direct defence offsets but also for getting political and economic benefits.

Although it is foreign policy that will essentially drive a defence relationship, defence diplomacy can and does invariably cement bilateral ties, simply because it creates linkages in the crucial field of security. One example is the vital role that substantial defence cooperation plays in holding together the overall India-Russia relationship. Another example is Israel, where growing Indian dependence on Israel for defence equipment exerts some pressure, albeit unacknowledged, on India to moderate its position on political issues like Palestine which matter to Israel. India's defence and foreign policies are closely inter-related. 'Defence' and 'diplomacy' are really two sides of the same coin. The goal in either case is the same—namely, defence of India's unity, territorial integrity and sovereignty from outside threats; only the means are different. In order to conduct successful diplomacy, India's foreign policymakers must clearly understand India's own military capabilities as well as those of India's adversaries. They must also understand the military way of thinking, for not only is the military the instrument of last resort for every state but it also wields political power in many countries, directly or indirectly. India's interests can be best served by much closer coordination and consultation between its defence and foreign policy establishments. Only then will India be able to optimally mesh its diplomacy with its military strength.

Economic Diplomacy

Economic issues have occupied a central place in the foreign policy of all countries, particularly during prolonged periods of peace. Historically, trade has generally been the wedge that has opened the door for empires, which were established with the primary purpose of protecting and furthering the imperial country's trade and economic interests. Even today, for most countries, foreign policy is guided by economic considerations: the search for markets for their goods, services and labour; for sources of raw materials and the latest technologies; and for making or receiving investments. India, obviously, needs to give high priority to its economic relationship with all countries. This is not to suggest that India should be complacent and naïve in pursuing only economic objectives while ignoring other traditional foreign policy concerns like security. Yet, even in strategic relationships, trade and economic interaction provides a solid foundation for relations, creates interdependencies that foster mutual trust and confidence, and gives people concrete stakes in the relationship. India's economic diplomacy will be most successful if official India encourages and promotes partnerships between the state- and privately-owned industry and businesses in order to ensure an all-round coordinated and optimal national effort involving close and purposeful cooperation with all stakeholders.

That is why there is greater emphasis today on the economic component of India's foreign policy. Global interdependence and the digital revolution have made trade and other economic interactions, including movement of capital and labour across countries, more important for India's development. Economic liberalization has raised the stakes and influence of businessmen, industrialists and entrepreneurs in foreign affairs. Foreign policy has to promote trade, create jobs, bring in civilian and defence technologies, and promote inward as well as outward investments. It also has to ensure India's energy security, since India depends hugely on imported oil, gas and coal, as well as many other raw materials and natural resources. Today, millions of Indians travel abroad for business, education or tourism. Large numbers of Indian citizens and people of Indian origin live and work abroad. Looking after the welfare of all these groups of Indians is a very important task of Indian foreign policy.

Before 1991, India's interaction with the outside world was marked by a defensive and protectionist mindset, which arose out of domestic economic policies that restricted imports and foreign investment, a very modest level of foreign trade (of which a fairly large share was rupee trade with the Soviet Union and countries of East Europe), and an undiversified export basket consisting mostly of raw materials and semi-finished products. The focus of India's economic diplomacy was on export promotion, on canalized imports of critical commodities and products through public-sector organizations, and on getting more bilateral and multilateral development assistance. At the multilateral level, it was focused on South-South cooperation through organizations like the G-77. India had a very marginal role in multilateral trade negotiations within the GATT framework.

With the onset of economic reforms in 1991, India's challenge was to convince other countries that its economic policies were changing. The priority task of economic diplomacy in the 1990s was to attract foreign direct investment, made much more difficult because of the opposition of powerful domestic lobbies. Considering themselves comparatively disadvantaged because special facilities were being given to foreign investors, many Indian industrialists (the so-called 'Bombay Club') wanted a level playing field, without which they feared they would be wiped out. This was a period of transition as India adjusted to the changed post-Soviet world. In India's quest for new investments, markets and technologies, the West became much more critical for it while the importance of the former Soviet bloc countries and the relevance of organizations like the Non-Aligned Movement (NAM), G-77 and the Commonwealth sharply declined. Over the subsequent three decades, India has forged a wide network of bilateral and regional partnerships.

It is only in the twenty-first century, as its economy matured, its business community gained self-confidence and India began to integrate with the global economy that the country began to see more opportunities than challenges in the ineluctable process of globalization. Within India, the dismantling of the 'licence raj' and the process of economic reforms gathered momentum, resulting in fundamental and irreversible changes in the economy, in government policies, and in the outlook of business and industry. A growing number of Indian companies became globally competitive and outward looking, and the new generation of Indians more ambitious and self-confident. Buoyed by comfortable foreign exchange reserves, both the public and private sectors of corporate India started making tentative forays into investing abroad. Gradually increasing inward flows of foreign direct investment and foreign institutional investment enabled India to cut back on its reliance on foreign aid for budgetary support and economic growth. The revolution in information technology opened up new opportunities for India's exports of services. From a primarily agro-based economy, India emerged as an increasingly service-oriented one. As India opened up, the rising numbers and purchasing power of the Indian middle class transformed India into a large and attractive market for foreign companies. The changed scenario required India's economic diplomacy to shift gears dramatically.

In addition to export promotion, India's new economic diplomacy priorities became more diversified. Now the stress was on different goals: attracting more foreign direct investment (preferably for greenfield infrastructure projects), as well as foreign institutional investment in India's stock markets; facilitating Indian investments and joint ventures abroad for profit as well as to gain access to much needed resources, raw materials and technologies; protecting and promoting India's economic and commercial interests in multilateral and regional trading arrangements; influencing other countries' economic and commercial policies to create a more favourable environment for Indian business; and using India's overseas development assistance programme more effectively to serve its larger foreign policy goals. Energy security, intellectual property rights, environmental issues and climate change became important new areas of economic diplomacy. The increasing role of the private sector in India's economic development and foreign trade required government and private industry to work in tandem in pursuing India's economic interests vis-à-vis the rest of the world. Decentralization of economic power required that the states also be taken on board in crafting an overall strategy of economic diplomacy.

The success or otherwise of economic diplomacy depends not merely on objective realities; perceptions are equally important. India has to leverage its 'soft power' effectively. The earlier stereotyped images of India—heat, dust, crowds, poverty, snake charmers, elephants, culture and spirituality—do linger, but they have been overtaken by the changed realities of twenty-first century India. There is a new image of India that has taken shape since 1998—as a nuclear weapons power, and as a politically stable, determined, technologically advanced and economically vibrant country. India's achievements in an increasingly digital world have caught the attention of the world. Where once the world saw India's teeming millions as a liability, today India's large pool of trained workforce and knowledge workers and its youthful demographic profile make India an attractive long-term partner. India's democratic systems and institutions, its legal system and the widespread use of English in business are seen as providing a stable, predictable and comforting framework for the rest of the world to engage with. India's entertainment industry testifies to the imaginativeness, dynamism and innovativeness of its people. Indians prospering abroad have helped to create a new image of Indian intellectual and managerial capabilities. Working together, the Indian government and private industry have also given high priority to burnishing India's image abroad.

WTO and Regional Trading Arrangements

Against the background of the Great Depression of the 1930s and the resultant trade wars, the West, after the end of World War II, established the General Agreement on Tariffs and Trade (GATT) as a treaty to promote trade and economic development by reducing tariffs and other restrictions. Under GATT rules, global trade was conducted on the Most Favoured Nation (MFN) basis, the essence of which is that all countries grant the same trade advantages, including tariffs, to all other countries. The agenda was clearly set by the West. The biggest beneficiaries were countries whose economies were tied to the West. Communist countries with non-market economies like the Soviet Union and China were excluded. The rest of the world was mostly either under colonial rule or had just become independent. Items of interest to the developing countries, like textiles and agricultural products, were excluded from the ambit of GATT. Gradually, as the developing countries' economies grew stronger, they sought greater market access from the West for their competitive, labour-intensive products. In the Tokyo Round of trade negotiations (1973–79) they managed to get two principal concessions in this regard—the non-reciprocity clause, which exempted developing countries from giving reciprocal tariff concessions to the developed countries, and the Generalised Scheme of Preferences (GSP), which permitted developing countries to export their products to the developed countries at less-than-MFN rates. In a quid pro quo, developing countries had to concede on some crucial matters, which reduced market access for their competitive products in the developed world. The 1974 Multi-Fibre Arrangement (MFA), also called the Agreement on Textiles and Clothing, established quotas for the quantities developing countries could export to the developed countries. Non-tariff barriers became the new instrumentality of the developed countries to protect their highly subsidized domestic agricultural sector from the competitive agricultural exports of developing countries.

India is a founder member of GATT, but till the Tokyo Round (1973–79) it played a passive role in its deliberations. India's limited agenda was to look for exemptions from the MFN principle through non-reciprocal concessions and market access for its products. As India, like other developing countries, had no experience in multilateral trade negotiations and little bargaining power, it had no realistic option but to accept the rules set by the more influential members of GATT. In the Uruguay Round of multilateral trade negotiations (1986–94), India participated more actively than before, but its approach remained defensive. India was still comparatively inexperienced and lacked clout, but there was a much better understanding both within the government as well as among the general public of the long-term stakes for India in the outcome of the negotiations. After seven and a half years of negotiations, at times marked by high drama and brinksmanship, the Final Act of the Uruguay Round trade negotiations was signed by 123 countries at Marrakech, Morocco, in April 1994. It was the most far-reaching and wide-ranging reform of the global trading system since the setting up of GATT in 1948. The traditional definition of international trade underwent a drastic change—international trade rules now covered not only trade in goods outside a country's national borders, but new areas that impinged on domestic policy choices. The backdrop to this aggressive attitude of the West was the hubris that had overcome it after the collapse of the Soviet Union.

The outcome of the Uruguay Round was not the best deal from India's perspective of the mid-1990s, since India was obliged to take on commitments in new areas such as services, agriculture, intellectual property and investment, for which it was not yet ready. However, India had no choice in the matter since the main players insisted that all the agreements were part of a whole and indivisible package (the so-called 'Single Undertaking'). Thus, India had to undertake commitments on opening up its economy to foreign investment, on intellectual property, on agriculture and services. There were some gains for India—greater market access, the commitment to end the MFA (thereby ending quotas) by 2005 and a new, more effective mechanism for settling disputes (through the Dispute Settlement Understanding, or DSU). The legal commitments of the Final Act provide the framework and the rationale for the considerable economic legislation, policies, rules and regulations introduced by India since the mid-1990s. The Uruguay Round also decided that GATT should be succeeded by the World Trade Organization on 1 January 1995. While GATT was a treaty that laid down a set of rules agreed to by its members, the WTO is an organization that is responsible for negotiating and implementing new trade agreements, and is in charge of policing member countries' adherence to all WTO agreements.

With every passing year since the setting up of the WTO, the battles within the organization have become progressively sharper over the divergent priorities of the developed and developing countries. While the developing countries want the focus to be on the unfinished business of the Uruguay Round and on getting the developed countries to meet the commitments they have already undertaken, the West pushes for inclusion of new areas like labour and environment in the trade agenda. However, it is no longer able to determine the agenda and outcome of trade negotiations as easily as before. Under the shadow of 9/11, the West did get its way and a new round of trade negotiations (Doha Development Agenda) was launched in Doha in 2001. This time, however, the developing countries managed to include many issues of interest to them in the Work Programme of the Doha Round. They also gained a psychological victory through the very nomenclature of the new round of trade negotiations, which emphasized an agreed focus on developmental issues. Thereafter, there has been a growing assertiveness on the part of the developing countries in pursuing their interests. There is much greater determination on their part not to let themselves be pushed around by the West and to put up a stiff resistance to systematic efforts by the developed countries to get control of their economies through the WTO system. Contrary to general expectations, the unity of the developing country coalitions has survived the pressure and blandishments of the West.

India has an important defensive interest in agriculture in the WTO negotiations. Even though it is a marginal player in the global trade in agricultural products, about 45 per cent of India's workforce is engaged in agriculture, many of them subsistence farmers without any safety nets.[9] India considers trade in agriculture not an issue of economics but of livelihood for hundreds of millions of its people, and is understandably resisting demands from developed countries to limit its use of the tools currently available to it to prevent a potential flood of subsidized agricultural commodities from the rich countries swamping India's markets. India's position on agriculture and fisheries in the WTO negotiations is guided by the three principles of ensuring food security, ensuring livelihood security and taking care of rural development needs. Although there have been many voices urging India to take a less defensive and more flexible position on agriculture, keeping in mind that over the long term India could emerge as an important exporter of agricultural products, this is not the kind of political risk that any government in India is likely to take. As a country more than half of whose GDP derives from services, India has become a 'demandeur', seeking more openings for its exports in the services sector, particularly in the so-called 'Mode 1' (cross-border supply) and 'Mode 4' (movement of natural persons) areas. From being a bit player in GATT/WTO, India has gradually emerged as one of the key players in WTO negotiations.

While by no means perfect, the WTO remains the most desirable structure for international trade. It already has 166 members and, notwithstanding the enormous economic and political hurdles that aspiring members have to overcome, more countries are striving to join it. All countries understand that a rules-based and transparent multilateral system is in their overall interest. The inefficient and cumbersome alternative, as countries outside the WTO painfully realize, is to negotiate separately with individual countries or groups of countries. In practice, the multilateral trading system has led to an enormous expansion of international trade over the last several decades. But there is disappointment that there have been no real breakthroughs in trade negotiations in recent decades. This is principally because the West is no longer interested in a more open trading regime as that goes against its interests. China has gamed the WTO rules so well that it has become the manufacturing hub of the world, thereby creating painful and disturbing dependencies which are difficult for the rest of the world to overcome. Another problem is that the United States, by blocking the appointment of new members to the WTO's Appellate Tribunal, has rendered dysfunctional the dispute settlement mechanism, a key element in the WTO's functioning. The 13th WTO Ministerial Conference held in Abu Dhabi in February–March 2024 (MC 13) was a disappointment, as it did not result in any breakthrough on outstanding issues. India held firm on not compromising on issues where its vital interests are at stake. On the whole, the long-term outlook for the WTO appears bleak.

While the WTO may be the optimal framework, as multilateral trade negotiations have faltered in recent years, pressure has been building up to permit plurilateral agreements (wherein WTO member countries would be given the choice to agree to new rules on a voluntary basis) within its framework. The move by some countries to go in for plurilateral agreements does not find favour with India for various reasons, including that it violates the WTO principle of 'Single Undertaking', which entailed significant compromises by India in the past.

The other alternative to the WTO multilateral framework consists of the Regional Trading Arrangements (RTAs) such as Free Trade Agreements (FTAs) or Preferential Trade Agreements (PTAs). WTO rules do permit RTAs under certain strict conditions to ensure that they complement rather than compete with the WTO multilateral regime. These have become more attractive and widespread, and well over half the world's trade is at present conducted through RTAs. RTAs are admittedly inefficient and messy. They often overlap; involve complicated rules of origin and value-addition norms to ensure that third parties do not take advantage of an FTA between two countries/regions; include negative lists for sensitive products; create difficulties in administering multiple tariff lines; and are widely regarded as a trade-diverting rather than trade-creating mechanism. Yet RTAs remain popular. In practice, RTAs have allowed groups of countries to negotiate rules and commitments that go beyond what was possible multilaterally. RTAs were considered a hedging strategy to guard against a crisis in the multilateral trading regime which is now upon the world.

Even though India's opening up has resulted in a sharp rise in the proportion of the country's overall trade in goods and services to its total GDP, India (which has about 2 per cent share of the global trade in goods and about 4 per cent in services)[10] is still not a major trading nation. Can India afford to be the only large and fast-growing economy that is not part of a major trade bloc? India has to anticipate future situations. Till recently, the thinking was that a passive approach by India carried the risk of it getting left behind or marginalized as other major economies integrate or, worse still, of its exclusion for economic as well as non-economic reasons. This was the economic rationale and main consideration for India's activism in the first decade or so of the twenty-first century in negotiating RTAs with a wide range of countries in Asia. When India signed FTAs/CECAs with ASEAN and East Asian countries of the region in the decade of the 2000s, there were both political and economic considerations. Politically, India wanted to consolidate its relations with these countries. In this India was successful. On the economic side, India hoped that opening up its market would spur its domestic industry to become more efficient and competitive, draw in foreign investment and give a fillip to exports of goods and services.

Sadly, these expectations have not been met. India's trade deficit with the Regional Comprehensive Economic Partnership (RCEP) countries (the ten ASEAN countries plus China, Japan, South Korea, Australia, New Zealand) has grown exponentially.[11] China, both directly as well as via ASEAN (by misusing rules-of-origin provisions), has deeply penetrated the Indian market, hollowing out many domestic industries. After careful consideration, India took the decision to stay out of the RCEP, as it is increasingly worried about its growing trade deficit with China and unhappy with the working of the existing FTAs and CECAs with countries that are part of RCEP. As relations with China have sharply deteriorated, the Indian government has taken a policy decision to restrict trade and investment with it. If India were to join the China-dominated RCEP, it would open the doors for China to penetrate the Indian market even more deeply, which is politically and strategically unacceptable to India. It also goes against the government policy of Atmanirbharta and Make in India. India is rightly focusing on increasing its manufacturing capabilities and its exports. India also needs some time to fix many difficult and politically controversial domestic issues (such as reforms in areas like agriculture, land, labour, energy, logistics and infrastructure) before it can think of joining the RCEP. Thus, the considerations behind India's decision to stay out of it are even more relevant today. It is noteworthy that today the RCEP signatories appear to need India more than the other way round, as they have kept the door open for India to join the organization at a later date. India is also seeking to renegotiate its existing FTAs and CECAs with the ASEAN and East Asian countries to ensure that the benefits to both sides are more balanced. While political considerations no longer have the same salience in India's decision-making on FTAs and CECAs as they did a decade or two ago, it is also true that India's aspiration to become a 10-trillion-dollar economy within the next decade and its ambitious vision of becoming a developed country (Viksit Bharat 2047) by the centenary of its Independence require vastly greater economic integration with the rest of the world.

That is why India is not shutting the doors to all FTAs. It is working on developing a comprehensive strategy for future FTAs and is now looking at a different set of countries for possible FTAs. There is already a Comprehensive Economic Cooperation and Partnership

Agreement with Mauritius, a Free Trade Agreement with the United Arab Emirates, a Trade and Economic Partnership Agreement with the European Free Trade Association and an Economic Cooperation and Trade Agreement with Australia. FTA negotiations are under way with Oman, Israel, the Gulf Cooperation Council (GCC), the European Union, the United Kingdom and Canada (currently suspended). Recently, India has become part of the US-initiated Indo-Pacific Economic Framework (IPEF) that brings together the major economies of the Pacific Ocean area comprising the seven ASEAN countries (excluding Laos, Cambodia and Myanmar), Japan, South, Korea, Australia, New Zealand, Fiji, India and the United States. The IPEF will contribute to economic rule-making in the Indo-Pacific region and promote the shared goal of a free, open and inclusive Indo-Pacific region. Structured around four pillars—trade, supply chains, clean economy and fair economy—the IPEF gives flexibility to partner countries to join only some of these pillars based on their respective priorities. For the moment, India has not joined and is only an observer in the trade pillar, as it is not sure what benefits it would get to advance its priorities of getting greater market access and protection for its agricultural, digital and labour sectors.

Chapter 13

The Way Forward

India's foreign policy strategy will be shaped by its assessment of the likely evolution of the world order. Predictions are fraught with uncertainty. A single unexpected event or a development in a seemingly unimportant part of the world could trigger off a chain reaction that draws in outside powers and leads to unforeseen consequences. There are many ongoing conflicts and flashpoints around the world that could become game-changers. Will the ongoing war in Ukraine destabilize Europe? Will the Israel-Hamas war in Gaza spread and become a wider regional conflagration? Will North Korea ever stabilize? Will China invade Taiwan? What is the future of Pakistan and Afghanistan? What of natural disasters and pandemics? Events often follow a non-linear path. The past is rarely a reliable guide, while present realities and trends are, at best, a rough guide to the future. For centuries, Europe dominated the world and the rivalries among European powers, both in Europe and in their far-flung colonies, had a global impact. Yet today, despite its economic strength, Europe is not a major military power or a serious global geopolitical player.

India's Geography Matters

India is already the world's fifth largest economy and is projected to become the third largest within less than a decade. By the mid-twenty-first century, it is likely to be a global power, if circumstances are propitious and India plays its cards right. Will India live up to its promise and potential, in the face of formidable internal and external challenges? India, which has given the Indian Ocean its name, is at the crossroads of Asia, with links to all the sub-regions of Asia. Its geographical location puts it at the vortex of what I call five arcs that carry both potential and peril. The first is the 'arc of prosperity', extending from India through South-east Asia to East Asia. This encompasses about half the world's population and many of the world's largest and most dynamic economies, accounting for a significant proportion of global trade and foreign exchange reserves. To India's west is the growing weight of the second, the 'arc of energy', extending from the Persian Gulf through the Caspian Sea to Russia's Siberian, Arctic and Far East regions. As three-fourths of the world's oil and gas reserves are located here, this region will remain a key strategic arena where the interests of major global powers will intersect, and probably clash. The already complex traditional geopolitics of this region, marked by myriad inter-state disputes and instability, have been further complicated by energy geopolitics, great power rivalry and potential conflicts. The third arc in Asia, 'the arc of instability', is perhaps the most dangerous one since it envelops India from Myanmar in the east, passing through the tinderboxes of Pakistan, Afghanistan, Iran, Iraq, Syria and Palestine in the west all the way to the Mediterranean. The fourth is the 'arc of uncertainty' north of India, encompassing Nepal, Tibet, East Turkestan and the Central Asian countries. Finally, there is the 'arc of communications'—the Indian Ocean, earlier the principal conduit for the colonization of Asia and eastern Africa, which today controls the trade and energy flows from the Persian Gulf and SLOCs between Europe and Asia. With the interests of so many powers at stake, it is little wonder that the area of the northern Indian Ocean, the Arabian Sea and the Persian Gulf has become the most militarized region in the world, much like Europe was during the Cold War era. The United States remains firmly entrenched at multiple locations on land and sea in the Persian Gulf-Indian Ocean region. China is also steadily increasing its military and economic presence in the Indian Ocean region.

Against this backdrop, India needs to be imaginative and agile in order to ensure its military, economic, energy and environmental security. The world is looking expectantly at India. Fortunately, today India is seen as a benign rising power, though that may not be necessarily true in the future. Thus, India has a window of opportunity to secure its due place in the world. How should India go about ensuring its interests? First, India must have a clear strategic vision. One could say that India has three security rings. The innermost ring is from the Hindu Kush through the Himalayas to the Irrawaddy, the natural geographical boundaries of the Indian subcontinent. What happens here is of direct and vital interest to India. This is India's immediate neighbourhood. The second ring, which constitutes India's extended neighbourhood, encompasses the choke points of the Indian Ocean—the Straits of Aden and Hormuz in the west and the Malacca Straits in the east. The outermost ring covers the extremities of the Asian continent, extending from Suez to Eurasia and the western rim of the Pacific Ocean, where other regional and global powers too have vital strategic interests.

India's Immediate Neighbourhood

Currently, India's immediate neighbours are not critically important economic partners, and India's main concerns with them are related to security. In order to ensure that it doesn't remain bogged down in managing relations with its neighbours and can devote greater attention to strategic engagement with the rest of the world, India needs a stable and friendly neighbourhood. The challenges are formidable. India's neighbours, fearful of India's overwhelmingly larger size and power, and hence influence over individual countries as well as over the region as a whole, are both envious and suspicious of it and do not fully cooperate on its political and security concerns. It does not help that Indians in these countries are regarded, not without some justification, as boorish and arrogant. Thus, India's neighbours have traditionally sought some countervailing force to balance India's all-round domination of South Asia. This has taken the form of seeking and using available leverages against India on the part of some nations, and their use of obstructionist, often openly hostile policies deliberately designed to hurt India economically and to deny India benefits, even if this means cutting off their own noses to spite their faces. India will need to deploy considerable attention, imagination and resources to develop relationships of mutual trust and economic interdependence with its neighbours.

Fortunately, the situation is now changing, at least on the economic front. Bangladesh, for example, is more open to giving India transit access to the North-east region. Nepal is less reluctant to cooperate with India for more effective harnessing of its hydropower potential. Sri Lanka and the Maldives seem to have shed their earlier inhibitions about Indian investment in their countries. Politically, however, India's neighbours continue to allow outside powers to exercise a degree of influence on their policies, and this makes India uneasy. India has to guard against the inevitable machinations of outside powers to exploit existing tensions and to create differences between India and its neighbours. India cannot allow outside powers to have too great a role and influence in India's immediate neighbourhood, since their principal objectives and interests, which are not necessarily benign, relate to India. India's neighbours have shied away from building very close relationships with India since that could blur their essential identity of projecting themselves as *not* Indian. But here is the conundrum: while they see India as a threat to their identity, all of India's neighbours except Pakistan also know, even if they do not openly acknowledge it, that India is the ultimate guarantor of their survival and well-being. Bangladeshis openly talk of how environmental refugees will come to India were Bangladesh to be affected by rising sea levels as a result of climate change. The same holds true of the Maldives. India is invariably the first, and often the only, responder to help when natural calamities strike its neighbouring countries.

India has to handle relations with its neighbours with great care and delicacy, mindful of their sensitivities, aspirations and dignity. It is not enough for India to consider itself the natural leader of South Asia. It is equally important that other South Asian countries accept it as such. India has to earn the right to leadership by setting an example, by showing magnanimity, and by successfully managing the growing challenges and contradictions of the region. No matter how difficult and hopeless a relationship may look at present, India must always keep its doors open for dialogue. Patience and an appeal to the self-interest of its neighbours have to mark India's attitude. Such an approach will earn India their respect, howsoever grudging it may be.

In order to foster greater mutual confidence and trust, India has to devote much more time and attention to its neighbours than it has in the past. Fortunately, Prime Minister Narendra Modi has recognized this shortcoming. In his early years in office, he made it a priority to have frequent and regular exchanges of high-level visits with India's neighbours within the framework of a 'Neighbourhood First' policy. Regrettably, this momentum seems to have been lost over the last few years. Official visits are not the only way to maintain contact and dialogue. There are many other mechanisms by which to engage with neighbours. There could be frequent telephonic conversations and informal contacts, using pegs like private visits, religious pilgrimages and transit halts in order to make personal assessments, exchange views, resolve problems and massage egos! Discussions with neighbours should not be confined to purely bilateral issues, but cover regional and global issues too. This would convey the message that India considers its neighbours sufficiently important for an exchange of views on a broad spectrum of global and regional issues. It only exacerbates the apprehensions and frustrations of India's neighbours if India ignores or looks down upon them.

Even though India has managed a respectable annual rate of economic growth in recent years, its continued future growth will to some extent depend on its ability to take along its neighbours. India cannot hope to remain prosperous if its neighbours languish. Growing prosperity and economic opportunities in India will inevitably generate cross-border flows of legal and illegal economic migrants across porous and laxly policed borders from South Asia's poorer parts. One sees how the open-border regime with Nepal facilitates a regular flow of Nepali immigrants to India. From Bangladesh, a steady stream of illegal migrants, estimated at over 20 million, has fanned out across India and changed the demographic profile in the neighbouring states of West

Bengal, Tripura and Assam, as well as in Delhi. Illegal immigration has severely compromised India's security. It has spawned many terrorist cells within India. But India has been unable to insulate itself from its neighbours by creating an effective *cordon sanitaire* around itself. Only along the India-Pakistan border has fencing worked, that too because a strip of land along the border has been cleared of population. Fencing on the Bangladesh border has been ineffective in stopping illegal Bangladeshi migrants from coming into India. Similarly, there is reason to be sceptical that the proposed border fencing with Myanmar will be effective. This is hardly surprising. Even the United States, with its vastly superior resources and technology, has been unable to control illegal migration from Mexico across a riverine border running through thinly populated, arid territory. Where is the hope that India can seal borders that cut through thickly populated areas with dense vegetation, particularly when local politicians and vested interests on both sides covertly encourage emigration for narrow and short-term political gains?

The government of Prime Minister Modi has rightly come to the conclusion that India's self-interest dictates the need for fresh thinking and a changed approach. India's bargain with its neighbours has to be that it will give them generous economic benefits provided the countries do not follow policies that pose a threat to India's security. Within its limitations, over the years, India has indeed given considerable assistance to its neighbours through concessional lines of credit for infrastructure and other projects, as well as technical-economic assistance and educational facilities. The focus has been on setting up high-visibility projects that improve the lives of the common people in the neighbouring countries, not projects that can be criticized as bringing benefit to India only.

India has to be magnanimous in stimulating the economic development of its neighbours. While fully respecting the sovereignty, independence and sensitivities of its neighbours, from an economic perspective, India has no alternative to treating them like its own states. Some of the steps that the Indian government could take is to encourage, through tax and other incentives similar to those given within India for certain regions and states, its private sector to invest in these countries to promote their industrial development, create local jobs and produce value-added products for export to India and elsewhere. Hopefully, this will reduce the pressure on the people in these countries to want to migrate to India in search of greener pastures. Reciprocally, India should welcome investment by businessmen from neighbouring countries. That would give their ruling elites a long-term stake in India's stability, growth and prosperity. Ultimately, India's objective should be maximum possible economic integration of its neighbouring countries with itself, which would tie their destinies with India regardless of the political predilections of the regimes in power. Economic interdependence leading to economic integration may also lead to a better appreciation of India's security concerns among its neighbours and greater cooperation in this respect. India must also give much greater attention to the development of its border regions, including road and rail links, and infrastructure relating to customs, immigration, etc. It is difficult to project the image of a strong and efficient India to its neighbours when the roads and other infrastructure, including symbols of the Indian state like customs and immigration offices on the Indian side of the border, compare poorly with those on the other side.

While India has to open its purse strings for its neighbours, it realistically realizes that its neighbours will never love it. The trouble is that they do not fear India—at least not enough. At times they tweak India's nose, just to make a point, and appear confident that India will do nothing. Such an attitude should not be acceptable to India. India's goal should be to get the respect of its neighbours, perhaps some admiration too if possible, and definitely some sensitivity to its red lines. Even as it must be visionary, large-hearted and sensitive to its neighbours, India needs to firmly and unambiguously define for its neighbours the goalposts of its non-negotiable security and other concerns. India should make it clear that it will be uncompromising on security issues and expects its neighbours to cooperate with it in combating terrorism by not giving shelter to extremist and separatist elements from India, and by not permitting outside powers to conduct anti-India operations from their territory. That has to be India's bottom line. Regrettably, an impression had gained ground among India's neighbours that India is a soft state whose interests can be ignored with impunity. Thankfully, of late, India has made it clear that its neighbours should respect India's core interests, and that if they do not, India would not hesitate to use its many leverages against them.

India's neighbours too need to rethink their traditional attitude towards India. Seeing that distant countries are planning long-term strategies to plug into India's impressive current and potential growth, logic would seem to dictate that India's neighbours too should be thinking along similar lines. Sharing many complementarities with India, they can become globally competitive if they take full advantage of their geographical proximity to India. They could exploit India's competitive advantages, such as easy availability of raw materials, economies of scale of a huge production base and a large market. All of them have a deep understanding of India and are well networked with key players in India. But they have to honestly answer some hard questions. Do they want to ride on the back of India's success and weight in the world? Will their global competitiveness improve if they are economically integrated with India? Or do they believe that their long-term development, prosperity and security could be autonomously generated, or perhaps by relying on a predatory China? Bhutan has traditionally been closely integrated with India. In a welcome change of attitude, Bangladesh in recent years has shed its earlier hesitations about economic cooperation and integration with India. The attitude of Nepal, the Maldives and Sri Lanka is fickle. Because of internal turmoil in these countries, there are limits to what India can do with Afghanistan and Myanmar at the present time. Unexpectedly, Pakistan is the odd one out. One hopes that all the South Asian countries can look beyond their existing political prejudices and think of what they must collectively do if they are not to be left behind in a fast-changing world.

The issue of democracy sometimes complicates India's relations with its neighbours. The problem is that while India is an established and vibrant democracy, its neighbours are not. Willy-nilly, the Indian model of democracy exerts a powerful influence on politics in the neighbouring countries. Unlike in the past, after the overthrow of Musharraf in Pakistan and the end of the caretaker government in Bangladesh, both in 2008, overt military rule is no longer practicable in these two countries. Experience has shown that authoritarian regimes in South Asia do not have long-term survivability. Sensing the changing winds, Bhutan has transformed itself into a constitutional monarchy, and the Maldives now has a multiparty system. From India's perspective, democratically elected governments accountable to the people in its neighbouring countries are preferable because policies towards India then would not be subject to the whims and fancies of a small ruling elite or clique.

This matter needs careful handling. India does not use democracy as an ideological stick with which to beat its neighbours. It is not in the business of 'export' of democracy and has been perfectly willing to deal with all kinds of regimes in its neighbourhood and around the world. Moral judgements need to be tempered by pragmatism and political realism. At times a strong hand is needed to keep a country united, secure and stable. However, where military regimes are in power, they are stable only if the military is seen as acting in the national interest, not self-interest. The use of military power must be legitimized by the explicit support of the people (as is done in democracies where there is civilian control over the military), or by the people's implicit acceptance of military rule. As a democratic country, India must speak out a little more, perhaps quietly, in favour of the desirability of democracy in its neighbourhood because the solutions to many of the social and political problems in those countries lie in greater democracy.

It is obvious that India cannot be seen as interfering in the internal affairs of its neighbours and must continue to deal with whoever is in power. At the same time, it does matter to India what kind of regime is in power in a neighbouring country. In general, non-democratic regimes in neighbouring countries have been more inimical towards India, principally because the narrow and often selfish interests of the ruling elites who are unaccountable to their own people invariably require a policy of aloofness if not hostility towards India, in contrast to the much greater meeting of minds and convergence of interests at the popular level. When there are elections, there exists a framework for correction of aberrations. Democratic governments also have to be mindful of legitimate popular grievances and need to have a respectful and tolerant approach towards religious and other minorities. Even if such governments are not necessarily more stable, they do foster greater harmony and peace. Non-democratic governments create a political void that is readily filled by religious obscurantists, extremists and fundamentalists.

India will always remain an unspoken factor in the domestic politics of its neighbours (and vice versa, though to a lesser extent). For the sake of its security, if nothing else, India cannot remain detached from the dynamics of the internal politics of its neighbours, and will always have to maintain close contact with the major political players there. It cannot afford to abdicate its responsibility to facilitate the resolution of such problems in its neighbouring countries because domestic strife there can have an effect on India itself, particularly on contiguous states where the population shares deep emotional, cultural and family links across the border. Whenever a divided community feels that its culture or identity is being threatened, the problem no longer remains domestic, the best examples being the widespread empathy for Sri Lankan Tamils in India's Tamil Nadu state. Some other noteworthy examples are: the millions of Bangladeshi citizens who sought refuge in India in 1971 and those who have illegally migrated into Assam and various other parts of India; the persecuted Tamils in Sri Lanka who have periodically migrated to India; the Nepali-origin people expelled from Bhutan, and refugees from Myanmar in Manipur and Mizoram. If the Madheshis in Nepal do not get a satisfactory political solution to their grievances, the problem spills over into India, as happened in 2015-16.

India has no alternative but to closely follow and deeply analyse political trends and discreetly try to influence the domestic political debate within these countries. All too often, political parties and groups in India's neighbouring countries too seek India's intervention in their internal political squabbles and rivalries. On many occasions over the last seven and a half decades, India has been a decisive player in domestic political crises in Bangladesh (1971), Sri Lanka (1987), Nepal (1950-51, 2005–08, 2015-16) and the Maldives (1988). The challenge for India lies in not getting drawn into situations from which there may be no safe and honourable exit, and in creating a national consensus on relations with it among the principal political actors in the country concerned.

India's Extended Neighbourhood

It is noteworthy that two of India's three rings of security, namely the middle one, from Aden and Hormuz to Malacca, and the outer one, from Suez to Shanghai, involve maritime security. This brings out the importance of maritime power in India's security and strategic perspective. It is India's geographical dominance that gives the Indian Ocean its name. It was across the seas and oceans that Indian people and culture spread both to the east and west. Nor can India forget that it was from the oceans that it was conquered by the colonial powers. Today it is in the oceans that China is crafting its 'string of pearls' strategy. India, fortunately, has unimpeded access to the open seas from multiple points on both its western and eastern coasts. The fact that a very large percentage of global energy and trade SLOCs are in the northern Indian Ocean, passing very close to Indian waters, gives India considerable leverage. There is now a welcome emphasis on developing India's sea power (though there are resource constraints) and on expanding cooperation with the littoral and island states across the Indian Ocean, like Sri Lanka, the Maldives, Oman, Seychelles, Mauritius, Kenya, Tanzania, Madagascar, Mozambique, France and Indonesia. India cannot prevent outside powers from having a presence in the Indian Ocean but, as before, it remains India's policy to try and prevent hostile powers from consolidating their presence in Sri Lanka and the Maldives, which are located very close to India. Hence India must intensify its engagement with its immediate island neighbours as well as with the Persian Gulf region, east Africa and South Africa, small island countries in the Indian Ocean, South-east Asia, Australia and Japan.

Across the Bay of Bengal, the countries of South-east Asia and India have had very close historical, cultural and people-to-people links, which is why this region was widely regarded in the nineteenth and early twentieth century as 'Greater India'. However, continuing wars in the region and the Cold War divide kept India and South-east Asia apart for many decades. Relations revived about three decades ago with the launch of the Look East policy, later renamed as the Act East policy. Initially, this policy had an economic dimension. However, over the years India has been disappointed that in practice the FTAs and CECAs it signed with ASEAN and other countries have not brought it the anticipated benefits. Originally, the ASEAN countries regarded India as a balancing power against China's strong presence in the region, but this is now much less so. The accelerated growth of China's economy and China's influence over the economically dominant Chinese communities in these countries have led to a growing China orientation among the ASEAN countries, even as they helplessly chafe at China's bullying and intimidating tactics in the South China Sea. ASEAN itself has become a divided house. 'ASEAN centrality' has turned out to be a myth and a bubble. ASEAN-centric structures like the EAS, ARF and ASEAN Defence Ministers' Meeting Plus (ADMM+) are ineffective in dealing with regional security issues. Today India is paying greater attention to security and strategic issues in this region because of growing concerns over China's aggressive behaviour in the Western Pacific and Indian Ocean. China's de facto takeover of the South China Sea is particularly troublesome, as that could enable it to interdict critical lines of communication, both on the sea and in the air, and thereby cut off access between the Pacific and Indian Oceans, as well as provide a base for its forays into the Indian Ocean. This is an important factor driving India's close defence and security ties with the United States, Japan and Australia in bilateral and trilateral formats, and within the framework of the Quad. France, Indonesia, the Philippines and Vietnam are other key countries partnering with

India in the Indo-Pacific region to help prevent China's control over the Western Pacific region and in developing counter-choke points for China in the Straits of Malacca as well as in the Sunda and Lombok Straits in Indonesian waters.

India's interests in the Indian Ocean are not merely defensive. With its access routes to and from the oil-rich Persian Gulf, the Indian Ocean is the new energy security heartland. It is also a major trading artery, a highly militarized region and a platform for power projection on the Eurasian landmass. The Indian Ocean rim is home to a significant proportion of the world's population, which is mostly poor. All these factors give enormous contemporary economic and strategic significance to the Indian Ocean. If India aspires to be a great power, then the only direction in which its strategic influence can spread is across the seas. In every other direction, there are formidable constraints. Thus, the Indian navy has to play a new, strategic role as a foreign policy tool, in tandem with India's growing weight in world affairs. India today is seen as a credible naval power, and its strategic location, which enables it to keep a watch on the major SLOCs in the northern Indian Ocean, is lost on no one.

At the same time, it cannot be denied that countries outside the Indian Ocean rim have important stakes in the Indian Ocean. The presence of foreign navies in the Indian Ocean is not a new phenomenon, and is likely to increase. The United States, France, China, Russia, Japan, Australia and some other countries have a significant presence in the Indian Ocean region. The UN General Assembly Resolution of December 1971 on declaring the Indian Ocean as a Zone of Peace was a utopian dream, which has predictably come to naught. With so many extra-territorial naval powers present in the Indian Ocean close to India's shores, it is only prudent that India should have a significant naval presence in the region, both for defensive purposes as well as to project force if needed. India's control of the Andaman and Nicobar Islands gives it a formidable presence in the Bay of Bengal. The setting up of the Tri-Services Command in the Andaman and Nicobar islands in 2001 was a shrewd move that gives credibility to India's regional naval capabilities and posture. India is steadily strengthening this outpost. In the Arabian Sea, India is also developing the Lakshadweep islands as a naval outpost.

With the Persian Gulf countries, India has had centuries-old deep cultural linkages and movement of people. Today there is an incredibly thick and diverse web of ties. Nearly half of India's oil and gas imports are from this region. More than 9 million Indians live and work in the Gulf, which gives India huge stakes and leverage there. Two-way trade, investment and travel are booming. With a lighter US military footprint now in the region, the GCC countries are keen on greater security cooperation with India, the most proximate large power. As a result, security and defence cooperation with all these countries has rapidly grown. Frequent exchanges of high-level visits have enhanced mutual confidence and understanding. At the same time, India, having overcome its traditional hesitation and self-imposed constraints arising from Arab-Israeli tensions, has managed to consolidate as well as diversify its ties with Israel while enhancing relations with the Persian Gulf countries, especially Saudi Arabia and the United Arab Emirates. With strong inherent strengths and capabilities, Iran is the other large regional player that India cannot and should not ignore. Iran is vital for India's access to Afghanistan and Central Asia and is an important proximate source of oil and gas. Unfortunately, US sanctions on Iran have imposed limitations on India's ability to develop closer relations with it. There is little doubt that in the coming years, the Persian Gulf region will occupy an increasingly important role in India's foreign policy.

Central Asia remains in a flux. The precipitate US withdrawal from Afghanistan has enabled the Taliban to regain control over Afghanistan. India is also unhappy with China's growing presence and influence in Afghanistan and the emergence of a Pakistan-China-Afghanistan axis. But while India enjoys considerable popular goodwill among Afghans, its ability to do more in and for Afghanistan is limited by its lack of direct access to land-locked Afghanistan. India faces similar limitations in its relations with the Central Asian countries, which hold strategic importance for it. India has to continue to work at developing ties with them so that they do not get completely sucked into China's sphere of influence. It would be wise for India to work together with Russia in Central Asia.

India and the Global South

As in the nineteenth century, capitalism in the twenty-first century continues to produce many discontents arising out of its fundamental weakness that it cannot ensure either sustainable or inclusive growth. The ills of capitalism in the modern era gave rise to socialism, the defining idea of the twentieth century. Even if the socialist and communist experiments around the world have left much to be desired, the idea of social justice remains firmly entrenched among hundreds of millions around the globe. The unprecedented massive bailouts of private financial institutions by governments all over the world during the 2008 financial crisis emphatically underlined the responsibility of the state to ensure social welfare and stability. The 'American Dream' is no longer achievable even for Americans, much less for the rest of the world. Nor can one be optimistic about authoritarian forms of governance. If there is to be any hope of peace, stability and harmony in an increasingly turbulent world where expectations have outstripped resources and now threaten to destabilize an iniquitous global political and economic order, the world needs a model of development that takes care of the interests of its underprivileged and dispossessed billions.

Sharing with other developing countries India's own capabilities, and assisting and cooperating with them in developing their own economies has been an integral part of Indian foreign policy from its very inception. India's independence was an inspiration and catalyst for many other countries under colonial rule, which got considerable political, moral and diplomatic support from India in their struggle for independence. India has projected itself as a Vishwamitra, or friend of the world. South-South cooperation represents the economic face of India's political support to anti-colonial struggles. As a poor and diverse developing country that has made impressive strides in all fields after Independence, India offers an alternative model of governance and development to the one being advocated by the West as the so-called universal one. Without India's support and leadership, there is little hope of bringing about a new world order that gives due importance to the imperatives of social justice and inclusive growth. India believes in the philosophy of *Vasudhaiva Kutumbakam,* or 'the world is one family'. Two recent examples bring this out forcefully. One is the supply of vaccines by India to numerous countries around the world during the Covid-19 pandemic. The other is India's successful initiative as chair of the G-20 to get the African Union accepted as a member of the forum in 2023.

From this perspective, India's policy of seeking friends and partners globally and offering them assistance does serve its interests. India's traditional source of standing and influence was as a leader of the non-aligned countries, often a synonym for developing countries that the West derisively called the 'Third World', an expression used as a psychological tool by a dominant rich and powerful West in order to engender a sense of inferiority among these countries. It brought out the disdain with which the West regarded this motley bunch of countries that were, in its world view, neither fish nor fowl, being neither part of the West (the so-called 'First World') and therefore not co-opted into Western institutions or ideologies, nor part of the communist bloc (the so-called 'Second World'), a competitor and opponent of the West. These so-called 'Third World' countries were unceremoniously lumped together and dumped into the global fishpond designed by the West. The affected countries were individually too weak to rebel against this concept, much less change it. It was India, principally because of its size and relative weight in the world, which provided political leadership to this group of countries. The successes on the ground were generally limited and ephemeral, but were invaluable in giving a sense of dignity and self-confidence to these countries.

It is this legacy that has enabled these countries, now called the Global South, to voice their demands and leverage their strengths in the twenty-first century. The Global South is India's natural constituency. India has to find its niche in the world. If India ever makes it as a permanent member of the UN Security Council, it will not be because the existing permanent members of the Security Council (P-5) wanted it there but because of the support of the Global South, based on their confidence that India would protect the interests of its members. It is noteworthy that India used its presidency of the G-20 in 2023 to project itself as a champion of the interests of the Global South. India organized two 'Voice of the Global South' summit meetings. Prime Minister Modi summed up India's assessment of its G-20 presidency in the following words: 'The global conversation had to evolve. The interests of the few had to give way to the aspirations of the many. This required a fundamental reform of multilateralism as we knew it . . . India amplified the voice of the Global South.'[1]

India's steady achievements in diverse fields have made it an increasingly influential international player. For countries that may be too weak to follow autonomous policies but remain ready to rally behind a stronger country that can be an independent global player, India has become a potential leader, even though it should not seek to project itself as one. In any case, India's strategic economic objectives (such as energy and other resources to sustain its economic growth, and new opportunities for exports and investments) require the support and goodwill of developing countries. India cannot afford to neglect the poorer countries of the world.

India's foreign assistance programme is a strategic tool with which to showcase its technical strengths and achievements and to harness them to promote its political and economic interests in the world. This valuable instrument of India's foreign policy has generated goodwill, brought economic dividends for India and built Indian brand equity. Technical and economic cooperation with foreign countries constitutes a substantial part of the budget of the Ministry of External Affairs. Many countries benefit from India's Technical and Economic Cooperation programme (ITEC) as well as other specialized training programmes in areas like agriculture and science and technology.[2] ITEC covers many aspects, both on the civil and defence sides—training of individuals in India; deputation of Indian experts abroad; the setting up of projects abroad; restoration of heritage projects abroad. One recent innovation has been the e-ITEC scheme, which uses digital technology and online training programmes. India also extends concessional lines of credit under the Indian Development and Economic Assistance Scheme (IDEAS) through Exim Bank of India. So far, a total of 306 lines of credit have been extended, worth over $30 billion, of which more than half go to India's neighbouring countries.[3] ITEC could be given a sharper strategic focus so that it can live up to its promise and realize its full potential. Apart from spending significantly larger sums of money on development assistance, India needs to leverage its core competencies more effectively and optimally and create a model of development assistance that matches its strengths with the changing needs of the beneficiary countries. Perhaps it is time to set up an autonomous entity to coordinate India's technical and economic assistance programme. That may help India to pursue its foreign policy goals more systematically and effectively.

It is understandable that India's neighbours should get the highest priority in India's development assistance to foreign countries. Outside India's immediate neighbourhood, Africa is the largest beneficiary of India's technical and economic cooperation. India's development assistance programme to Africa goes back nearly half a century, immediately after the African countries gained their independence from colonial rule. India's economic and technical assistance to developing countries in Africa at a time when India itself was a recipient of foreign aid was premised both on principle and on the reality that the political independence of newly independent countries would be unsustainable without a matching economic autonomy. India's forthright support of the struggle of African countries against colonialism and apartheid, and the assistance India has given them has generated genuine goodwill and trust for India across Africa. India's projects in Africa are geared towards creating value addition for Africa's natural resources, generating local employment, transfer of technology, and developing Africa's human resources through training in Indian institutions as well as by deputation of Indian experts to Africa. Africans find Indian technology appropriate for their level of economic development, and India's experience in developing the small and medium sectors of its economy as particularly useful and relevant.

India has not thrust projects on African countries but has tried to take into account their developmental priorities and environmental concerns. India gives Africa not just official assistance; the Indian private sector too is involved in Africa in a big way. Indian companies have invested in many sectors of African economies such as transport, power generation, telecommunications, other areas of infrastructure development, horticulture and agriculture.

A few years ago, India waived many debts owed by African countries under the World Bank's Heavily Indebted Poor Countries (HIPC) Debt Relief Initiative. Recently, India decided to give phased duty-free market access to fifty Least Developed Countries (LDCs) from Africa and Asia. India is also undertaking an ambitious Pan African e-network project for tele-education and tele-medicine. In the twenty-first century, India has begun to give much more focused attention to Africa through its regional bodies. India has organized three representative India-Africa Forum Summits. Defence and security have also become a growing area of cooperation between India and African countries. Another welcome change has been that India now has more and better-staffed resident diplomatic missions in Africa. It is encouraging that there are now more frequent high-level visits exchanged between India and Africa.

India's Global Challenges

As of now, the United States is the only great power, because it has all the essential attributes of one. Firstly, it has power—in terms of population, resources, technology, economic and financial strength, the military, its leading role in the management and control of international bodies, as well as cultural and social influence. Secondly, with interests across the world and the will and capability to pursue and protect them, it behaves like a great power. Finally, it is recognized as a great power and is treated as such by other countries. Nevertheless, the relative weight of the US has diminished and it is less self-assured and more anxious about its ability to preserve its global hegemony beyond the next two or three decades. China is an aspiring great power with some, but not all, of the required attributes. It is the new pretender that relentlessly pursues its 'China Dream' of Asian, and eventually global, domination. Russia (as the core of the Soviet Union) was a great power, a status that it lost with the breakup of the Soviet Union. It has regained much of its self-confidence and seeks to reclaim great-power status. A more activist and less pacifist Japan is playing a greater role in Asia matching its economic and technological strengths.

While India has never been an aggressive, expansionist power, it has not been a passive or a status quo power either. India fought against colonialism and apartheid, resisted pressures to join blocs and did not accept the iniquitous nuclear regime of the NPT. Today India has a more ambitious and positive agenda. India is not content to remain a second-rung player, a mere 'balancer' or 'swing state'. Its goal is to become a 'leading state' with a place at the global high table, on an equal basis with other great powers. India seeks to become a permanent member of the UN Security Council; to be a recognized nuclear weapons power enjoying the same rights and responsibilities as the five nuclear weapons powers under the NPT; and to be completely liberated from technology denial regimes like those imposed by the NSG. This will not be easy, since those wielding power do not give it up voluntarily or easily. Many influential circles among the present-day 'haves' oppose India's rise and will work to keep India down. History shows that emerging or rising powers have rarely been smoothly co-opted into existing power structures.

For India to rise, the existing powers must become relatively weaker. This is indeed happening in the world today. The power and influence of the West are waning. The five-centuries-old political, military, economic, financial, cultural and psychological domination of the world by the West is coming to an end. The G-7 countries no longer dominate the global economy. International financial institutions like the World Bank and IMF are much less influential than they used to be. Russia too has been weakened. It lost its empire with the collapse of the Soviet Union, and the sanctions imposed on it as a fallout of the ongoing conflict in Ukraine will continue to bleed it for some time. While China's economic and military power has increased phenomenally over the last couple of decades, the world is trying to reduce its economic dependence on China, which is also facing serious political, demographic and economic challenges. With the P-5 countries fighting among themselves, the UNSC has become ineffective, almost paralysed, in its primary task of ensuring peace and security. On the economic side, the WTO has become progressively less relevant as RTAs are now increasingly popular.

The door is open for India to assume a greater role in global affairs. Clearly, India has an opportunity to break into the ranks of the most exclusive club of great powers. At this time, when it is being seriously viewed by the rest of the world as a country that will inevitably play a much greater role in world affairs in the coming years, India must evolve a strategy that will enable it to become a global player in all respects—economically, politically, militarily and technologically. Does India want to be co-opted into the existing international structures that have been fashioned by and are dominated by the West in general and the United States in particular? Or does India see itself as one of the 'poles' in a multi-polar world? Understandably, the West would like India to become a responsible stakeholder in the current global system that has been fashioned and is dominated by it. The question is whether it can be suitably changed to accommodate India. External Affairs Minister Jaishankar made India's position clear with these pithy remarks: 'For India, when we confront a largely Western-created architecture, we would like to encourage, facilitate, induce and pressurize changes that are badly needed. But it is done to add a non-Western layer as an input. I make this very important distinction. India is non-Western but it isn't anti-Western.'[4]

In a shifting global kaleidoscope, a more self-confident and ambitious India is fortunate to have in Prime Minister Narendra Modi a strong, bold and clear-headed leader who thinks strategically. His imaginative and dynamic handling of foreign affairs has galvanized Indian foreign policy, which is now, more than ever before, an integral and critical element of an overall national strategy. India is no longer seen as a weak country that can be easily manipulated and arm-twisted. In dealing with existing and potential great powers, India must retain its strategic autonomy. Politically, India has always sought to preserve its independence of action and autonomy of decision-making. It has also shown that it has the capacity to do so. Various factors, including its sense of pride and self-worth based on its rich heritage of civilization and culture, its past achievements and its multi-faceted successes as an independent nation impel it to seek its due place in the comity of nations. India is too big, too proud and too steeped in the anti-colonial mindset to become a camp follower of any power. The highest priority has to be given to building India's own comprehensive national power. India must leverage its comparative advantages, such as its size, its geographical location, its demographic dividend, its large and growing market, its robust economic growth, its cultural attractiveness, and the talent, financial and political clout of its large diaspora.

India's principal long-term geopolitical challenge is China. The relationship is essentially competitive because there is a clash between the 'core interests' of the two countries. Even if there is a change in China's thinking, the outlook is pessimistic. The Galwan clashes of 2020 were a turning point. India no longer trusts China to abide by any agreement it may conclude with it. China aspires to become the world's leading power, but for this to happen it first must have unquestioned primacy in Asia, where India is the principal obstacle. China is not prepared to treat India as an equal, while India will never accept an inferior status in a Sino-centric Asia. In order to keep India pinned down in South Asia, China is steadily and unremittingly encroaching on India's security space in the Indian Ocean rimland, with Pakistan playing the role of a handmaiden.

One of the most significant decisions that India has taken is to openly and boldly reject the Belt and Road Initiative (BRI), Chinese leader Xi Jinping's grand, personal, strategic project, which is a key element in China's global strategy. There are many reasons for this. Firstly, India is the only country whose sovereignty is impacted by the China-Pakistan Economic Corridor (CPEC), the flagship project of the BRI which passes through Pak-occupied Kashmir. Secondly, India has sent a clear message to China—and the world—that it rejects Chinese pretensions to hegemony in Asia and eventually the world. Finally, and most importantly, it is not in India's interest that the BRI should succeed. Given the ongoing US-China technological competition and an increasingly wary Europe, the success of the BRI becomes very important for China. A wider global understanding of the perils of the neo-colonial BRI model and growing pushback by countries that have joined the BRI portends its ultimate failure, which suits India. Already, many countries that had joined the BRI have realized that they had signed on to economically unviable projects financed by loans on quasi-commercial and opaque terms. Unable to repay the loans, they find themselves in a debt trap. China's spectacular rise is based on its economic growth fuelled by its exports. Any significant economic slowdown would threaten China's internal social and political stability. Were the BRI to succeed, there is a real possibility of the world becoming Sino-centric, with China determining the fate of a large number of countries, setting new standards and controlling global institutions. China's ability to squeeze India regionally and bilaterally would increase exponentially. As the global ramifications of a Sino-centric world are immense, India must do its best to frustrate China's imperial BRI project, in which Pakistan has a key role, similar to that of India in the British empire. Once Britain lost India, its empire quickly crumbled. The same could happen to the BRI if the CPEC fails. China also has its eye on India's growing market. India has to restrict this access—by diversifying its imports, curbing Chinese investment in sensitive areas, using tariff and non-tariff barriers, not giving China market-economy status, influencing Indian public opinion to curb the people's appetite for Chinese products, and preventing China from routing its exports to India via other countries.

India has certainly shed its earlier diffidence in dealing with China. This is most welcome. If India aspires to be a serious regional and global player, it has to behave in a more dignified manner worthy of a great power, particularly in relation to a country like China. The eagerness, even anxiety, that India in the past tended to convey about reaching an early settlement of the boundary question sent a regrettable signal of weakness. That is hardly a sensible approach when dealing with a growing power that has traditionally looked at the world with a sense of superiority and condescension. Fortunately, under Prime Minister Modi, India's approach towards China has become more hardline, realistic and reciprocal. It is good that India has eschewed its earlier defensive, timid and somewhat legalistic approach in dealing with China. India now has a more focused and activist policy and is more willing to stand up to China, as well as test and probe China's weaknesses. There is no need to be in awe of China. It may be militarily and economically stronger than India today, but India too has its long-term comparative advantages vis-à-vis China. China's growth has slowed down, while India's has accelerated. India also has an important, albeit somewhat diminished, Tibet card in its hand that must be skilfully played. As a country with aspirations to a larger regional and global role, India has to do some hardheaded scenario-building, including the possibilities of a relentlessly rising China or a disintegrating China. India must be alert, imaginative and quick-footed in order to protect its national interests and be on the lookout for new strategic opportunities that may come its way.

In addition, India needs to craft a strategy of psychological warfare against China. Historically, China did not figure in India's consciousness because interaction with it was minimal. India's northern neighbour is Tibet, with which India has had close and friendly religious, cultural and people-to-people ties based on mutual respect. Secondly, India should undertake a systematic campaign to puncture the Chinese concept of itself as being the 'Middle Kingdom'. It should be argued that this is merely China's self-perception born out of its ignorance and isolation from the rest of the world for centuries. As the other civilizations with which China came into contact were not so developed, China came to regard all foreigners as 'barbarians' who were expected to kowtow to the 'Middle Kingdom'. The concept of equality of sovereign states was not known to China. The reality is that India was arguably more developed than China, which borrowed hugely from India's religion and culture. Thirdly, India should make a conscious effort to project its culture and achievements in a positive light, including for the sake of its own self-esteem. Prime Minister Modi and his government are now doing this actively. India's intellectual and spiritual advancements can be seen in the fact that India gave birth to sophisticated religions and philosophies that had wide appeal in other parts of Asia. India is the home of Buddhism, which later spread to Tibet, China and other parts of Asia. The attractiveness of India's developed culture can be seen in the sprawling Buddhist and Hindu kingdoms that flourished in South-east Asia. India also had a more advanced form of political organization that was inclusive and consensual—so essential to preserving harmony in multicultural countries like India and China. India borrowed freely from other civilizations with which it came into contact, thereby enriching its own. It is these traits of flexibility and openness of character among its people that equips India to deal with the challenges of globalization much better than China, which has been a closed civilization. It is noteworthy that persons of Indian origin are heading many large global companies in diverse fields, whereas the Chinese have been unable to make a similar impact. Finally, through the media, intellectual and academic circles, India must create greater public awareness of the myriad challenges that China faces.

No matter what it does, India would find it extremely difficult to counter China on its own without the support of weighty friends. This is where the United States comes in. India and the United States have shared concerns about China. It would be unrealistic to expect the United States to get militarily involved if there were to be an India-China border conflict but, by sharing advanced defence and technology systems and equipment, as well as intelligence, the United States can help India build up military deterrence to cope with the China challenge. A century ago, the famed British geographer Sir Halford Mackinder put forth his theory about the Heartland and the Rimland. In essence, it posited that if the Eurasian landmass—the Heartland—is dominated by one power, that power could dominate the world, unless it was countered by other powers on the periphery of Eurasia—the Rimland. Its basic premise remains valid even today. With Russia as its junior partner and the BRI spreading its tentacles all over Eurasia, China is trying to control the Heartland. It is also trying to establish its presence in the Rimland space through its control of the South China Sea and its forays in the Indian Ocean. This must be resisted.

Hence India is closely cooperating with major Indo-Pacific maritime powers like the United States, Japan, Australia and France, and key countries in South-east Asia like Indonesia, the Philippines and Vietnam.

China is not the only reason why India and the United States should come closer. Despite its relative decline, the United States is still the world's preeminent power in most respects—economic, financial, scientific, technological and military. If it is to grow rapidly, India needs a supportive, or at least not a hostile, United States. As open societies with extensive people-to-people contacts, the United States and India are indeed 'natural partners.' There is now more trust between the two countries. The large and influential Indian diaspora in the United States has played an important role in favourably shaping US public and political perceptions about India and Indians. As for the United States, India is no longer peripheral to its global interests because of shared perceptions of military, economic and technological threats from China, the lure of the Indian market, access to India's large and growing talent pool, and as a partner in developing supply-chain resilience. Strategic and defence cooperation, including extensive military and naval exercises, intelligence sharing, supply of high-end weaponry, countering of terrorism, has boomed. Gradually, at times painfully, the two countries have managed to overcome decades of mutual mistrust, suspicion and hostility. Over the last couple of decades, despite occasional setbacks, the overall trajectory of relations between the two in all respects has been upward. Unquestionably, the United States has become India's most important foreign partner. The relative decline of US global power and the corresponding rise of India have made it a more equal relationship. There is now greater Indian self-confidence in dealing with the United States. As India's minister of external affairs Jaishankar has remarked: 'At a global level the United States will need partners and India will need opportunities and possibilities.'[5]

Notwithstanding all the factors that make for closer relations between India and the West, in particular the United States, some unpalatable truths should not be swept under the carpet. Differences remain on many issues, such as policy towards Russia, Iran and Bangladesh, as well as on trade, digital services and intellectual property issues. Many influential US administrators and lawmakers have an ingrained prejudice against India and remain obstructive and unhelpful. India also has to deal with the vagaries of US electoral politics, which can make US foreign policy hostage to narrow domestic agendas and can throw up fickle and unpredictable leaders. Indo-US relations will continue to grow if India is willing to accept the United States as the premier global power. It will be difficult to get the United States to treat India as an equal, seeing that it rides roughshod over even its closest allies. India should be aware that the United States and its allies like the United Kingdom and Canada would never tolerate India becoming so powerful as to pose a threat to US global dominance. They will always keep multiple weapons in their toolkit as useful leverages against India. For decades, Pakistan has been and will remain one such pressure point. Hosting and encouraging anti-India terrorists, separatists and criminals is another way of keeping India off-balance. For a long time now, Canada has been a particularly troublesome country in this respect. India has accused Canada of interfering in its domestic politics. There has been a sharp downturn in relations following Canadian prime minister Justin Trudeau's unfounded allegation about India's complicity in the murder of a separatist Sikh-Canadian wanted terrorist. One can expect the United States and the West to continue to use their domination of the international mainstream media to hector India and spread false narratives and negative perceptions about it. Some of the sticks that are being used to beat India with are alleged human rights violations, religious intolerance, and lack of democracy and transparency in governance. On the economic side, the United States is already using its control over the global financial systems and its unilateral sanctions regime to restrict India's trade with Russia, Iran and Venezuela. This control can also be used to manipulate India's stock markets and currency. If the United States continues to follow tactics that keep India down and humiliate it, the hard-won trust between the two countries and Indian public support for closer ties with the United States could rapidly erode. The fact that India under Prime Minister Modi has begun to push back forcefully on these fronts irritates the West, which would ideally prefer a weak Indian leadership that is amenable to arm-twisting.

Hence, it would not be wise for India put all its eggs in the US basket. The United States can do little on the ground to help India tackle the China threat on its borders, and military cooperation with Russia will remain vital for India's security, at least for some time into the future. Then there is always the danger of the United States and China cutting a deal at the expense of the rest of the world, of which there were signs during the Clinton and Obama administrations. These realities impose limitations to the growth of Indo-US relations. The best approach for India would be to expand areas of cooperation wherever possible and avoid needlessly annoying the United States where India's vital interests are not threatened. Seeing how the United States is dealing with Russia, India also needs to slowly and cautiously move away from excessive reliance on the US dollar in its international transactions and for its reserves.

Even as it negotiates the complex inter-relationship between the putative superpowers, United States and China, India must not ignore the growing importance of other countries that are influential regional powers. Among these, Russia is the most important, as it continues to retain significant global influence, though on a much smaller scale compared with the former Soviet Union. Russia's nuclear and military capabilities, sheer size, geographical location, large population, rich natural resources, permanent membership of the UN Security Council, and its strategic culture and experience as a former superpower enable it to have global impact. While Russia remains a close and valued partner for India, the relationship is now a more transactional and equal one compared with what it was in Soviet times. India's significant dependence on Russia in the defence field cannot be wished away for the foreseeable future. Russia has also become an important partner for India's energy needs, as well as for critical raw materials, including uranium and diamonds. As a member of the UNSC P-5, Russia (earlier the Soviet Union) has provided crucial political and diplomatic support to India in the past and could be helpful in the future too. Neither country poses a threat to the other in their respective neighbourhoods—South Asia in India's case and the 'near abroad' in Russia's. Some important differences do remain. India is concerned about the growing closeness in Russia-China relations, while Russia rejects the concept of the 'Indo-Pacific' and views the Quad as a threat. India must continue to have a strong relationship with Russia to prevent it from slipping under China's domination. India also needs Russia to deal with the situation in Afghanistan and Central Asia. It would certainly not be in India's interest were a China-Pakistan-Afghanistan-Iran-Russia axis to develop. Russia too would like India as a balancing factor to reduce its dependence on China and to restrain India in its current Westward orientation. Thus, both India and Russia have their compulsions to have friendly and cooperative bilateral relations.

India cannot, and rightly did not, 'cancel' Russia on account of the Russia-Ukraine war. Contrary to the wishful thinking of the West, Russia is not collapsing because of sanctions by the West. In the long term, the world cannot isolate Russia or wish it away. Sooner rather than later, Europe and the United States will have to come to terms with Russia. As Napoleon and Hitler learnt at considerable cost, it is never wise to underestimate Russia's strength and resilience. Rational thinking dictates that the nuclear overhang and Europe's geographical proximity to Russia should push Europe towards eventually working out a mutually satisfactory European security arrangement with Russia, as happened at the end of the World War II and during the Cold War period. Thus, it would not be prudent for India to jeopardize its relations with Russia. The eclipse of Russia as a significant power (admittedly an unlikely scenario) would be most undesirable from India's point of view. It does not suit India to have either a unipolar world dominated by the West or a bipolar world dominated by the West and China.

Europe, which ruled the world for centuries, has become strategically marginal. It has been content to let the United States take over responsibility for its security and is not a serious global power. Perhaps this is the inevitable result of a deliberate US policy after the end of World War II to ensure that Europe remains militarily defanged. It does seem an anachronism that US troops remain stationed in Europe nearly eight decades after the end of World War II! Germany has meekly accepted the destruction in 2022 of the Nordstream-II gas pipeline from Russia and does not show the slightest interest in getting to the bottom of this brazen, monumental terrorist act against civilian infrastructure, widely suspected of having been done, or at least instigated, by the United States. Europe's ruling elite, with the possible exception of France, is unwilling or unable to defend Europe's interests in the face of US pressure. European integration hasn't lived up to expectations. It has not created a credible strategic entity. Whatever the other successes of the European Union—a common negotiating platform at the WTO, a single market, a common currency, freer movement of people, and common standards on issues like food quality, environment and agriculture— individual European countries have been loath to give up control of political, military and security issues. Strangely, it is not major powers like Germany and France but the relatively smaller and weaker Russophobe states in east Europe, like Poland and the Baltics, who are setting the European Union's agenda. This is not a tenable situation in the long run. It is not ruled out that some day in the future Germany may get out of its shell and start to flex its muscles, not only vis-à-vis other European countries but perhaps vis-à-vis the United States too. This process could be accelerated were Donald Trump to return as US President and take steps, as he has indicated, that would weaken NATO.

Europe's preoccupations are internal and regional. It is grappling with internal divisions and rivalries, the shock of Brexit, coping with the rise of right-wing nationalism, managing the societal tensions resulting from the flood of Muslim immigrants and Ukrainian refugees, and finding reliable and economically viable energy alternatives to cheap Russian oil and gas. Europe has also cut itself off from Russia. There is now a new 'Iron Curtain' in Europe, this time drawn not by Russia but by the West. European states like Switzerland, Austria, Sweden and Finland have abandoned neutrality as they clamber on to an anti-Russia bandwagon. The perception of the European elites, who appear to be disconnected from the public, that Europe is a 'garden' while the world outside is a 'jungle' reflects a skewed mindset that is out of touch with contemporary realities. Europe has been happy to be a kind of moral superpower, focusing on an idealist and woke agenda, dominated by issues like the environment, human rights and LGBTQ rights, rather than based on considerations of realpolitik. Given its long tradition and rich experience of statecraft and diplomacy, Europe's policies and priorities do not appear to be rational. It would be in India's interest if Europe were to regain its strategic autonomy.

For now, Europe remains important for India principally as a valuable trade and investment partner and as a source of high technology. For Europe, India has not been very important from an economic perspective, at least till now, since Europe's principal economic attention has been on China. Its approach to China has been purely mercantilist, the focus being on exploiting the Chinese market while ignoring political and strategic considerations. The coronavirus pandemic and China's burgeoning geopolitical ambitions have compelled Europeans to revisit their strategy and try to reduce their dependence on China. Hence, Europe is now starting to look at India with greater interest, which India welcomes. If Europe were to regard India as an equal partner, and not merely as a market or a resource, India-Europe relations could rapidly develop.

Access to advanced technologies as well as reliable, affordable energy supplies will be two key factors that can spur India's growth. On technology, it is welcome that India now has a focused strategy to develop indigenous technologies and to give importance to manufacturing. Success in this endeavour will take time and persistence. Meanwhile, India has to look to other countries for assistance. In order not to be too reliant on the United States, India would do well to tap other countries that have advanced technologies and are willing to share them with India. Some of the more important countries in this respect are Russia, France, Germany, Japan, South Korea, Taiwan and Israel. India should also view its talented diaspora in the United States as an asset that could be of great assistance in propelling it forward technologically if a suitable ecosystem were to be put in place domestically. As far as energy security is concerned, India is unfortunately poorly endowed with hydrocarbons, which will remain a critical source of energy for at least a decade or two. Hence the importance of proximate oil and gas-rich countries like Saudi Arabia, Iran, Iraq, United Arab Emirates,

Kuwait and Qatar in the Persian Gulf region, as well as of Russia and Venezuela. India is rightly focusing much more on non-conventional sources of energy, especially solar energy, as well as accelerating its fast breeder programme for nuclear energy.

India is a member of various regional organizations, but the importance of many of those, like the G-77, NAM, Commonwealth, SAARC and IBSA, has gone down. The SCO, EAS, ARF, ADMM+ and IORA have regional agendas. Among the global organizations in which India is a member, the most important is the G-20, which brings together the most important global and regional powers. Even that is divided into two broad groups—the Western bloc and the more independent-minded non-Western countries, including the BRICS nations. BRICS emerged a decade and a half ago as a non-Western grouping of large and influential rising economies (Brazil, Russia, India, China, South Africa) to counter a unipolar world. Its progress has been slow and uneven, the major achievement being the setting up of the New Development Bank in 2014 for the purpose of mobilizing resources for infrastructure and sustainable development projects in emerging markets and developing countries. China has been trying since 2017 to expand the group by including other countries to constitute a BRICS Plus framework. India will have to be proactive to ensure that BRICS does not become a group dominated by China. Over the last year or two, global interest in BRICS has certainly increased. In 2023, six regionally important countries—Argentina, Egypt, Ethiopia, Iran, Saudi Arabia and the United Arab Emirates—were cleared for membership with effect from 2024. Even as Argentina under a new government has rejected BRICS membership, no doubt under US pressure, there are plenty of other countries aspiring for membership. This shows that there is a widespread global yearning for an effective balance to a Western-dominated world. However, it is doubtful if BRICS, whose agenda is economic rather than political, can emerge as an effective counter to the West. Russian President Putin did not participate in person in the last BRICS summit in South Africa and may not be present at the next summit in Brazil, because both these countries are under pressure from the West to arrest Putin, who has been charged with war crimes by the International Criminal Court. India-China tensions and India's orientation towards the West also limit the ability of BRICS to emerge as an anti-West grouping. Nevertheless, BRICS does serve a useful, though limited, purpose for India insofar as it gives it some leverage over the West.

Conclusion

I have described in this book some of the principal foreign policy challenges before India today. As India's recent high-level interactions with other major powers and its role in the G-20 have shown, India's views are sought and taken seriously across the world. Given India's size, population and its self-perception that it was historically, is today. and will be in the future a global player, piggybacking is not a viable option for it. India has to continue to follow a policy of strategic autonomy. Secondly, to be a truly credible leading power, India must accelerate its economic growth, build up its military strength and be more self-reliant militarily and technologically. Hence the importance of Atmanirbharta, which is no longer a mere slogan but a policy that has begun to be seriously implemented in practice. Thirdly, India must maximize the advantages of its geographical location and overcome its geopolitical weaknesses. With its proximity to abundant sources of energy and raw materials, large markets, access to the open seas, India is favourably located. As the biggest threat to India's rise is an unstable and unfriendly neighbourhood that could keep India preoccupied with handling threats to its security from its immediate neighbours, the highest priority has to be given to an imaginative 'Neighbourhood First' policy. Fourthly, India must have good leaders. India is fortunate to have in Prime Minister Modi, now in his third consecutive term in office, a leader with ambition, drive and a clear vision. One hopes that political leaders in the coming decades will continue to have a similar perspective. Finally, influential sections of India's political and intellectual elite must overcome their regrettable tendency to run down India, often in active collaboration with foreign vested interests, and thereby undermine its unity, stability and progress.

India's overall approach should be guided by hard-nosed national interest. Its thinking needs to be clear and long term, its options diverse and its diplomacy skilful and nimble. Perhaps then, India will finally be able to translate its much-vaunted potential into reality, and become a strong, prosperous and globally influential country.

Notes

Chapter 1: The World Today

1 Robert Kagan, *The Return of History and the End of Dreams* (Atlantic, 2009).
2 'NK Singh, Lawrence Summers Co-Conveners of G20 Expert Group on Strengthening MDBs,' *Hindustan Times*, 28 March 2023, available at https://www.hindustantimes.com/india-news/nk-singh-lawrence-summers-co-conveners-of-g20-expert-group-on-strengthening-mdbs-101679998187746.html.
3 Samuel P. Huntington, *The Clash of Civilizations and the Remaking of World Order* (Simon & Schuster, 2011).
4 'Population Trends,' UNFPA Asiapacific, 2022, available at https://asiapacific.unfpa.org/en/populationtrends.

Chapter 3: Pakistan and Afghanistan

1 'India Withdraws Most Favoured Nation Status to Pakistan: What It Means,' India Today, 15 February 2019, available at https://www.indiatoday.in/india/story/india-withdraws-most-favoured-nation-status-to-pakistan-what-it-means-1456746-2019-02-15.
2 'The 'generals' elections' in Pakistan that turned against the military', France 24, 9 February 2024, available at https://www.france24.com/en/asia-pacific/20240209-the-generals-elections-that-turned-against-pakistan-s-military.
3 "Pakistan Has Learnt Its Lesson . . .': PM Shehbaz Sharif on Wars with India,' India Today, 17 January 2023, available at https://

www.indiatoday.in/world/story/pakistan-has-learnt-its-lesson-pm-shehbaz-sharif-on-wars-with-india-2322445-2023-01-17.

4 M.K. Gandhi, 'Kashmir Issue (Speech at the Prayer Meeting on 4th January 1948', *Collected Works of Mahatma Gandhi*, Vol. 90, pp. 356–58. Also available at https://www.mkgandhi.org/speeches/kashmir_issue.htm.

Chapter 4: Bangladesh and Myanmar

1 Article XXIV of the General Agreement on Tariffs and Trade (GATT 1947), World Trade Organization, available at https://www.wto.org/english/tratop_e/region_e/region_art24_e.htm.

2 'We have transformed Northeast to 'abundant region, says PM Modi', *Business Standard*, 8 April 2024, available at https://www.business-standard.com/elections/lok-sabha-election/we-have-transformed-northeast-to-abundant-region-says-pm-modi-124040800977_1.html.

Chapter 5: Sri Lanka and the Maldives

1 'Lanka declares pause on foreign research vessels amidst Indian concerns over Chinese surveillance', *Deccan Herald*, 20 December 2023, available at https://www.deccanherald.com/world/lanka-declares-pause-on-foreign-research-vessels-amidst-indian-concerns-over-chinese-surveillance-2819435.

2 Aftab Ahmed and Uditha Jayasinghe, 'India plans no more funding for Sri Lanka as IMF talks progress – sources', Reuters, 15 September 2022, available at https://www.reuters.com/world/asia-pacific/india-plans-no-more-funding-sri-lanka-imf-talks-progress-sources-2022-09-15/.

3 Mohammed Sinan Siyech, 'Poverty, Criminality, Extremism: The Interrelated Sources of Insecurity in Maldives', Observer Research Foundation, 16 August 2023, available at https://orfonline.org/

research/poverty-criminality-extremism-the-interrelated-sources-of-insecurity-in-maldives.

4 'China says 'firmly opposes external interference' in Maldives as Muizzu winds up visit', *Economic Times*, 12 January 2024, https://economictimes.indiatimes.com/news/international/world-news/china-says-firmly-opposes-external-interference-in-maldives-as-muizzu-winds-up-visit/articleshow/106733712.cms?utm_source=contentofinterest&utm_medium=text&utm_campaign=cppst.

5 Vignesh Radhakrishnan and Sonikka Loganathan, 'With China's help, Maldives plans to lower dependence on India in tourism, trade and healthcare: Data', *The Hindu*, 16 February 2024, available at https://www.thehindu.com/data/with-china-help-maldives-plans-to-lower-dependence-on-india-in-tourism-trade-and-healthcare-data/article67821326.ece.

6 Amiti Sen, 'Development of India, Maldives ties based on mutual interests, reciprocal sensitivity: Jaishankar', *Hindu Business Line*, 9 May 2024, available at https://www.thehindubusinessline.com/economy/development-of-india-maldives-ties-based-on-mutual-interests-reciprocal-sensitivity-jaishankar/article68157246.ece.

Chapter 8: 'Act East' Policy and the Indo-Pacific

1 Matthew Robert Carnell, 'India from Colony to Nation-State: A Re-Reading of India's Foreign Policy in Southeast Asia, c.1945-1955', doctoral thesis, September 2012, available at https://etheses.whiterose.ac.uk/3274/1/thesis-matt-carnell.pdf.

2 K.M. Panikkar, 'India and the Indian Ocean: An Essay on the influence of Sea Power on Indian History', *Life*, 2019.

3 'India aiming to become maritime power: Pranab', *Hindustan Times*, 30 June 2017, available at https://www.hindustantimes.com/kolkata/india-aiming-to-become-maritime-power-pranab/story-sDCNab50ZeJAAgUV5UfZVP.html.

Chapter 9: Persian Gulf and West Asia

1 'QUESTION No. 583 INDIAN WORKERS IN GULF COUNTRIES,' Ministry of External Affairs, Government of India, available at https://www.mea.gov.in/lok-sabha.htm?dtl/35979.

2 'India, Saudi Arabia Ink Haj Agreement with over 1.75 Lakh Pilgrim Quota for 2024', *The Hindu*, 8 January 2024, available at https://www.thehindu.com/news/national/india-saudi-arabia-ink-haj-agreement-with-over-175-lakh-pilgrim-quota-for-2024/article67717128.ece. See also, 'At 18 Lakh, Indian Muslim Umrah Performers Third Highest In 2023: Saudi Arabia', NDTV, available at https://www.ndtv.com/india-news/at-18-lakh-indian-muslim-umrah-performers-third-highest-in-2023-saudi-arabia-4752447.

3 Rezaul H. Laskar, 'India, Saudi Arabia to Speed up Kingdom's $100-Billion Investment Plan', *Hindustan Times*, 11 September 2023, available at https://www.hindustantimes.com/india-news/india-saudi-arabia-to-speed-up-kingdom-s-100-billion-investment-plan-101694444845438.html. See also 'Saudi Arabia's Vision 2030 Fuels Order Books of India's Infrastructure Companies', Moneycontrol, 2024, available at https://www.moneycontrol.com/news/business/saudi-arabias-vision-2030-fuels-order-books-of-indias-infrastructure-companies-12375211.html.

4 'Indian Community in UAE', Embassy of India, available at https://www.indembassyuae.gov.in/indian-com-in-uae.php#:~:text=Indian%20expatriate%20community%20is%20the,2021%20as%20per%20UAE%20records.

5 'India-UAE Trade Agreement Cementing Long-Standing Economic Ties: UAE Envoy', *Business Standard*, 1 May 2024, available at https://www.business-standard.com/industry/news/india-uae-trade-agreement-cementing-long-standing-economic-ties-uae-envoy-124050100882_1.html.

6 'Comprehensive Economic Partnership Agreement (CEPA) between the Government of the Republic of India and the Government of the United Arab Emirates (UAE) - Mcommerce,' Mcommerce, 2023, available at https://commerce.gov.in/international-trade/trade-agreements/comprehensive-economic-

partnership-agreement-between-the-government-of-the-republic-of-india-and-the-government-of-the-united-arab-emirates-uae/.

7 'Brief on India-UAE Commercial Relations', Embassy of India, available at https://www.indembassyuae.gov.in/bilateral-eco-com-relation.php.

8 Ibid.

9 'Ongc-Led-Lndian-Consortium-Acquire-Zakum-Concession-Offshore-Abudhabi', Oil and Natural Gas Corporation Ltd, available at https://ongcindia.com/web/hi/w/ongc-led-lndian-consortium-acquire-zakum-concession-offshore-abudhabi.

10 'I2U2', United States Department of State, July 2022, available at https://www.state.gov/i2u2/#:~:text=The%20I2U2%20Private%20Enterprise%20Partnership,of%20Understanding%20is%20available%20here.

11 Ibid.

12 'India Reassures Aid for War-Torn Iraq's Rebuilding Process', *Hindustan Times*, 14 February 2018, available at https://www.hindustantimes.com/india-news/india-reassures-aid-for-war-torn-iraq-s-rebuilding-process/story-TJlZwXCe04rDZw8aM1EoAJ.html.

13 Mahatma Gandhi, 'The Jews in Palestine', Counter Currents, available at https://www.countercurrents.org/pa-gandhi170903.htm.

14 'Why India Has Not Designated Hamas as a Terrorist Organisation', Firstpost, 26 October 2023, available at https://www.firstpost.com/explainers/why-india-has-not-designated-hamas-as-a-terrorist-organisation-13301442.html.

15 'Bilateral Economic Relations', Embassy of India, Tel Aviv, Israel, available at https://www.indembassyisrael.gov.in/pages?id=nel5a&subid=7ax9b.

Chapter 10: Russia and Eurasia

1 Ivan Shchedrov, 'India-Russia relations: Seeking to overcome the 'oil fever'', Observer Research Foundation, 11 March 2024, available at https://www.orfonline.org/expert-speak/india-russia-relations-seeking-to-overcome-the-oil-fever.

2 Schmidt Helmut and Brzezinski Zbigniew, 'The Grand Chessboard: American Primacy and Its Geostrategic Imperatives', *Foreign Policy* 110 (1998): 179, available at https://doi.org/10.2307/1149289.

Chapter 11: United States and the West

1 'How Will the EU Carbon Border Adjustment Mechanism Impact India?', India Briefing News, 2023, available at https://www.india-briefing.com/news/eu-carbon-border-adjustment-mechanism-impact-india-business-exports-27901.html/.

Chapter 12: Strategic, Military and Economic Constraints

1 Shyam Saran. *How India Sees the World: Kautilya to the 21st Century* (New Delhi: Juggernaut Books, 2020).

2 Sardar Patel's Letter to Prime Minister Jawaharlal Nehru of 7 November 1950 warning India about dangers from China. Available at https://www.friendsoftibet.org/sardarpatel.html.

3 'Text of Notes exchanged between the delegations of India and China on 29 April 1954', *Foreign Policy of India, Texts of Documents 1947–1959* (New Delhi: Lok Sabha Secretariat, 1959). See also, Nehru's reply to debate in Rajya Sabha on 24 December 1953 on closure of Indian Consulate in Kashgar, reproduced in *Selected Works of Jawaharlal Nehru*, second series, vol. 24 (Jawaharlal Nehru Memorial Fund, 1972), p. 581.

4 Nehru in Lok Sabha on 14th August 1962, reproduced in *Selected Works of Jawaharlal Nehru*, vol. 78 (Jawaharlal Nehru Memorial Fund, 2019), p. 623.

5 Sujit Nath, 'Nehru Rejected Offer to Make Nepal Province of India, Indira May Have Taken It: Pranab in Autobiography', News18, 5 January 2021, available at https://www.news18.com/news/politics/nehru-rejected-offer-to-make-nepal-a-province-of-india-indira-may-have-taken-it-pranab-in-autobiography-3249731.html.

6 Shania Mathew, 'Abdul Ghaffar Khan was no Gandhi—he was the powerhouse Pathan who mobilised Indian Muslims', The Print, 20 January 2023, available at https://theprint.in/theprint-profile/abdul-ghaffar-khan-was-no-gandhi-he-was-the-powerhouse-pathan-who-mobilised-indian-muslims/1325088/. See also 'Report by Henry Grady, US Ambassador to Delhi to US Secretary of State on 9th July 1947', reproduced in *Selected Works of Jawaharlal Nehru*, second series, vol. 3 (Jawaharlal Nehru Memorial Fund, 1972), pp. 392–93.

7 Anil Kumar Lal, 'Did Balochistan accede to India during partition, but India refused to accept this and turned a blind eye? Part-1', *Times of India*, 12 October 2020, available at https://timesofindia.indiatimes.com/blogs/rakshakindia/did-balochistan-accede-to-india-during-partition-but-india-refused-to-accept-this-and-turned-a-blind-eye-part-1/. See also, *Selected Works of Jawaharlal Nehru*, second series, vol. 5 (Jawaharlal Nehru Memorial Fund, 1972), pp. 299–300.

8 Sushim Mukul, 'Gwadar, now Pakistan's, was offered to India in 1950s', India Today, 7 April 2024, available at https://www.indiatoday.in/sunday-special/story/gwadar-port-offered-to-india-by-oman-pakistan-cpec-china-bri-jawaharlal-nehru-balochistan-2523885-2024-04-07.

9 Nikhil Rampal, 'Only Half of India's Working-Age Population Works, Most Still in Agriculture, Shows ILO Report,' The Print, 30 March 2024, available at https://theprint.in/economy/only-half-of-indias-working-age-population-works-most-still-in-agriculture-shows-ilo-report/2020831/.

10 Rimjhim Singh, 'India Global Services Export to Reach $800 Billion by 2030: Goldman Sachs', *Business Standard*, 30 April 2024, available at https://www.business-standard.com/industry/news/india-global-services-export-to-reach-800-billion-by-2030-goldman-sachs-124043000713_1.html.

11 'India Has Trade Deficit with 10 Regional Comprehensive Economic Partnership (RCEP) Members', *Economic Times*, 17 June 2018, available at https://economictimes.indiatimes.com/

news/economy/foreign-trade/india-has-trade-deficit-with-10-regional-comprehensive-economic-partnership-rcep-members/articleshow/64620160.cms.

Chapter 13: The Way Forward

1 'Towards a Brighter Tomorrow: India's G20 Presidency and the Dawn of a New Multilateralism', Prime Minister's Office, 30 November 2023, available at https://pib.gov.in/PressReleaseIframePage.aspx?PRID=1980993.
2 'ITEC: Indian Technical and Economic Cooperation', available at https://www.itecgoi.in/about.
3 Abhijit Mukhopadhyay 'India's Lines of Credit, Development Cooperation, and G20 Presidency: A Primer', Observer Research Foundation, 17 August 2023, available at https://www.orfonline.org/research/india-s-lines-of-credit-development-cooperation-and-g20-presidency-a-primer#:~:text=More%20than%20306%20LOCs%2C%20cumulatively,277%20more%20are%20under%20implementation.
4 'EAM Jaishankar on global architecture: India non-western but not anti-western', *Economic Times*, 29 September 2023, available at https://economictimes.indiatimes.com/news/india/eam-jaishankar-on-global-architecture-india-non-western-but-not-anti-western/videoshow/104050599.cms?from=mdr.
5 Prashant Jha, 'Convergences, divergences: Jaishankar outlines crux of US relations', *Hindustan Times*, 30 September 2023, available at https://www.hindustantimes.com/india-news/convergences-divergences-jaishankar-outlines-crux-of-us-relations-101696013869228.html.

Selected Bibliography

Books

Amrith, Sunil S. 2013. *Crossing the Bay of Bengal: The Furies of Nature and the Fortunes of Migrants.* Cambridge: Harvard University Press.

Asia Centre Bangalore. 2013. *India's Security Environment: Proceedings of Select Seminars Held by Asia Centre Bangalore.* New Delhi: Konark Publishers.

Bhagwati, Jagdish. 2004. *In Defense of Globalization.* New Delhi: Oxford University Press.

Bisaria, Ajay. 2024. *Anger Management: The Troubled Diplomatic Relationship between India and Pakistan.* New Delhi: Aleph Book Company.

Brzezinski, Zbigniew. 1997. *The Grand Chessboard: American Primacy and Its Geostrategic Imperatives,* New York: Basic Books.

Brzezinski, Zbigniew. 2004. *The Choice: Global Domination or Global Leadership.* New York: Basic Books.

Chakravarty, Pinak. 2024. *Transformation: Emergence of Bangladesh and Evolution of India-Bangladesh Ties.* New Delhi: Knowledge World.

Chaudhuri, Rudra. 2014. *Forged in Crisis: India and the United States since 1947.* New Delhi: HarperCollins Publishers India.

Chawla, Shalini (ed.). 2023. *India's Neighbourhood: Challenges and Opportunities.* New Delhi: Knowledge World.

Chinoy, Sujan, Vijay Chauthaiwale and Uttam Kumar Sinha (ed.) 2023. *Modi: Shaping a Global Order in Flux.* New Delhi: Wisdom Tree.

Daulet Singh, Zorawar. 2019. *Power and Diplomacy: India's Foreign Policies during the Cold War.* New Delhi: Oxford University Press.

De, Prabir (ed.). 2023. *Thirty Years of ASEAN-India Relations: Towards Indo-Pacific.* New Delhi: Knowledge World.

Debroy, Bibek, and Ashok Malik (ed.). 2017. *India @ 70 Modi @3.5: Capturing India's Transformation under Narendra Modi.* New Delhi: Wisdom Tree.

Devare, Sudhir. 2006. *India & Southeast Asia: Towards Security Convergence.* Singapore: Institute of Southeast Asian Studies.

Dixit, J.N. 2003. *India's Foreign Policy 1947–2003.* New Delhi: Picus Books.

Dogra, Rajiv. 2020. *India's World: How Prime Ministers Shaped Foreign Policy.* New Delhi: Rupa Publications.

Dubey, Muchkund. 2012. *India's Foreign Policy: Coping with the Changing World.* New Delhi: Pearson.

Dutt, V.P. 1999. *India's Foreign Policy in a Changing World.* New Delhi: Vikas Publishers.

Dutt, V.P. 2007. *India's Foreign Policy since Independence.* New Delhi: National Book Trust.

Emmott, Bill. 2008. *Rivals: How the Power Struggle between China, India and Japan Will Shape Our Next Decade.* London: Allen Lane.

Foreign Service Institute, New Delhi. 1998. *Indian Foreign Policy: Agenda for the 21st Century (2 volumes).* New Delhi: Konark Publishers.

Foreign Service Institute. 2007. *Indian Foreign Policy: Challenges and Opportunities.* New Delhi: Academic Foundation.

Friedman, Thomas. 2005. *The World Is Flat: A Brief History of the Globalized World in the Twenty-First Century.* London: Allen Lane.

Fukuyama, Francis. 1992. *The End of History and the Last Man.* London: Penguin Books.

Ganguly, Anirban, Vijay Chauthaiwale and Uttam Kumar Sinha (ed.). 2016. *The Modi Doctrine: New Paradigms in India's Foreign Policy.* New Delhi: Wisdom Tree.

Ganguly, Sumit (ed.). 2010. *India's Foreign Policy: Retrospect and Prospect.* New Delhi: Oxford University Press.

Ganguly, Sumit, Nicolas Blarel and Manjeet S. Pardesi (ed.). 2018. *The Oxford Handbook of India's National Security.* New Delhi: Oxford University Press.

Gokhale, Vijay. 2021. *The Long Game: How the Chinese Negotiate with India.* New Delhi: Penguin Random House India.

Gupta, Arvind, and Anil Wadhwa (ed.). 2020. *India's Foreign Policy: Surviving in a Turbulent World.* New Delhi: SAGE Publications India.

Gupta, Arvind. 2018. *How India Manages Its National Security.* New Delhi: Penguin Random House India.

Guruswamy, Mohan, and Zorawar Daulet Singh. 2009. *India China Relations: The Border Issue and Beyond.* New Delhi: Viva Books.

Heimsath, Charles H., and Surjit Mansingh. 1971. *A Diplomatic History of Modern India.* Calcutta: Allied Publishers.

Huntington, Samuel P. 1996. *The Clash of Civilizations and the Remaking of World Order.* New Delhi: Penguin Books India.

Jaishankar, S. 2020. *The India Way: Strategies for an Uncertain World.* Noida: HarperCollins Publishers India.

Jaishankar, S. 2024. *Why Bharat Matters.* New Delhi: Rupa Publications.

Kagan, Robert. 2008. *The Return of History and the End of Dreams.* London: Atlantic Books.

Kaplan, Robert D. 2010. *Monsoon: The Indian Ocean and the Future of American Power.* New York: Random House.

Kaplan, Robert D. 2012. *The Revenge of Geography: What the Map Tells Us about Coming Conflicts and the Battle against Fate.* New York: Random House.

Karnad, Bharat. 2008. *India's Nuclear Policy.* New Delhi: Pentagon Press.

Kennedy, Paul. 1989. *The Rise and Fall of the Great Powers.* London: Fontana Press.

Kennedy, Paul. 1994. *Preparing for the Twenty-First Century.* London: Fontana Press.

Kissinger, Henry. 2014. *World Order: Reflections on the Character of Nations and the Course of History.* London: Penguin Group.

Kumar, Mohan. 2023. *India's Moment: Changing Power Equations around the World.* New Delhi: HarperCollins Publishers India.

Kumar, Surendra (ed.). 2015. *India and the World through the Eyes of Indian Diplomats.* New Delhi: Wisdom Tree.

Kumar, Yogendra. 2015. *Diplomatic Dimension of Maritime Challenges for India in the 21st Century.* New Delhi: Pentagon Press.

Kux, Dennis. 1993. *India and the United States: Estranged Democracies*, Washington D.C.: National Defense University Press.

Lambah, Satinder Kumar. 2023. *In Pursuit of Peace: India-Pakistan Relations under Six Prime Ministers.* New Delhi: Penguin Random House India.

Lintner, Bertil. 2012. *Great Game East: India, China and the Struggle for Asia's Most Volatile Frontier.* New Delhi: HarperCollins Publishers India.

Lok Sabha Secretariat. 1959. *Foreign Policy of India, Texts of Documents, 1947–59*. New Delhi: Lok Sabha Secretariat.

Mackinder, Halford J. 2009. *Democratic Ideals and Reality.* London: Faber and Faber.

Malone, David M. 2011. *Does the Elephant Dance? Contemporary Indian Foreign Policy*. New Delhi: Oxford University Press.

Malone, David M., C. Raja Mohan and Srinath Raghavan (ed.). 2015. *The Oxford Handbook of Indian Foreign Policy.* New Delhi: Oxford University Press.

Menon, Shivshankar. 2016. *Choices: Inside the Making of India's Foreign Policy.* New Delhi: Penguin Random House India.

Muni, S.D. 2009. *India's Foreign Policy: The Democracy Dimension*. New Delhi: Cambridge University Press.

Nehru, Jawaharlal. 1961. *India's Foreign Policy: Selected Speeches, September 1946–April 1961*. New Delhi: Publications Division, Ministry of Information and Broadcasting, Government of India.

Pande, Aparna. 2017. *From Chanakya to Modi: The Evolution of India's Foreign Policy.* New Delhi: HarperCollins Publishers India.

Panikkar, K.M. 1956. *The Principles and Practice of Diplomacy*. Bombay: Asia Publishing House.

Pant, Harsh V. (ed.). 2009. *Indian Foreign Policy in a Unipolar World.* New Delhi: Routledge.

Prasad, Bimal. 1973. *Indo-Soviet Relations: 1947–1972*. New Delhi: Allied Publishers.

Rachman, Gideon. 2016. *Easternisation: War and Peace in the Asian Century.* London: Penguin Random House UK.

Rae, Ranjit. 2021. *Kathmandu Dilemma: Resetting India-Nepal Ties.* New Delhi: Penguin Random House India.

Raghavan, Srinath. 2010. *War and Peace in Modern India: A Strategic History of the Nehru Years.* Ranikhet: Permanent Black.

Raja Mohan, C. 2013. *Samudra Manthan: Sino-Indian Rivalry in the Indo-Pacific.* New Delhi: Oxford University Press.

Ram, Amar Nath (ed.). 2012. *Two Decades of India's Look East Policy: Partnership for Peace, Progress and Prosperity*. New Delhi: Manohar Publishers and Distributors.

Sanyal, Sanjeev. 2016. *The Ocean of Churn: How the Indian Ocean Shaped Human History*. New Delhi: Penguin Random House India.

Saran, Shyam. 2020. *How India Sees the World: Kautilya to the 21st Century*. New Delhi: Juggernaut Books.

Schaffer, Teresita C., and Howard B. Schaffer. 2016. *India at the Global High Table: The Quest for Regional Primacy and Strategic Autonomy*. New Delhi: HarperCollins Publishers India.

Sikri, Rajiv. 2009. *Challenge and Strategy: Rethinking India's Foreign Policy*. New Delhi: SAGE Publications India.

Sikri, Veena. 2013. *India and Malaysia: Intertwined Strands*. New Delhi: Manohar Publishers and Distributors.

Singh, Jaswant. 1999. *Defending India*. New Delhi: Macmillan.

Singh, Jaswant. 2013. *India at Risk: Mistakes, Misconceptions and Misadventures of Security Policy*. New Delhi: Rupa Publications.

Sirohi, Seema. 2023. *Friends with Benefits: The India-US Story*. New Delhi: HarperCollins Publishers India.

Stiglitz, Joseph. 2002. *Globalization and Its Discontents*. New York: Penguin Books.

Tellis, Ashley J., Bibek Debroy, C. Raja Mohan (ed.). 2022. *Grasping Greatness: Making India a Leading Power*. New Delhi: Penguin Random House India.

Thant, Myint-U. 2011. *Where China Meets India: Burma and the New Crossroads of Asia*. London: Faber and Faber.

Tharoor, Shashi. 2012. *Pax Indica: India and the World of the 21st Century*. New Delhi: Penguin Books India.

Tripathi, D.N. 2013. *India, Central Asia and Russia: Three Millennia of Contacts*. New Delhi: Indian Council of Historical Research, and Aryan Books International.

Vivekananda International Foundation. 2017. *Securing India*. New Delhi: Wisdom Tree.

Zakaria, Fareed. 2008. *The Post-American World*. New York: W.W. Norton & Company.

Journals

Strategic Analysis, bimonthly journal of the IDSA

India Quarterly, quarterly journal of the Indian Council of World Affairs.

Indian Foreign Affairs Journal, a Quarterly of the Association of Indian Diplomats

U.S.I. Journal, the Journal of the United Service Institution of India

Journal of Indian Ocean Studies, tri-annual publication of the Society for Indian Ocean Studies

Himalayan and Central Asian Studies, journal of Himalayan Research and Cultural Foundation

Internet Resources

www.mea.gov.in	Ministry of External Affairs, India
www.idsa.in	Manohar Parikkar Institute for Defence Studies and Analyses
www.icwa.in	Indian Council of World Affairs
www.orfonline.com	Observer Research Foundation
www.vifindia.org	Vivekananda International Foundation
www.ris.org.in	Research and Information System for Developing Countries
www.ipcs.org	Institute of Peace and Conflict Studies
www.isas.nus.edu.sg	Institute of South Asian Studies, Singapore
www.delhipolicygroup.org	Delhi Policy Group

Scan QR code to access the
Penguin Random House India website